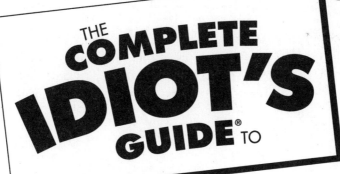

THE COMPLETE IDIOT'S GUIDE® TO

Eating Well on a Budget

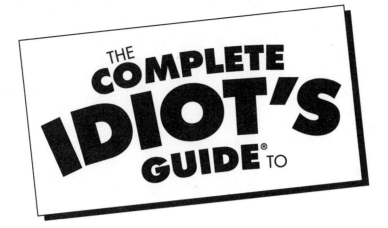

THE COMPLETE IDIOT'S GUIDE® TO

Eating Well on a Budget

by Lucy Beale and Jessica Partridge

ALPHA

A member of Penguin Group (USA) Inc.

Lucy: To my husband and best friend, Patrick.
Jessica: To Schabe and my Momar, for everything.

ALPHA BOOKS

Published by the Penguin Group

Penguin Group (USA) Inc., 375 Hudson Street, New York, New York 10014, USA

Penguin Group (Canada), 90 Eglinton Avenue East, Suite 700, Toronto, Ontario M4P 2Y3, Canada (a division of Pearson Penguin Canada Inc.)

Penguin Books Ltd., 80 Strand, London WC2R 0RL, England

Penguin Ireland, 25 St. Stephen's Green, Dublin 2, Ireland (a division of Penguin Books Ltd.)

Penguin Group (Australia), 250 Camberwell Road, Camberwell, Victoria 3124, Australia (a division of Pearson Australia Group Pty. Ltd.)

Penguin Books India Pvt. Ltd., 11 Community Centre, Panchsheel Park, New Delhi—110 017, India

Penguin Group (NZ), 67 Apollo Drive, Rosedale, North Shore, Auckland 1311, New Zealand (a division of Pearson New Zealand Ltd.)

Penguin Books (South Africa) (Pty.) Ltd., 24 Sturdee Avenue, Rosebank, Johannesburg 2196, South Africa

Penguin Books Ltd., Registered Offices: 80 Strand, London WC2R 0RL, England

Copyright © 2010 by Lucy Beale

International Standard Book Number: 978-1-59257-980-8
Library of Congress Catalog Card Number: 2009932962

12   11   10   8   7   6   5   4   3   2   1

Interpretation of the printing code: The rightmost number of the first series of numbers is the year of the book's printing; the rightmost number of the second series of numbers is the number of the book's printing. For example, a printing code of 10-1 shows that the first printing occurred in 2010.

Printed in the United States of America

Note: This publication contains the opinions and ideas of its authors. It is intended to provide helpful and informative material on the subject matter covered. It is sold with the understanding that the authors and publisher are not engaged in rendering professional services in the book. If the reader requires personal assistance or advice, a competent professional should be consulted.

The authors and publisher specifically disclaim any responsibility for any liability, loss, or risk, personal or otherwise, which is incurred as a consequence, directly or indirectly, of the use and application of any of the contents of this book.

Most Alpha books are available at special quantity discounts for bulk purchases for sales promotions, premiums, fundraising, or educational use. Special books, or book excerpts, can also be created to fit specific needs.

For details, write: Special Markets, Alpha Books, 375 Hudson Street, New York, NY 10014.

Publisher: *Marie Butler-Knight*
Editorial Director: *Mike Sanders*
Senior Managing Editor: *Billy Fields*
Acquisitions Editor: *Tom Stevens*
Development Editor: *Nancy D. Lewis*
Production Editor: *Kayla Dugger*
Copy Editor: *Amy Lepore*

Cartoonist: *Steve Barr*
Cover Designer: *Bill Thomas*
Book Designer: *Trina Wurst*
Indexer: *Heather McNeill*
Layout: *Ayanna Lacey*
Proofreader: *Laura Caddell*

Contents at a Glance

Part 1:   Creating and Managing Your Budget   1

   1   The Best Nutrition at the Best Price   3
Use budgeting to eat plenty of healthy, delicious food using the Plate Method, based on recommended nutritional standards. Budget for extra treats and avoid money wasters.

   2   The Budget   15
Become familiar with budgeting terms and principles as you write down your goals or use accounting software on your computer. Manage monthly expenses and adjust your budget based on your family's needs and lifestyle preferences.

   3   Managing Your Eating Style   25
Learn your basic eating style to help you determine where to cut costs and where not to cut back on spending. Teach your family about the budget so that they collaborate with you to eat and spend responsibly.

   4   Food and Menu Planning   35
Plan your family's weekly menus to include variety, snacks, and special occasions. The Big Pot Theory gives you multiple meal options for cooking convenience and saving money.

   5   Food Preparation   45
Choose the cooking strategy that works for you—cook daily, once a week, or once a month. Learn about neighborhood cooking co-ops. Use food wisely to avoid throwing food away.

Part 2:   Shopping for Groceries and Saving on Food   57

   6   The Shopping List   59
Write your shopping list from your weekly menu plan while utilizing foods already in your pantry. Supply your kitchen with basic cooking and food storage equipment. Save money on household cleaners and supplies.

   7   The Well-Informed Shopper   75
Use all the cost-saving tools available: shop sales, use coupons, check out in-store unadvertised specials. Adopt a guerilla-style shopping attitude to avoid impulse purchases and to navigate around the money wasters in each aisle.

   8 Eating Out on a Budget   85
      Enjoy eating out while carefully managing your menu
      choices. Learn ways to handle school lunches and work
      cafeterias. Entertain comfortably and enjoy potlucks, too.

   9 More Ways to Save on Food   95
      Find ways to enjoy cooking. Grow your own fresh herbs or
      produce. Preserve in-season food by freezing, canning, or
      drying.

Part 3:   **Recipes for Eating Well**   **105**

  10 Breakfasts   107
      Cook up quick, easy, and nutritious meals for this most
      important meal of the day. Choose eggs, cereal, or fruit
      parfaits for all-day energy.

  11 Lunches   121
      Prepare light meals for lunchboxes or at-home eating.
      The recipes provide balanced nutrition to sustain family
      members until dinner or their late-afternoon snack.

  12 Soups and Stews   137
      Provide savory comfort to your family while saving money
      with these high-nutrition soups. You'll appreciate the wide
      variety of tastes and textures.

  13 Snacks and Appetizers   153
      Serve these light foods for late-afternoon snacks, in lunch-
      boxes, or while watching the big game. They're substantial
      in taste and variety.

  14 Salads   167
      Enjoy the light, fresh taste of cost-conscious salads while you
      treat your body with important antioxidants and delicious
      flavors.

  15 Beef and Pork Main Dishes   185
      These meat recipes offer affordable cuts cooked luxuriously,
      with a variety of flavor options to keep your menu lively.

  16 Poultry Main Dishes   197
      Chicken and turkey are mainstays of economical cooking.
      Try both the fruity and savory offerings in these recipes.

17 Seafood Main Dishes   209
    Purchase seafood on sale or in cans and treat your family to
    these scrumptious recipes.

18 Ground Meat Main Dishes   221
    Serve ground beef or ground turkey in these recipes for
    high nutrition and hearty food with superb cost savings.

19 Vegetarian Main Dishes   233
    Prepare these substantial and filling vegetarian meals that
    offer great taste and balanced nutrients.

20 Vegetable Side Dishes   245
    These recipes make eating your vegetables delectable. The
    recipes call for frozen, fresh, or canned vegetables, based on
    what's most economical that week.

21 Grains and Side Dishes   261
    Add these filling and hearty recipes to any meal to satisfy
    hungrier appetites.

22 Desserts   271
    Satisfy your sweet tooth with these cost-saving desserts.
    Your choices include cookies, chocolate pâté, and fruit-
    flavored breads.

Appendixes

    A Glossary   283

    B Resources   297

       Index   299

Contents

Part 1:   **Creating and Managing Your Budget**   **1**

1   **The Best Nutrition at the Best Price**   **3**

Money-Wise Delectable Meals...4

Budgeting Makes Cents 5

What Budgeting Is and Isn't 6

Calories Per Dollar 6

    Eating the Basics...8

    The Plate Method...10

    Money Wasters 11

    Possible Extras..12

2   **The Budget**   **15**

Budgets Are Your Friend...16

Pick a Number..16

Types of Food Purchases..18

Starting to Budget 19

    Put It in Writing...20

    Computer Solutions...20

Managing Your Budget 21

Helpful Budgeting Tools 22

3   **Managing Your Eating Style**   **25**

What's Your Style? 26

    Where to Cut Back 27

    Where Not to Cut Back 29

The Budgeting Family 30

Actual vs. Expenses...32

4   **Food and Menu Planning**   **35**

Planning Weekly Menus 36

    Menu Planning Worksheets 36

    Choosing Family Favorites...36

    The Big Pot Theory 37

    Creating Your Menus...39

Sample Menus 39

Avoiding Boredom...44

5   Food Preparation   45

Cooking Strategies 46
   Cook Once a Month 47
   Cook Once a Week 48
   Cook Almost Daily 49
   Baking 51
Neighborhood Cooking Co-Ops...51
Wise Use of Food...53
Food That Expires Slowly 54

Part 2:   Shopping for Groceries and Saving on Food   57

6   The Shopping List   59

The First Ingredient List..60
Make a Shopping List 64
Budget-Wise, High-Nutrition Foods.....................................66
Staples for Your Pantry and Refrigerator 66
   Spices...67
   Ingredients Used in This Book 68
   Basic Cooking Equipment You Need 72
   Food Storage Containers 73
Saving Money on Household Supplies....................................73

7   The Well-Informed Shopper   75

Shop First at Home..76
Shopping the Sales 76
   Looking for Sales 77
   In-Store Unadvertised Specials..78
   Coupons...78
Choosing the Grocery Store..79
Your Weekly Shopping Trip 81
   In-Store Tactics..82
   Purchasing Guidelines...83
Prepared Foods..84

8   Eating Out on a Budget   85

Essential Meals Out 86
   School Lunches...86
   Lunches at Work..89

Eating Out for Fun 90
   Restaurant Choices *91*
   Money-Saving Ways to Eat Out *92*
Entertaining 93

9 More Ways to Save on Food   **95**

Your Cooking Skills 96
More Flavorful Foods 97
Fresh from the Garden 99
Stocking Your Pantry with Preserved Food 100
   Freezing *100*
   Canning *101*
   Drying *102*

Part 3: Recipes for Eating Well   **105**

10 Breakfasts   **107**

   Chile Egg Puff *109*
   Savory Spinach and Bacon Bake *110*
   Poached Eggs on Turkey *111*
   Just Right Cheese Omelet *112*
   Zesty Breakfast Burritos *113*
   Baked Scotch Eggs *114*
   Banana Honey Oatmeal *115*
   Baked Cranberry Apple Oatmeal *116*
   Baked French Toast with Honey Walnut Syrup *117*
   Cottage Cheese and Fruit *118*
   Fresh Fruit with Tangy Yogurt Sauce *119*
   Nutty Fruit Parfait *120*

11 Lunches   **121**

   Mediterranean Veggie Pockets *122*
   Bottom-of-the-Bag Chicken *123*
   Tuna Salad with Vegetables *124*
   Chili-Stuffed Potato Skins *125*
   Grown-Up Peanut Butter and Jelly *126*
   Rarebit and Turkey Sandwich *127*
   Turkey and Cranberry Wrap *128*
   Cheese Wraps with Vegetables and Herbs *129*

Baked South-Of-The-Border Tortillas 130

Creamy Chicken and Raisin Salad 131

Baked Salmon and Asian Cabbage Salad 132

Garbanzo and Cottage Cheese Salad with Pita Chips 133

Egg Salad with Red Pepper and Walnuts 134

Hawaiian Ham Rollups 135

12 Soups and Stews   137

Nine Vegetable Soup 139

Chicken Noodle Soup with Vegetables 140

Ham and White Bean Soup 141

Lentil Soup 142

Creamy Clam Chowder 143

Chicken Tortilla Soup 144

Southwestern Corn Chowder 145

Stout Potato Cheese Soup 146

Split Pea Soup 147

Tomato Soup 148

Miso Soup 149

Beef Stew 150

Red Chili 151

White Chili 152

13 Snacks and Appetizers   153

Baked Hot Drumsticks 154

Asian Chicken Appetizers 155

Hummus 156

Crunchy Jicama Snack 157

Guacamole 158

Deviled Eggs 159

Oven-Baked Potato Chips 160

Avocado Kraut Cups 161

Hot Spinach and Artichoke Dip 162

Warm Onion and Mushroom Dip 163

Cool Dill Dip 164

Quick Fruit Salsa 165

14 Salads   167

Spring Salad 169

Summer Salad 170

Autumn Salad...*171*
Winter Salad..*172*
Mexican Vegetable Salad...*173*
Greek Salad...*174*
Creamy Potato Salad...*175*
Crunchy Coleslaw *176*
Sour Cream Cucumber Salad...*177*
Warm or Cold Bean Salad *178*
Seven Layer Salad *179*
Curried Fruit and Spinach Salad....................................*180*
Mint and Melon Salad *181*
Tossed Chef's Salad *182*
Chef's Choice Salad...*183*

15 Beef and Pork Main Dishes 185

Orange Spiced London Broil...*186*
Slow-Cooked Pot Roast..*187*
Oven Barbecued Beef *188*
Roast Beef..*189*
Pan-Seared Skirt Steak *190*
Quick Beef Fajitas *191*
Pork Chops with Rosemary...*192*
Mustard-Glazed Ham *193*
Ham and Noodle Casserole...*194*
Baked Italian Sausage and Peppers with Spaghetti *195*

16 Poultry Main Dishes 197

Baked Chicken with Apples and Sweet Potatoes...........................*198*
Lemon Pecan Stuffed Chicken *199*
Curried Chicken and Rice Casserole...............................*200*
Chicken with Vegetables and Tarragon *201*
Southern Spiced Chicken..*202*
Tangy Chicken and Fruit Kabobs....................................*203*
Turkey and White Bean Skillet.......................................*204*
Herb Roasted Turkey..*205*
Leftover Turkey and Vegetable Stir-Fry...........................*206*
Caesar Turkey with Mushrooms......................................*207*
Apricot Glazed Turkey Thighs *208*

17 Seafood Main Dishes   209

Gumbo with Shrimp and Sausage...*211*

Herbed Salmon Cakes...*212*

Tuna with Olives and Pasta...*213*

Lemon Halibut Kebabs..*214*

Oven-Sautéed Catfish...*215*

Paella-Style Seafood Bake..*216*

Baked Seafood Casserole..*217*

Fish Tacos...*218*

Fish Baked in Bags..*219*

Fish Stew with Potatoes and Tomatoes.....................................*220*

18 Ground Meat Main Dishes   221

Honey Mustard Glazed Meatloaf...*222*

Enchilada Pie..*223*

Lasagna with Meat and Cheese..*224*

Turkey Meatballs with Spaghetti Marinara.................................*225*

Easy Sloppy Joes...*226*

Beef and Potato Casserole...*227*

Spicy Turkey and Vegetable Burritos...*228*

Stuffed Turkey Burgers...*229*

Creamy Beef Stroganoff..*230*

Turkey Goulash..*231*

19 Vegetarian Main Dishes   233

Baked Macaroni with Two Cheeses..*234*

Nutty Brown Rice Burgers...*235*

Vegetable and Tofu Stir-Fry...*236*

Nutty Fruity Lentil Loaf...*237*

Pick-Your-Own Pita Pizzas...*238*

Vegetarian Barbecue Bake..*239*

Barley-Stuffed Peppers..*240*

Zucchini Lasagna...*241*

Mushroom Ragout on Spaghetti Squash.....................................*242*

Five Bean, Tofu, and Vegetable Bake...*243*

20 Vegetable Side Dishes   245

Fruit-Glazed Carrots..*246*

Black Bean and Sweet Potato Bake...*247*

Herbed Roasted Roots...*248*

Rosemary Spaghetti Squash...249
Slow-Cooked Onions with Apples and Sour Cream 250
Tart and Nutty Green Beans..251
Basil Broccoli with Cashews..252
Broccoli with Oranges and Rhubarb......................................253
Southwestern Succotash..254
Spinach and Carrot Kugel...255
Cheesy Vegetable Polenta..256
Baked Zucchini with Mozzarella..257
Hot Caraway Cabbage 258
Red Cabbage and Zucchini Skillet 259
Mashed Cauliflower with Cheese..260

21   Grains and Side Dishes   261

Barley Pilaf with Mushrooms...262
Sweet Potato Oven Fries 263
Risotto with Green Peas and Parmesan 264
Baked Beans 265
Grandma's Rice and Beans with Spinach 266
Quick Drop Biscuits 267
Buttermilk Corn Bread...268
Cheese Grits Casserole..269

22   Desserts   271

Pear Cobbler...272
Baked Stuffed Apples 273
Sweet Potato Fritters with Apples...274
Sweet Fruit and Noodle Pudding 275
Raspberry Banana Bread...276
Slow-Cooked Pudding and Fruit Cake 277
Brown Sugar Ginger Shortbread 278
Cookies Flavored with Tea..279
Chocolate Chip Cookies..280
Chocolate Not-Quite-Fudge Pâté..281
Brownies with Walnuts 282

Appendixes

A   Glossary   283

B   Resources   297

Index   299

Introduction

Eating well is important for your health and physical well-being. Budgeting is important for your financial health and peace of mind. In this book, we've combined the two—eating well and budgeting. Your body, mind, and spirit will benefit, and your family will benefit, too.

Initially, budgeting can seem intimidating, complicated, and restrictive. However, as you use our step-by-step process, you'll soon be confident and in control. You'll learn how to budget for meals at home, eating out, and school lunches. If you choose, you can even budget for impulse purchases.

You'll learn ways to adapt the budget to your lifestyle and personal preferences—and how to gain buy-in from family members to assure your budgeting success.

The recipes don't taste as if you're eating on a restricted budget, they just cost less to prepare and are designed to save you money. You won't be eating fewer vegetables, fruit, or meat. In fact, you may be eating more healthful foods as you learn how to shop sales and spend wisely. We've even included a chapter of vegetarian main dishes to give you more money-saving options.

You can cook these recipes with confidence for guests and potlucks—they are delicious. And if you like, you can brag about how you saved money while preparing such delectable foods.

Eating well works for everyone—and so does budgeting. No matter what shape your financial situation, you're bound to benefit from budgeting, careful shopping, and delicious, healthy eating. As we've written this book, we've benefitted from using the concepts presented in this book. We hope you do, too.

What You'll Find in This Book

This book is divided into three parts:

Part 1, "Creating and Managing Your Budget," shows you step by step how to set up a budget. You'll determine what amount to spend every month based on the size of your family and your net income and how to write a weekly menu plan. You'll adapt your budget to fit your eating style and review options for cooking meals—once a week, once a month, daily, or in a neighborhood cooking group.

Part 2, "Shopping for Groceries and Saving on Food," explains how to create a shopping list before you go to the store. At the store you'll know how to avoid the emotional and impulse pitfalls that inflate your food bill and perhaps your waistline.

You'll be comfortable eating out within your budget guidelines and find ways to add gourmet touches to your meals with gardening, fresh herbs, and preserving food.

Part 3, "Recipes for Eating Well," offers you delicious recipes that fit your budget and satisfy your food and taste desires. You'll avoid wasting food and avoid taste boredom. The recipes provide varied tastes—some traditional, some ethnic, some pop culture. The recipes call for basic and healthy foods—vegetables, meat, fruit, butter, cheese, and legumes. Each recipe contains nutritional counts so you can adapt the menu to meet your dietary preferences and restrictions.

Extras

Budgeting while eating well requires careful balancing. To help you accomplish your goals, we've added special messages that offer tips, suggestions, and warnings. Look for these sidebars to help hone your skills.

Kitchen Wise

With these suggestions, you'll save time and money when eating well.

Money Matters

You'll spend your money wisely when you use these tips.

Don't Get Burned

Gain information to avoid budgeting, spending, and cooking mistakes.

Tasty Tidbits

Use these suggestions to create delicious meals.

Acknowledgments

Lucy thanks her husband, Patrick, for his encouragement and enthusiasm. She thanks her mother, Ann, who cooked and baked for their family of seven on a tight budget while teaching Lucy how to cook. Lucy is thrilled to have written this book with her daughter-in-law, Jessica Partridge. She enjoyed Jessica's enthusiasm and joyful can-do participation.

Jessica thanks the love of her life, Patrick, and her mother, Trish, for all their support and encouragement, for all the meals enjoyed together so far, and for all the meals to come. Many thanks to Lucy, who believed in Jessica's love of food and made a terrific writing partner. Thanks also to Dr. Rebecca Hunt and Dr. Cynthia Wong of the University of Colorado at Denver for helping her find her path.

Lucy and Jessica thank their terrific agent, Marilyn Allen, and knowledgeable editor, Tom Stevens, for guiding this book from inception to publication. Special thanks to their recipe editor, Jennifer Anderson, who reviewed every ingredient and procedure to assure that the recipes are technically correct.

Special Thanks to the Technical Reviewer

The Complete Idiot's Guide to Eating Well on a Budget was reviewed by an expert who double-checked the accuracy of what you'll learn here, to help us ensure that this book gives you everything you need to know about eating well on a budget. Special thanks are extended to Jennifer Anderson.

Trademarks

All terms mentioned in this book that are known to be or are suspected of being trademarks or service marks have been appropriately capitalized. Alpha Books and Penguin Group (USA) Inc. cannot attest to the accuracy of this information. Use of a term in this book should not be regarded as affecting the validity of any trademark or service mark.

Part 1

Creating and Managing Your Budget

Sharpen your pencil, get out a spiral notebook, and keep your calculator close at hand. It's time to create your family food budget.

First of all, don't be intimidated. Even if math isn't your favorite pastime, you can easily create a workable and realistic budget. The calculator does the arithmetic, and we show you where to write the numbers.

Having a clear food budget focuses you and allows you to spend your food money wisely and feed your family well. That means eating healthy food that provides energy, well-being, and mental acuity.

The Best Nutrition at the Best Price

In This Chapter

- ◆ Making the best use of your food dollar
- ◆ Good nutrition is a good investment
- ◆ Enjoying your food preferences
- ◆ Using business principles

Eating is fun, enjoyable, and important. It's a life essential. Eating fulfills our primitive need for sustenance, but it does so much more. It defines ethnicities, socioeconomic background, and regional cultures. The thought of food and eating elicits strong emotions. People can fear food because overeating can lead to weight gain, they can love food for its delicious flavors, and they can carefully select foods based on their health-giving potential—sometimes all at once!

One thing none of us can do very well is ignore food. Even if we try to ignore it, our stomach gives us hunger pangs when we haven't eaten for several hours. Thankfully, good health—and common sense—means listening to our hunger and eating when our stomach signals that it's time to eat.

Money is just as powerful as food. We need it, we love it, and we may fear it (or fear the lack of it). Money stirs up just as many strong emotions, and our need for money is equally impossible to ignore.

The connection between food and money is basic—we need money to eat. In this chapter, we discuss how to begin managing the money-food connection in your life so that you can eat well and nutritiously while on a budget.

Money-Wise Delectable Meals

Budgeting can be fun and interesting as you gain expertise and experience. Keep a forward-thinking attitude, knowing that you are mastering how you and your family spend money. Whether you need to cut back on spending money or simply want to manage your household income better, budgeting is a great skill to develop.

> **Money Matters**
>
> Don't let yourself be a victim of "having" to live on a budget. That self-defeating attitude usually leads to failure. When a person feels deprived, it's easy to "blow off" the budget and overspend. Instead, view budgeting as a fun challenge. The reward is that you'll gain control of your finances and your life.

Many people budget regardless of how large or small their income. It makes sense to control spending—that way, there can be more money left over at the end of the month for other uses.

Budgeting is usually thought of as a business-related concept. Businesses budget costs down to the penny so that they can be profitable and, in a sense, bring home more bacon for owners and shareholders. Budgeting is also important for households and families. A well-budgeted household provides long-term financial gains and both short- and long-term peace of mind.

Thinking of your family or just yourself as a business may seem outlandish, but the truth is that using business principles works to stay happy, healthy, and solvent. In the language of business, money is a resource; food is an operating expense. Financial stability and success come when a business uses resources wisely and manages operating expenses.

You'll use the same way of thinking as you budget for food and other operating expenses such as housing, clothing, and entertainment. In the beginning, you'll analyze how many resources—money—you can allocate to food and how much food you need. This will take a couple months of tracking unless you've already been saving all of your eating and meal receipts for 2 to 3 months.

You'll determine how much food you need by such factors as the number of family members, your current eating lifestyle, the types of foods you prefer, and the nutritional value of those foods.

Budgeting Makes Cents

If you're reading this book, you've already decided to get serious about a budget. Congratulations! We love budgeting. While it may seem scary and ominous at first, budgeting is actually a relief. You'll know where the money is going, how much you can spend on food and eating, and how to pay for some treats without guilt or fear of overspending.

Budgeting brings with it emotional rewards. The corporate model of budgeting doesn't consider the emotional rewards, as shareholders are more interested in the bottom line. But as you budget yourself, you'll love those perks. You may feel less guilt about your spending because you'll know how much you can afford and how much you can't. You'll enjoy a deep sigh of relief because you won't be going into debt.

What's more, sticking to a budget can help control household splurges. When a family member asks for money or a special food, you can easily say no by blaming the budget, as in, "It's not in the budget this month, but perhaps we can add it in next month" or "It's not in the budget, but would you like to trade out another budget expenditure this month so you can have your treat?"

Yes, we're talking about delayed gratification. We all need to learn how to accept it eventually. That means you, the family, all of us. The sooner the better.

Budgeting has value in both the tough times and the good times. It makes the tough times easier and the good times even better. So keep on budgeting even when the money tide shifts for you.

 Money Matters _____

When financial times are good and one's money flow is abundant, instant gratification is so much fun. When the tide shifts, it can be hard to adjust to the need to plan purchases. You may need to save money for purchases, postpone buying luxuries, and reduce spending on entertainment and travel.

What Budgeting Is and Isn't

Budgeting sounds restrictive and boring. It certainly can be. It's a discipline and a great life skill. It can also be fun, enlightening, challenging, and satisfying. Your point of view will make the difference.

Here's what a budget and budgeting are:

♦ Information to use in making spending decisions.

♦ A factual way to gather and organize expenses for food and eating.

♦ An impartial planning tool. You'll be using numbers, not your emotions.

♦ A time investment of several hours monthly.

♦ A money-saver.

♦ A decision-making tool that gives you criteria for food and eating decisions.

♦ A tool that may let you eat more nutritionally than you do now.

Here's what budgeting is not:

♦ Going with your intuition. Your intuition is valuable in spending, but a budget doesn't account for intuition.

♦ A straightjacket with no flexibility. As a tool, budgets still leave you as the decision-maker. The budget merely gives you information.

You'll get started on the actual budgeting process in Chapter 2. Before you do, you'll identify your eating style and learn how to count calories in a whole new way.

Calories Per Dollar

When you shop for food, you're trading dollars for calories. Each person needs a certain number of calories per day to sustain life. The number of calories a person needs per day is based on height, weight, age, gender, activity level, and muscle mass. You can go to www.caloriecount.about.com to calculate how many calories you need per day. Multiply that amount by 7, and that's how many calories you need to purchase that week. If you need 2,000 calories per day, then you need 14,000 calories per week for yourself.

As a generalization, you could figure that most people need about 2,000 calories per day. To feed a family of four for a week, you'll need to purchase $2,000 \times 7 \times 4 = 56,000$ calories per week. Teenagers may require more calories; young children may need less.

Don't Get Burned

When money's tight, it's tempting to eat cheap and filling foods such as macaroni and cheese or stuffed baked potatoes. They provide many calories per dollar, but these foods are high in fat and starch. Such foods aren't nutritious and, if eaten often, can lead to health complications such as high cholesterol, high blood pressure, obesity, diabetes, and autoimmune disorders.

When you shop for groceries you don't need to count weekly calories, but knowing this information is useful.

♦ You and your family members won't gain weight if you each eat about 2,000 calories a day per adult.

♦ You don't need to purchase more food than your target number of calories for the week. This will save you money because chances are you currently purchase more food than you actually need.

♦ The formula for purchasing a certain number of calories for each week works whether you shop weekly, monthly, or stock up on special purchases.

Don't Get Burned

In this book, we won't be recommending how many dollars specifically you should spend on groceries and eating out. The price of groceries differs regionally and changes annually. Instead, we'll be recommending guidelines based on percentage of take-home income.

♦ You won't be wasting food or letting it rot in the refrigerator. If it rots because no one eats it, be wary if you consider purchasing that food in the future.

Next we'll look at how to divide those calories among the vital food groups so that you obtain the best nutritional value.

Eating the Basics

To eat well, you first need to eat the basics. Most of your calories will come from these foods:

◆ **Protein.** An adult needs 3 to 4 ounces of complete protein per meal. This amount is the size of a deck of playing cards. Complete protein contains all eight essential amino acids. They are easily obtained in ideal ratios in animal protein such as eggs, meat, fish, poultry, and cheese.

◆ **Dairy products.** Milk, cheese, yogurt, and cottage cheese provide protein, fat, and other nutrients. Milk, yogurt, and cream cheese are not as high in protein as cottage cheese and harder cheeses. To save money, use dry powdered milk in cooking.

◆ **Legumes.** You'll find vegetable protein and fiber in the wide variety of legumes: black, pinto, kidney, and navy beans, lentils, and many others. Legumes offer incomplete protein and are best eaten with small amounts of animal protein or with whole grains, such as corn or rice, to provide complete protein. Purchase canned or raw.

◆ **Vegetables and fruit.** An adult needs 5 to 10 servings of vegetables and/or fruit per day. A serving size is $\frac{1}{2}$ cup cooked or 1 cup raw. Fruits and vegetables provide vitamins, minerals, fiber, and antioxidants. The most nutritious forms are fresh and frozen. You may want to keep a couple cans of vegetables in your pantry for convenience, but plan to purchase vegetables and fruits weekly.

◆ **Starchy vegetables.** Starchy vegetables are white potatoes, red potatoes, and sweet potatoes. Pass on the white and fluffy potatoes because they're high-glycemic, high in starch, and provide little nutritional value. Use sweet potatoes or red potatoes instead. Baked sweet potatoes are fabulous! High-glycemic foods are carbohydrates that are quickly digested by the stomach into simple sugars. These cause a quick lift in blood

Don't Get Burned

Processed soy products such as tofu, soy protein powder, and soy milk don't provide complete protein. Eat these foods with whole grains, dairy, or animal protein to obtain your body's daily need for protein.

Money Matters

Tomatoes, olives, green chiles, pineapple, crushed garlic, and tomato paste in cans or jars are usually good buys and are an exception to the "fresh or frozen" rule.

sugar levels and in insulin levels. Eating high-glycemic foods, such as simple starches, high-fructose corn syrup, and sugars causes weight gain and leads to insulin resistance, metabolic syndrome, and may lead to type 2 diabetes.

> ### Kitchen Wise
>
> Whether or not to purchase organic produce is a challenging decision. It usually costs more but not always. It's usually a healthier choice than conventionally grown produce. When you can afford it, go organic, but don't feel guilty if you can't. If you can only purchase some organic produce, opt for soft-skinned items such as strawberries, spinach, pears, peaches, and nectarines.

- **Whole grains.** Wheat berries, barley, steel-cut oats, and rice are healthy forms of starch. Serve in casseroles or as a side dish for lunches and dinners. Serve for breakfast with protein and fruit.

- **Butter and olive oil.** Keep these two fats on hand and you won't need any others. Use olive oil for coating pans, light sautéing, and dressing salads and vegetables. Use butter for baking, on cooked vegetables, and to spread on bread or cooked grains.

- **Stone-ground bread.** This is the best bread for the value. It's rich, highest in fiber, hearty, and filling. The taste is nutty and the aroma enticing. Purchase genuine stone-ground bread that doesn't contain additives or wheat flour. You'll eat less and be more satisfied.

> ### Money Matters
>
> White bread is okay to eat, but it's not as nutritious as stone-ground bread. Fluffy white and whole-wheat breads, with the exception of sourdough bread, are high-glycemic, making them a poor choice for health or eating well.

- **Nuts.** Purchase in the shell for snacking. Taking the time to remove the shell slows you down, so you'll eat a smaller serving of nuts and get more pleasure from eating. Nuts are high in good fats and offer vegetable protein. Keep packaged walnuts on hand for cooking.

- **Condiments.** Some offer nutritional value, others add zest to your meals. Purchase these when the price is right: olives, pickles, salsa, chutney, fruit preserves, relish, ketchup, mustard, mayonnaise, horseradish, barbecue sauce, dried fruit, and other flavorful meal additions.

◆ **Coffee and tea.** If you enjoy these and consider them a necessity, make them at home and include them in your budget.

To plan a meal, start with the protein and then add 2 to 3 servings of vegetables and fruit. Use the Plate Method, discussed in the next section, to ensure that you eat the correct amounts of the basic foods.

The Plate Method

Knowing how much food to put on your plate is easy when you use the Plate Method. Fill everyone's plate in the kitchen before you bring the plates to the table. You'll know that everyone is obtaining a good balance of the most important foods.

If you are so inclined, you can figure the amount of calories you're placing on each plate. While the total for the day should be about 2,000, breakfast and lunch may contain fewer calories than dinner. Here's what to put on each plate:

The Plate Method.

- Fill about half of your plate with nonstarchy vegetables such as green beans, peas, carrots, lettuce, cucumbers, tomatoes, zucchini, and onions.

- Fill about one eighth of your plate with low-glycemic starches, fruit, or dairy products.

- One fourth of your plate is for lean protein, including meats, seafood, eggs, cheese, or poultry. That's enough room for about 3 to 4 ounces, or 15 to 20 grams.

- The remaining wedge of your plate, or about one eighth, is for healthy fats such as olive oil, avocados, and nuts and seeds.

Kitchen Wise

By filling almost half your plate with vegetables and having another quarter for fruit, you'll be sure to eat the recommended amount of 5 to 10 servings of vegetables and fruit every day.

In actuality, your plate won't look exactly like this. Usually, the fats will be part of your foods—such as dressing for your vegetables—and protein may include nuts and seeds sprinkled over your salad. And, as you know, oils run and spread over the plate.

You may be wondering where dessert fits on the plate. Figure it goes into the spot reserved for fruit/starchy vegetables or for fat. This reminds you to save room in your stomach for dessert, if you plan to eat some. It also helps keep your dessert portion size small but adequate.

Money Wasters

The ingredients listed here offer virtually no nutrition. They are in packaged foods, and purchasing them can waste money. In other words, buy these and you'll end up paying lots of money for no food value.

Before we list the ingredients, you need to know that we eat these foods from time to time, and you will, too. We know that. Just weigh the value based on your budgetary and food needs.

- **High-fructose corn syrup.** Check the ingredient list on sodas, candy, cookies, cakes, pastry, muffins, and electrolyte replenishment beverages. Your body doesn't want HFCS—high-fructose corn syrup. New research on the health concerns about this ingredient indicates it's a factor in metabolic syndrome and diabetes.

◆ **Artificial sweeteners.** Aspartame, Equal, sucralose, and Splenda are added to many products such as yogurt, beverages, baked goods, and candy.

◆ **Funny colors.** Think of the colors in jelly beans. Nature didn't supply those. They are created with dyes. Biologically, your body doesn't quite know what to do with them. But they sure are pretty.

◆ **Mystery ingredients.** They have unpronounceable names and are usually food additives used as preservatives, flavorings, and we're not sure what else. If you can't pronounce it, chances are good your body doesn't require it for nutrition.

The preceding ingredients are in many processed foods. Yet you can also find delicious processed foods that don't contain these no-no's. Become an ingredient-list reader and choose only those foods that provide you with value for your money—both economic and nutritional.

Possible Extras

Some foods are fun to eat and enjoy but may not be nutrient dense. They add a certain zest to a meal or snack. When your budget can afford these foods, enjoy small amounts. Think of them as add-ons, not the main course.

◆ Corn chips, potato chips, and dips.

◆ Bottled full-fat salad dressings. Low-fat dressings usually contain mystery ingredients and high-glycemic ingredients.

◆ Chocolate.

◆ Ice cream. Pure ice cream contains good nutritional value, but it's in this list because it's a treat food.

◆ 100% fruit juice. Avoid purchasing fruit "cocktails" or juices with added sugar or high-fructose corn syrup. We added juice to this list because nutritionally it's better to eat the fruit than drink the juice.

◆ Pasta. Pasta is a starch and can be nutritionally neutral or not, based on how you cook it. If you stop the cooking process before the pasta reaches the al dente point—almost crunchy—the pasta is low-glycemic and a viable addition to your meal. If you cook pasta longer, it's best not to eat it; it becomes a fattening starch. Eat pasta moderately as it offers little nutritional value.

◆ Foods high in nitrates—such as some cured bacon, packaged luncheon meats, and sausage—should be consumed in moderation.

Money Matters

Notice we haven't included alcoholic beverages in our lists. For the purposes of your budget, categorize them as entertainment and not food. Beer, wine, and spirits don't contain enough nutritional value to be considered a food.

Include these foods in a meal after you've eaten the basics and have room left in your stomach for more food—and room left in your budget for treats.

The Least You Need to Know

◆ Budgeting is an important life skill to use in managing your household.

◆ Purchase enough calories per week to feed your family and not more.

◆ Choose foods that provide the best nutritional value and avoid those that don't.

◆ Avoid filling up on starchy and fatty foods that don't provide nutrition.

2

The Budget

In This Chapter

- ◆ Setting a realistic food budget
- ◆ Committing to a budget
- ◆ Managing your food budget

Right now, sticking to a food budget may seem like a huge challenge. You want to manage your money wisely, but you also want the benefits of a healthy lifestyle, including delicious, wholesome foods.

It's true that a food budget combines some seemingly opposing concepts. On one hand, eating satisfies your body's basic need for sustenance, strength, health, and energy while also satisfying your palate and providing sensory satisfaction. On the other hand, budgeting is about controlling expenses, counting, accounting, and responsibility.

In this chapter, we focus on your household needs for the productive and exacting task of managing a budget. In later chapters, we'll show you how to use your food budget to provide both sustenance and pleasure.

Don't be put off by being accountable. You'll have newfound confidence in your food choices when you manage your money. You'll be certain that your purchasing decisions will keep you and your family well fed and keep you "in the black"—a financial term that means you're making more money than you're spending.

Budgets Are Your Friend

Often you'll hear folks talk about needing to go on a food budget for groceries, eating out, and treat foods. That declaration can sound like someone vowing to go on a diet and watch what they eat. Unless a person has a workable plan, those good intentions won't produce weight loss. In fact, they could produce guilt and regret and, in some cases, weight gain.

So, too, the person who's budgeting needs a concrete food and eating budget plan. When you use this valuable tool—the budget—you can rest comfortably knowing that you are in control. This makes you powerful—money doesn't control you; you control your money. You control the food budget, and food costs don't control your life. You may even like the peace of mind and financial rewards of budgeting so much that you'll continue to budget in both your prosperous and lean money times.

Most people have a money supply that changes based on life circumstances and income. A family may feel quite prosperous with ample disposable income for the fun things. Then, when twin daughters graduate from high school and enter college, the fun money gets used for textbooks, tuition, and room and board. They may find themselves in a cash crunch. Job transitions, relocations, promotions, downsizing, and retirement will change your budget numbers and require a budget review and appropriate adjustments. Budgeting is an important life-management tool no matter what your current financial situation.

Here's the good news: budgeting will make you money. Perhaps not your first year, but if you keep a budget year after year and stay faithful to that budget, you'll end up with more money than if you didn't budget. The reason is that you'll think twice before you splurge on a frivolous dinner out unless it's in the budget. In addition, your monthly budget review will remind you to adjust your spending when needed.

Pick a Number

Your very first step is setting a preliminary budget amount. After you use your budget for a couple of months, you'll be able to come up with a reasonable amount. You'll learn where you actually spend your food money, how many treat and luxury items you need, and how many you can live without. Then you can choose what type of eating and food lifestyle works best for you and your family.

A friend phoned recently with the news that he and his wife could eat for $30 a week. Huh? Sounds terrific, but let's examine the facts. That amounts to 71¢ per meal per person for 3 meals a day, or 21 meals a week, without paying for snacks. On that very limited budget, they couldn't order in pizza, eat at a fast-food joint, purchase a latte at the coffee shop, or go out to lunch with friends. If two people needed to eat on $30 a week, they could do it. But it would take commitment and very careful shopping.

Think carefully when you read about saving money on food. One recent article showed how to feed a family of four on $10 per meal. Sounds good, but if you do the numbers, at 90 meals per month, that family of four is spending $900 a month on food, not including snacks. Ten dollars per meal is not so economical. In fact, it's a very high food budget.

Before you choose your budget number, let's look at some methods that could work for you.

If you have grocery store and restaurant receipts from the past few months, add them up to determine what you're currently spending. Choose your monthly budget number based on what's reasonable or on how much you need or want to cut back. If you don't have past receipts, start saving each receipt from every food, eating, dining, and treat purchase. Keep them in one place, like an envelope or a drawer, so you know where they are when you need them.

 Money Matters _____

Without tracking your food budget, you could still overspend when using only cost-cutting tips. Request sales receipts for all cash purchases as well as those made with checks and credit cards. You'll use these to keep track of your budget.

The Bureau of Labor Statistics figures that, on average, people spend 12 to 13 percent of their take-home income on food. To calculate a monthly budget, use this equation: Monthly income less taxes times 0.125 equals monthly food budget. If your net monthly income is over $6,000 a month, this number is probably too high.

If you aren't currently employed, you need to figure your preliminary budget differently. In 2009 dollars, you can feed two adults luxuriously for $500 per month. Figuring 90 meals per month, not including snacks, that's $5.50 per meal. Eating conservatively, that amount could be $300 ($3.34 per meal) or even $250 ($2.78 per meal). A family of four could eat well but conservatively for $500.

If you have no idea what your budget should be, pick a number that seems practical for you. After a couple months of tallying up your spending on food items, you'll know how much you're spending and what adjustments you need to make to your budget.

"Pick a number" works because budgeting allows for changes as you gain new information or as your financial circumstances change.

Types of Food Purchases

As you budget, notice which types of food purchases you make. We've listed some possibilities in this section. You can include each of these types of purchases in your food budget as subcategories. You may find that you can eliminate or cut back on some of these purchases with no compromise in nutrition or satisfaction.

Habitual purchases. You may stop at the coffee shop every day for specialty coffee or tea. Or perhaps you tend to always purchase a soda at the gas station. These purchases are habit forming and don't contain dietary value. Which of these can you cut back on or eliminate?

Takeout. Some days you can't cook dinner, and yet you need to eat and feed your family. When you want takeout and you have takeout as a budget item, go for it. Otherwise, make another plan. Have some dinners cooked ahead or waiting in the freezer for a takeout day.

Junk foods. Junk foods are packaged and processed items from the grocery store that don't contain much if any nutritional value. Rather, they contain plenty of calories, starch, sugar, and/or fat. These include sodas, diet sodas, electrolyte beverages, and caffeine-powered drinks. Add cookies, candy, crackers, muffins, pastries, popcorn, doughnuts, chips, and pretzels. Fruit juice beverages that contain high-fructose corn syrup or added sugar are also considered junk food.

Don't Get Burned

The next time you dine at a sit-down restaurant, notice the price of coffee, tea, and a glass of wine. They're probably higher than you thought. You may choose not to order them again.

Restaurants. Eating out is a part of your food budget. This includes fast-food places, lunch carts, buffets, and seated dining eateries. When you're eating out, be careful not to order food you don't need. Take a pass on dessert, appetizers, and fancy beverages if they aren't in the budget.

Core foods. These are the food items that you and your family enjoy eating, and they are the core foods of your menus. They are the "meat and potatoes," so to speak, of your daily food intake. Think eggs, lean meats, cheese, fruit, vegetables, and healthy fats.

Luxury foods. These are the crème-de-la-crème of culinary delights. They're pricey and highly desired. Examples are gourmet cheeses, salted mixed nuts, rib eye steaks, and fancy chocolates.

> **Tasty Tidbits**
>
> We all love luxury foods, so check out grocery store sales and purchase them when you can get a good deal. Even luxury is sometimes affordable.

If you're on a tight budget, focus on purchasing core foods and reduce or eliminate the other purchase categories. If you really want a specialty food item, such as a latte or gourmet chocolate, be sure to include it in the budget.

Starting to Budget

Budgeting is a process. To use your budget effectively, you'll be working with it at least once a week and again at the end of the month. Your weekly budget sessions involve recording all of your purchases. At the end of the month, you'll evaluate how well you stuck to your budget and determine what changes to make the next month.

Make sure you have these items when you do your budget:

1. Every receipt for food purchases from grocery stores, fast-food restaurants, gas stations, restaurants, ball games, and other entertainment centers. The snack dispenser at work doesn't give receipts, so make a note of how much you spent on those snacks.

2. A notebook in which you'll record all purchases. A bookkeeping notebook with six columns is nice but not necessary.

3. A calculator.

> **Don't Get Burned**
>
> Don't get lulled into thinking that the soft drink you purchase when you fill up your gas tank doesn't count. It does. So does the frozen latte you enjoy at the coffee shop. By being rigorous with yourself early in the budgeting and accounting process, you may be able to enjoy those treats within your budget—and without guilt—once you do the accounting.

Keep all receipts, the notebook, and the calculator where you can find them. Place all receipts for the month together in an envelope, file folder, or shoe box. You need to be able to locate them easily when you do the bookkeeping.

Put It in Writing

Label your notebook with your name, phone number, and "Food Budget Notebook." On the first page, write your starting-point budget. Then turn to the second page. You'll be using a new page for each week. At the top of the page, write the date and your weekly budget amount. Draw five vertical columns on the page. Label the columns:

> Date purchased
> Store or location
> Type of food purchase
> Cash, check, or credit card
> Amount
> Totals

Record each receipt from that week in your notebook. Be sure to include the type of food purchase (i.e., junk food, restaurant, luxury foods, etc.) so you can easily review how you're spending your food dollars. At the end of the week, total your purchases. Do this for each week in the month. Since the beginning and ending weeks of a month usually don't contain 7 days, you may have five or even six pages per month.

At the end of the month, label the next page "Actual vs. Budget." On that page, record your total food expense for the month and your budget number. If the two numbers are close, congratulations. You've met your budget goals.

If your expenses exceeded your budget, you're not alone. Most people who read this book will be amazed that they overspent by "that much." Don't feel bad. It's not time to get upset with yourself or your family. It's time to make adjustments and corrections. In other words, it's time to manage the budget.

Computer Solutions

If you have access to a computer, you'll love using money management software. You still need to enter your receipts accurately, but after that the computer takes over. It can ...

- Tally your expenses.

- Figure actual expenditures versus budget.

- Sort totals by store to let you know how much you spent at the grocery store or how much you spent at the coffee shop.

- Suggest a budget number after you've input several months of expenditures.

- Store budget vs. actual information for each month and for each year so that you can make changes as your life changes.

- Assist you in managing your entire household budget items—not just your food budget.

Tasty Tidbits

Our favorite accounting and budgeting software is Quicken. We've used it for years to manage our entire household budget. However, there are many very good money management software programs available. They are worth every cent you pay, provided you learn how to use the software and use it every month.

- Calculate your food budget as a percentage of take-home income.

Whether you use a manual system or a computer system to record your purchases, only you can do the management strategizing that puts you in charge of your food and eating.

Managing Your Budget

Now is the time to take charge and control your expenditures. You have power because you have knowledge. You also have clarity. Your next steps include managing and making spending decisions:

1. Determine how much less you need to spend every month on food to meet the budget.

2. Figure out what types of food purchases you can reduce or eliminate: habitual, takeout, junk food, or luxury items.

3. Plan how to prepare and eat your core foods.

Kitchen Wise _____

If you want cooperation, don't "cold turkey" everyone from their favorite fluff and junk foods. That breeds rebellion and sneaking. Instead, offer fluff and junk treats less frequently and prepare some at home instead. Home-baked cookies actually taste better.

4. Educate your family about the budget and your plans for eating and meals. Ask what foods they want you to prepare and which ones they don't like or won't eat. Enlist their cooperation in limiting fluff food and junk food purchases.

5. Continue to track food, grocery, and dining-out expenses weekly and compare to your budget.

6. If you're spending too much early in the month and think you won't meet your budget goal, figure out how to cut back for the remainder of the month.

Put your specific budget management plan in writing on the next page of your budget notebook. Include items like "prepare meals five evenings a week," "cook ahead and freeze some meals to replace takeout," or "bake cookies once a week." You may want to pack lunches more often or ask other family members to cook on a regular schedule.

Helpful Budgeting Tools

You'll find plenty of outside support for managing the food budget. Become a well-informed shopper and take advantage of these tools and techniques:

♦ Plan weekly menus. You'll find plenty of great choices in our recipe chapters. Enlist other family members in creating a meal plan for a day or an evening meal.

♦ Add variety to your meals to satisfy your palate and your family's. Too much of the same taste gets boring. Even if you love Mexican food, a steady diet of it becomes tasteless.

♦ Gather grocery store sale fliers from the newspaper and Internet. Shop the sales for core foods and special foods.

♦ Use coupons. Clip from magazines and newspapers. Find coupons online for foods you'll eat.

♦ Schedule how often you'll eat out or get takeout. Spontaneity is fun, but it can quickly blow the budget.

Initially, managing the food budget can seem like too much work. We empathize. If you've never budgeted before, this is quite a change. But budgeting is a worthwhile activity. Taking on this kind of responsibility and accountability propels you toward your personal and financial goals. The discipline required extends into many other areas of your life.

The Least You Need to Know

- ◆ Determine your food budget based on past purchases for groceries and eating out.

- ◆ Reduce your consumption of fluff and junk foods to save money.

- ◆ Enlist the entire family's support in managing the food budget.

- ◆ Use a manual or computer system for tracking food and eating expenses.

Chapter 3

Managing Your Eating Style

In This Chapter

- ◆ Evaluating your food preferences
- ◆ Making food-style and lifestyle changes
- ◆ Solutions for cutting back
- ◆ Budgeting is a family project
- ◆ Revising the budget

Cutting back on food purchases and spending less money on food sounds simple in principle. But reality is a whole different matter. Your eating style is tied to many complex lifestyle choices, some that you control and some that you don't.

For a moment, set aside the issues of emotional eating or dieting. Most likely, you control what food goes in your mouth when you're eating alone. At that time, it's easy to stick with your budget. But things become much more challenging on your lunch break with friends, when your children demand treats at the grocery store, and when family members complain or refuse to respect the food budget. Research shows that a person's food consumption increases when eating with one or more people. If dining with five or more people, a person may consume as much as 75 percent more food than if they ate alone.

In this chapter, we guide you through making food and eating lifestyle changes. Then we explain how to compare your actual expenses to the budget so you can make evaluations and adjustments.

What's Your Style?

Honoring your food preferences is important for your budgeting success. Research has shown that people who eat foods they don't enjoy won't receive optimal nutritional value. The foods, though, need to have real nutritional value to begin with.

We've grouped food preferences in the following categories to help you determine your current eating style:

Gourmet all the way. You prefer the fancier and usually more expensive foods available at specialty and health food groceries. This type of eating is hard to support on a limited budget. Consider cooking with the wide variety of spices and condiments that may already be in your pantry. Opt for simple preparation with elegant presentation of lean meats, vegetables, fish, fruit, and healthy fats.

Fast food and takeout is my nirvana. You're busy, you hate to cook, no one likes the meals you cook, or you don't know how to cook. Whatever the reason, you prefer fast food or takeout convenience. You can still budget, but your costs will be higher than cooking at home. Consider encouraging a family member to take up cooking, joining a neighborhood cooking co-op, or taking a cooking class in everyday meals.

The kitchen is my haven. You're already comfortable in the kitchen and love to prepare food. It's still possible to overspend when cooking at home, especially if you regularly cook elaborate meals with pricey ingredients. You can make changes to the way you purchase, prepare, and store foods to lower your total food costs. Be sure to include nutrient-dense ingredients to get the most value from your food dollars.

Tasty Tidbits

Some foods may taste good to you but are virtually devoid of nutritional value, such as popcorn and diet soda. We don't consider them food preferences; we consider them nonfood preferences. You can budget for them, but they don't qualify as "eating well."

Kitchen Wise

Nutrient-dense foods contain more healthful nutrition than other foods. Whole fruit is more nutrient dense than fruit juice. Corn on the cob is more nutrient dense than popcorn. Stoneground bread is more nutrient dense than white bread.

All of the above. You love gourmet foods, you get takeout or eat out some of the time, and you cook some of the time. Your flexibility will make it easier to choose your budgeting priorities, but you may be tempted to stray from your budget because you enjoy so many options. Sticking to a food and eating plan is the best way to avoid losing sight of your budget.

No matter what your eating style, you can save money with budgeting. It may be easiest if you already love to cook, but in this book, you'll learn ways to cut costs no matter what eating style you prefer.

Where to Cut Back

Your eating lifestyle probably contains a strong social aspect. This makes it difficult to budget or cut back spending. Read through the following list and find the events you enjoy that involve food. Then read our recommendations for making changes.

Lunch at work. The easiest way to save money is to pack a lunch and eat in the lunchroom or outdoors in warm weather. If you often eat out with your colleagues, arrange to meet them only one or two days a week and brown bag it the other days.

Coffee breaks. If your workplace provides coffee and hot water, that's great. If not, bring a thermos of your favorite brew. Not realistic? Then budget for how many cups of coffee or cans of soda you'll pay for each week.

Kitchen Wise

Eating your sack lunch at your desk saves money, but it may not give your mind a break or give you a chance to refresh your energy for the afternoon work ahead. As best you can, eat somewhere else.

The soda habit. Drinking sodas often or continually throughout the day isn't a good idea for lots of reasons. They don't provide food value and don't improve your health, but they can certainly harm it. The harm can be slight, such as developing sensitive teeth, or it can be severe, such as increasing your risk of developing diabetes and heart disease. If you can't stop completely, start by cutting back to one or two sodas a day. Be sure to include the cost in your food budget.

The coffee shop. One friend figured that at $5 per visit, her daily latte habit was costing $150 per month. She was living on a limited budget and had never tallied the coffee-shop damage to her budget. If she added in a luscious pastry, the cost soared further. If you love the coffee shop, visit less frequently, perhaps once or twice a week.

Another solution is to pack your own tea bag, ask for a cup of hot water, which is free, and leave a dollar tip in the jar. Even so, you'll be saving money.

After-school snacks. These can be a fun part of family time and an important opportunity for your children to refuel before they go outside to play or tackle homework. Rather than open containers of fruit-flavored drinks and individually packaged cookies and cakes, serve homemade foods that provide healthy nutrition, such as peanut butter and celery sticks, apples, oranges, and cheese. For a beverage, choose diluted juice, water, or milk.

TV eating. We've known folks who polish off an entire bag of potato chips while idly watching evening sitcoms. Eat your food and snacks at the kitchen or dining room table. Your budget and waistline will thank you.

At the movies. Check out the prices of popcorn, candy, and sodas at movie theaters. They'll break your budget. Theaters generally don't allow you to carry in snacks from home, so eat before or after you go to movies.

Event eating. Food and snacks at sporting and cultural events are pricey because you're a captive audience. Many ballparks check bags and confiscate any food you attempt to bring in, even bottled water. If you can't make it through a ballgame without brats and lemonade, enjoy. But make sure to add the cost of event eating into your food budget.

Fast-food meals. A friend added up her fast-food expenses for one year for herself and her two young sons. The tally: over $5,000. It seems impossible, but it sure was convenient. Telling this to her husband wasn't fun. Thank goodness her guilt changed their eating habits quickly. The guilt wasn't only about the money she spent; she was also involved in the wellness business and knew better than to feed her children that much junk food. Limit fast-food meals and include them in the weekly budget.

Social expectations. Does your social group eat out often and spend plenty of money doing it? If so, you may need to find ways to curtail dining out while still seeing your friends. You may want to meet them at the theater and forego dinner or even pass on some outings. Explain that you're watching your food budget. You may be able to suggest other activities that don't require eating, such as visiting a museum or enjoying outdoor sports.

Money Matters _____

Research shows that people who eat with one other person eat 35 percent more food than if they'd eaten alone. When eating with four or more people, a person's intake increases about 75 percent. If you eat with a large group, your food intake can increase by 95 percent. Take care not to overeat when you eat with others. It can ruin your budget and your waistline.

Emotional eating. When you aren't hungry and you eat to soothe emotional stress, you're likely to blow the budget. Adding to the inclination toward bingeing is the fact that tough economic times are emotionally stressful. Develop good stress-management habits now. Learn to relax, exercise, and pursue other interests such as reading books from the library, sewing, or gardening to soothe your troubled emotions.

These money-saving suggestions can work for you and family members. Enlist everyone's support and ask for suggestions to manage these eating situations.

Where Not to Cut Back

Budgeting is about being realistic. You can set yourself up for failure and even more expense if you don't take into account the human factor. Your bodily needs and your emotional health are vital to budgeting and eating well.

◆ Don't cut back on nutrition basics. It's tempting to cut out the foods that seem pricey and fill up on heavy-duty starches and cheap fats. They will sustain life but not well. To be a healthy person, you need vegetables and fruit, lean protein, and good fats. Surprisingly, a person doesn't need high-starch foods at all for health. In later chapters, we'll tell you how to purchase produce and lean protein on a budget.

Money Matters _____

Each recipe in this book was graded by a nutritional-standards website. All of the recipes received either an A or B for healthy meals. They supply good nutritional value and will save you money, too.

◆ Don't eliminate special foods required for special diets, such as those for allergies, diabetes, and other chronic health conditions.

- Eat at the table. Eating meals and snacks sitting down at the kitchen or dining room table makes meals more valued and important. This saves money indirectly by eliminating mindless snacking and overeating on the run.

- Don't give up all your treat foods. If you cut back too much on your favorite foods, you may experience a backlash in which you overspend and overeat. Instead, use moderation. Have some, but not as much as before.

- Don't deprive yourself and your family. Budgeting doesn't require eating at near-to-starvation levels. If you cut back everyone's calorie intake too much or serve undesirable foods, all sorts of weird things can happen, such as food hoarding, bingeing, and the creation of a food black market in your own household.

- Don't think budgeting will help you diet or lose weight. External events seldom motivate a person to lose weight and keep it off. Losing weight is a personal choice and requires motivation from within. If the timing's right for you and you are ready to be a thin person, then you can use budgeting and calorie management as a tool in your endeavor.

- Don't use budgeting as a way to put others on a diet. For the same reasons just mentioned, it won't work. And people don't like being manipulated.

Your budgeting will work best when you manage these items for yourself and your family members.

The Budgeting Family

Most likely, your family has diverse eating and food preferences. Some members love vegetables; others think that the only acceptable green food is a green M&M. Others crave meat and lots of it. Some will only eat brand-name boxed breakfast cereal. Others are more easy-going about what they eat.

Kitchen Wise _____

It's important to ask for the support of everyone in the family when you cut back on food expenses and go on a budget. Otherwise, you could end up with rebellion and unpleasant meals.

Just the thought of managing a food budget with so many different needs sounds tiring. Don't give up. Sort. We'll help you sort through everyone's needs so that you can then begin to win your family over to eating on a budget.

With paper and pen, list each person in the family.
Then interview them one at a time. If you consider their needs as important at this stage in the planning, you'll get more "buy in" later when you need it.

Here's how to have the budget conversation:

◆ Explain to each person that the family needs to cut back on spending on food and other items. They'll be cutting back on specialty foods, treats, and eating out. Emphasize that you want to eat very healthfully. You need their support and want to know if they'll help you plan how the family can eat on a budget.

◆ Ask them which foods they can give up and which ones they most enjoy eating. Find out what foods they would refuse to eat. Write down their responses. This will be helpful in menu planning.

◆ Ask for their support and ask them to be cheerful and accepting of this challenging situation. You're asking them to sacrifice some of their personal needs for the good of the whole family. This isn't easy to do because each person has personal food attachments. Let them know you understand. By empathizing with their emotions about food budgets, you'll find it easier to gain support. After all, you do empathize. You yourself need to make similar sacrifices to live within the budget.

Part of managing a food budget is being able to say no to yourself and family members. If you aren't great at this, practice. Strengthen your "no" muscle. If you receive lots of resistance, remind them of the family group effort.

You may also become skilled in negotiating as you budget. What expenditures would a person trade to gain a treat food? Is the trade really worth it?

Because food has a nurturing aspect, find other satisfying ways to nurture yourself and your family. Bake birthday cakes instead of purchasing them. Decorate gingerbread man cookies together. Hold family game nights. Read the entertainment section of the paper carefully to scout out free entertainment events. Attend free concerts, hot air balloon shows, and free days at the zoo or botanical gardens.

Create a reward for meeting the budget each month. Don't make the reward about food, though. That would send a confusing message. Make it a reward that is nurturing and special.

Actual vs. Expenses

For each month, record your food and eating expenses in your notebook or on the computer. Add them up and you have your actual expenditures.

Now comes the moment of reckoning. You've set your monthly food and eating spending goal. You have a month's worth of expenses tallied. Compare the two numbers. How did you do?

- ◆ **On the money.** The two numbers are within 5 to 10 percent of each other. For example, if you budgeted $100 and your actual expenditures ranged between $90 and $110, you're close enough. If you went over, you may want to cut back some for the next month, but overall you and your family performed very well to keep costs in budget.

- ◆ **Money left over.** For example, you budgeted $100 and spent less than $90. This can be a cause for celebration or a cause for concern. Extra money doesn't mean it's time to splurge. It's time to understand why you underspent and make adjustments, if necessary. Be concerned if you didn't eat adequate amounts of the three major nutrient groups: vegetables and fruit, lean protein, and good fats. If that's the case, you need to spend more money next month on these foods.

- ◆ **Deficit spending.** You overspent the budget by more than 10 percent. This means that if your budget was $100, you spent over $110. You need to make one of two adjustments: either increase the budget because it was unrealistically low or study your expenditures to find the reason you overspent. Some possible causes are too much eating out, too many treats, having guests over for meals, wasting food, impulse purchases, or too much junk food. Figure out what adjustments you need to make and incorporate them into next month's budget plan.

Turn to the next page in your budget notebook, record your adjustments, if any, and you're ready to record next month's expenses.

Household budgeting is an ongoing process for families, just as it is for businesses. After several months, budgeting will become a regular part of your management style.

The Least You Need to Know

- ◆ Understand your eating and food style as you design your budgeting strategies.
- ◆ Don't fill up on cheap empty and fattening calories to cut your food expenses.
- ◆ Cut back on food and eating situations that are habitual and pricey but not necessary.
- ◆ Involve your family in food and eating budget decisions.
- ◆ Compare actual spending to the budget and make adjustments.

Food and Menu Planning

In This Chapter

- Choosing hearty meals on a budget
- Saving money by planning
- Varying flavors and ingredients

You've heard of penny-pinching college students who survive on ramen noodles and cola during the last semester before graduation. They sustain life on a very limited budget by eating a highly unpalatable—and unhealthy—diet.

After 3 or 4 months of that diet, we'll bet they never do it again. Beyond the fact that eating probably became nightmarish, they weren't obtaining enough nutrition to think clearly, have high stamina, or score well on those challenging finals.

You don't need to impoverish your meals or starve yourself in order to save money. But you do need to plan. Overall, unplanned eating is costly. The simple act of planning will save you money, and planning cost-saving meals takes you one step further toward meeting your overall budget goals.

Planning Weekly Menus

Now that you know your eating style and have set a weekly food budget, it's time to plan. Creating weekly menus is the next step in eating well on a budget. Plan before you make a grocery list and before you go shopping.

Planning may seem boring or challenging—after all, you don't know specifically what you'll be hungry for at each meal. So be sure to include some flexibility in your meal schedule.

Menu Planning Worksheets

The tools you need are simple. Use a spiral notebook, print off a weekly calendar from your computer, or use the weekly menu planning worksheet provided later in this chapter. Save your planning sheets or notebook pages so you can refer to them as you plan meals in the future.

Kitchen Wise _____

In this book, we've chosen to use a week as the basis of planning menus and meals. You can also plan by the month if that works best for you. But we don't recommend that you plan by the day. Daily food planning is ultimately more costly.

Money Matters _____

The Internet offers many menu planning sites. Some will even do the calorie computations for you. Take advantage of these free offerings by searching for "menu planning."

Here's how to use the menu planner:

1. Enter the dates for the week in the upper-left column.

2. Check with your own and family members' calendars to categorize each meal for the week. Which meals will you eat out, which meals require a sack lunch, which will you eat at home? How much time do you have to prepare meals each day? Mark these on your planner. For the meals you'll eat at home, write how many family members will eat at each meal.

3. Count the number of breakfasts, lunches, dinners, and snacks you'll need for the week. If some family members won't be eating at home for a particular meal, you can prepare less food.

Choosing Family Favorites

Now make a list of your family's favorite meals. You'll need to ignore the lobster and drawn butter and other special meals to save money, but include your everyday favorites.

Does your family like Italian? Mexican? Asian? Do they prefer stir-fry or casseroles? Which vegetables will they eat? Think about what meals you and your family will like to eat when making your plan. Page through the recipes in this book if you need some ideas.

Think, too, about breakfast. Does your family prefer eggs and bacon or breakfast cereal with milk and fruit? Do they like peanut butter on toast before work or school? Plan each meal, including breakfast, according to what your family will eat.

Group recipes by their main protein ingredient—if not on paper, then at least in your mind. What dishes use beef roast? Ground beef? Turkey? Cheese? Legumes? You can save money by making several meals from one chuck roast or one turkey.

If your family likes to eat new flavors and new cuisines, add some of those into your preferred foods list. If you have picky eaters, you may need to provide some of their acceptable foods at each meal.

When you give your family members the tastes they prefer, they're less likely to be dissatisfied with eating on a budget. An inexpensive cut of beef can be as tasty as sirloin if it's seasoned the same and cooked to similar tenderness.

 Money Matters

Breakfast is an important meal for nutrition and energy. If some family members tend to skip breakfast, suggest—but don't demand—that they eat. Stuffing down food to please a parent creates more resentment than it's worth.

 Kitchen Wise

One friend manages the budget and eating with the picky eaters in her family by always having peanut butter, cheese, and bread in the kitchen. That way, the children can make themselves a sandwich for dinner if they don't want to eat the entrée she's prepared.

The Big Pot Theory

You're not quite ready to fill in your menus for the week. Before you think about buying individual ingredients for each meal, you should consider the Big Pot Theory.

Cooking a large amount of meat or soup early in the week, then saving it for the main ingredient in later meals, can save you money and make it easier to plan.

One example of the Big Pot Theory is to cook a large turkey breast in the slow cooker for 4 to 6 hours with simple seasoning, such as salt and pepper. You'll have enough meat for four meals for a family of four. You don't need to add liquid to the slow cooker because the long, slow cooking lets the turkey braise in its own juices.

1. Serve sliced turkey with gravy for dinner that evening with vegetables and a tossed salad.

2. Make a turkey stir-fry with chopped celery and green peppers over cooked rice. Season with soy sauce and ginger and sprinkle with toasted sesame seeds.

3. Make tacos with shredded or chopped turkey topped with lettuce, tomatoes, shredded cheese, and salsa.

4. Make turkey sandwiches with mayonnaise and lettuce. Add a cooked green vegetable.

In a slow cooker, or in a large covered baking pan in the oven, cook a beef chuck roast in low heat (250°F) for 2 to 3 hours, or longer based on the size of the roast. You don't need to add any liquid because the roast will braise in its own juices. This makes the meat exceptionally tender. Add carrots and red potatoes during the last 45 minutes of roasting. Here are four meals you can make from this single meat purchase:

1. Pot roast with carrots and potatoes. Serve with pan juices on the side.

2. Baked enchiladas in soft wheat or corn tortillas with cheese and enchilada sauce.

3. Shredded beef salad with lettuce, beets, shredded cheese, tomatoes, and other salad fixings. Serve with your preferred bottled salad dressing or tossed with a simple homemade oil and vinegar dressing.

4. Beef sandwiches served with horseradish or mustard. Add coleslaw and a dill pickle to finish the meal.

Kitchen Wise _____

When planning multiple meals from one roast, follow our suggestions or create your own meal plan based on your food preferences and creativity.

Purchase a bone-in ham on sale. Roast in oven per package directions and serve in the following ways:

1. Sliced ham with baked sweet potatoes topped with butter and cinnamon. Serve with a vegetable like broccoli or cauliflower.

2. Ham sandwiches with sliced tomatoes, Swiss cheese, mustard, and mayonnaise.

3. Omelets with ham and cheese for breakfast or dinner. Add herbs such as basil, oregano, or rosemary to vary the taste.

4. Hearty bean soup flavored with meaty ham bone.

After you cook the meat and eat your meal that day, freeze the remainder in bags labeled for the recipes you'll be using. If you plan to use the remaining meat later that same week, you can store it in the refrigerator.

Creating Your Menus

Fill in the menu planner for the week. As you do, consider the time you have available to prepare meals each day. When you don't have much time, use one of the preceding big pot suggestions or plan meals that are simple to prepare. Factor in which meals other family members can prepare and cook.

Preparing enough food is important so that everyone has enough to eat. If you prepare too much food, don't throw it out. Store it in the refrigerator for snacks, breakfasts, or lunches.

Sample Menus

Here's what your weekly menus could look like for three weeks. As you read through the menus, you'll find they offer many different tastes and flavors each week. Adjust them to meet your needs. But as they say, variety is the spice of life, and varying your meals is definitely one of the keys to eating well on a budget. The blank one at the end is for you to copy and use to plan your menus.

The planned menu lists don't take into account eating left-over foods for lunch or snacks. The suggested snacks are substantial, and you may prefer lighter fare. We also didn't include beverages such as juice, coffee, or tea. Add those to your menus because you'll use your planning sheets when you write your grocery list. In Chapter 6, we show you how to compile a grocery list.

 Money Matters _____

Some "left-over" foods almost taste better when eaten the next day. Think of lasagna, apple cobbler, and frittatas. When reheated or even eaten cold, they hardly make you feel like you're scrounging.

Sample Week 1:	Breakfast	Lunch	Dinner	Snacks
Sunday	Brunch: Savory Spinach and Bacon Bake, sliced apples and bananas, toast.		Pot roast with red potatoes and carrots, ice cream with chocolate sauce.	Hummus and crackers, celery sticks.
Monday	Scrambled eggs, sliced pears, toast.	Sack lunch: ham sandwiches, apple, dill pickle, potato chips.	Beef tacos, tossed salad, cookies.	Graham crackers with peanut butter.
Tuesday	Steel-cut oatmeal with raisins, milk or yogurt.	Green salad with tuna, cheddar cheese, and green beans; Caesar dressing.	Fish cooked in bags with ginger carrots and broccoli, Dutch apple pie.	Seasoned cottage cheese on crackers.
Wednesday	Fried eggs, sliced apple, toast.	Beef sandwiches with mustard, sauerkraut, raw sliced carrots.	Eat out before soccer game.	Easy eggrolls.
Thursday	Oatmeal with cottage cheese.	Lentil soup, oranges.	Quesadillas with shredded beef and vegetables, cookies.	Deviled eggs.
Friday	Fresh Fruit with Tangy Yogurt Sauce, toast.	Left-over lasagna, frozen, then reheated; tossed salad.	Homemade pizza with cheese, pepperoni, and green olives; rice pudding.	Peanut butter with apples or other fruit.
Saturday	Eat out before soccer game.	Fast-food chicken sandwiches.	Hamburgers with sweet potato fries and tossed green salad, ice cream.	Granola bars.

Weekly menus.

Sample Week 2:	Breakfast	Lunch	Dinner	Snacks
Sunday	Poached eggs on ham, muffins.	Chicken Noodle Soup with Vegetables, crackers.	Lasagna with ground beef. Make two recipes, freeze one. Tossed salad, fresh fruit.	Swiss cheese and ham rollups.
Monday	Scrambled eggs, sliced bananas, toast.	Sack lunch: turkey sandwiches, pears, dill pickle, corn chips.	Ham and bean soup, green peas, whole-wheat crackers, cookies.	Tuna salad, potato chips, raw carrots.
Tuesday	Steel-cut oatmeal with dried apricots, milk or yogurt.	Turkey and cranberry wrap.	Bottom-of-the-Bag Chicken, baked sweet potatoes, green beans, pear crumble.	Celery stuffed with cream cheese, olives.
Wednesday	Poached eggs, sliced apple, toast.	Veggie wrap.	Meatloaf. Make two recipes, freeze one. Spinach salad, ice cream.	Creamy Potato Salad, whole-wheat crackers.
Thursday	Oatmeal with fruit and spices, cheese.	Baked chicken fingers, tomato soup.	Oven-Sautéed Catfish, coleslaw, lemon bars.	Three-bean salad.
Friday	Huevos rancheros, sliced tomatoes, green bell peppers.	Left-over lasagna, frozen, then reheated; tossed salad.	Oriental pork stir-fry, rice, flan.	Herbed Salmon Cakes.
Saturday	Cheese Grits Casserole, oranges.	Broccoli and cheese bake.	Skirt steak, baked red potatoes, carrots, ice cream.	Greek Salad.

Sample Week 3:	Breakfast	Lunch	Dinner	Snacks
Sunday	Egg soufflé with cheese and green chiles, mixed fruit bowl.	Southwestern Corn Chowder, green beans.	Pork chops with sauerkraut, broccoli, carrot cake.	Ham and cheese rollups.
Monday	Omelet with ham and Parmesan, bananas.	Sack lunch: turkey sandwiches, apple, dill pickle, corn chips.	Creole gumbo, rice, sliced cucumbers and tomatoes, peanut butter cookies.	Celery stuffed with peanut butter, topped with jelly.
Tuesday	Steel-cut oatmeal with pecans and cinnamon, cottage cheese, pineapple.	Baked chicken drumsticks, coleslaw.	Slow-cook turkey breast with gravy and baked sweet potatoes, tossed green salad, vanilla pudding.	Guacamole with corn chips.
Wednesday	Scrambled egg and bacon sandwich, apple.	Tuna cheese wrap, three-bean salad.	Turkey tacos, Mexican Vegetable Salad, cookies.	Split Pea Soup.
Thursday	Boxed breakfast cereal, cottage cheese, oranges.	Stout Potato Cheese Soup, fruit salad.	Tuna with Olive and Pasta, tossed green salad, chocolate chip cookies.	Cucumber, bell pepper, and cauliflower crudités with yogurt dressing.
Friday	Granola, milk, celery sticks.	Five-bean bake, Mexican Vegetable Salad.	Creamed turkey with mushrooms, tossed green salad, cookies.	Raspberry Banana Bread with cheese spread.
Saturday	Baked French Toast with Honey Walnut Syrup, melon in season.	Tuna fish sandwiches, potato chips, apple.	Spaghetti with tomato sauce, Rosemary Spaghetti Squash, green peas, ice cream.	Chicken salad, crackers, celery sticks.

Week of: ____	Breakfast	Lunch	Dinner	Snacks
Sunday				
Monday				
Tuesday				
Wednesday				
Thursday				
Friday				
Saturday				

Avoiding Boredom

If you prepare the same cost-saving meals too often, beware taste boredom. You'll get complaints and plenty of pressure to purchase more costly foods and treats.

It's a challenging balancing act to provide healthy and nourishing foods for your family when their taste buds are accustomed to costlier fare. Not everyone thinks a home-baked brownie is better than store bought. Ditto pizza, fried chicken, and burgers.

Explain to your family that purchasing store-bought processed foods needs to fit in the budget. Sometimes you'll find that double cheeseburgers and fries cost less at the fast-food restaurant than if you cooked them. In that case, purchase and enjoy—but keep your health in mind.

Human beings are always seeking new tastes and flavors. It's natural and part of our biology. Even "meat-and-potatoes" people want the occasional variation. Provide it for them by using different spices and condiments with your meals.

For example, you can cook a pot roast with basil or soy sauce or lemons or hot red chili flakes. Each of those adds variety to the common pot roast. The same holds true for most main course dishes and salads.

Don't get caught in the tomato/onion/garlic food traps. You can season virtually any protein—from beans to beef to eggs—with these seasonings and make them taste fabulous. But don't use these for every meal or even every day. If you do, you and your family will end up with jaded tongues and expensive cravings.

The Least You Need to Know

◆ Plan menus weekly to save money and make shopping easier.

◆ Vary the menu to keep the eating interesting.

◆ Cook larger roasts so you can make three to four meals from each roast.

◆ Use the recipes in this book to add cost-saving variety to your meals.

Chapter 5

Food Preparation

In This Chapter

- ◆ Cooking to save money
- ◆ Preparing in quantity, eating in moderation
- ◆ Making delicious use of leftovers
- ◆ Keeping prepared foods on hand

Get out the pots and pans. Grab the cutting boards and your bake ware. Bring out your weekly or monthly menus. Now's the time to plan how you're going to cook your meals.

Yes, you do have options. Some families cook once a month, some once a week. Some families are members of a neighborhood meal cooperative, in which each family cooks one meal a week for all the other families. You can also cook as most of us do—nearly every day.

In this chapter, we explain your options and make recommendations for saving money no matter how you plan to cook.

Cooking Strategies

Remember, you're not alone. Many of us are preparing more meals at home these days. When a person needs to cut back on spending, it's natural to cut back first on unnecessary purchases such as restaurant meals. This decision leads to a renewed interest in cooking.

As the national economy has slowed, grocery sales have increased. Analysts tell us that sales of meat, produce, dry pasta, and cheese are up, while sales of candy are down.

You're ready to get back into the habit of cooking and the daily habit of eating at home. For some people this is easy, while for others it can be a challenge. You may need to reorganize your priorities, spend more time at home, and essentially change your lifestyle. Rather than dinner out with friends, you may be inviting friends to your home for entertainment.

You may need to organize your family in order to eat more meals together, or you may need to keep food warm for when they arrive home. There is a fabulous advantage to eating meals at home. You can enjoy more family time. You can even turn off the media, ban cell phones and iPods, and have conversations, tell jokes, and enjoy laughter together. There's more to eating at home than just the additional labor and cleanup. You may find eating well on a budget more enriching than you anticipated.

Plan time to cook and clean up. It probably takes a half hour to an hour on average to prepare a meal, based on your choice of recipe. Some people find this a creative and relaxing time, though many of us don't. At the very least, the extra labor is satisfying when it lets you eat well and save money. Start making time in your schedule to cook.

Ask your family members to set the table and do the dishes. Some may be willing to be your assistant and take on tasks such as cleaning and chopping produce and making salads. Food preparation time is an opportunity to teach your children and spouse how to cook so that they can prepare meals, too.

Your weekly menu plan is important to spending less. We urge you to use it and continue to improve it each week. You'll learn how your family really likes to eat, what foods are favorites, and which you can avoid preparing.

Make sure you have some food for quick meals on hand for when schedules change and unanticipated events and situations arise.

Kitchen Wise _____

Keep sandwich fixings on hand for quick meals or meals on the run. You'll need bread, mayonnaise or mustard, and fillings such as cheese, sliced meats, tuna, or peanut butter. Add an apple or other piece of fruit, and you have a balanced meal.

Cook Once a Month

Imagine doing all of your meal preparation for a whole month in one day. Many families set aside a day, usually a Saturday, and cook for hours. Overall, they spend less time on cooking, save money, and have more time on a daily basis for other activities.

Here are some of the advantages:

◆ It saves time on meal preparation during the rest of the month.

◆ It accommodates different eating times of family members.

◆ It optimizes savings on grocery store sales by purchasing in quantity.

◆ You always have food on hand for family members who aren't available at meal times.

Here's how cooking one day a month works:

◆ Prepare a list of menus for the month, just as we recommended that you do for each week.

◆ Shop for groceries a day or so before your cooking day. Shop carefully, looking for sales on meats, produce, and canned goods. Warehouse membership stores and grocery outlet stores are good for bulk purchases.

◆ Make sure you have enough food storage containers for the freezer and refrigerator, including freezer bags. Keep freezer tape on hand to label the containers with the date, meal, and number of servings.

 Money Matters _____

In the long term, you'll save money and the environment by owning reusable food storage containers. Purchase sizes for casseroles, stews, soups, as well as 9×13-inch containers for lasagnas and frittatas. Purchase only after you know with certainty that you want to cook one day a month.

◆ Use the Big Pot Theory by purchasing large beef roasts, turkeys, and/or hams. Some people purchase many chickens, too. Use the meats for preparing entrées such as enchiladas, stews, soups, sandwich spreads, and casseroles.

Start cooking early in the morning and make sure you have fun. Be sure to plan your meal for that evening, too.

Cooking one day a month has some possible disadvantages. First, it requires adequate freezer space. If you don't already own a second refrigerator or deep freezer, this may not be the best plan for you.

It also requires superb organization. You'll want buy-in from other family members to help you with some of the food prep and cleanup during the day.

If you use this method, you'll still need to spend time in the kitchen every day. You'll be reheating the entrée and preparing fresh produce for salads and vegetable side dishes. The cooking-one-day-a-month method isn't great for most breakfasts, so you'll still be cooking eggs or serving cereal.

Kitchen Wise

Be sure you like the idea of spending a whole Saturday cooking. One friend gave up on monthly cooking day when he was missing his children's soccer games and other activities.

When shopping for groceries in the cooking-one-day-a-month method, your monthly shopping needs to be supplemented with later trips to the store during the month for fresh produce, milk, eggs, fish, and fruit.

If you're interested in learning more about how to cook one day a month, research online to answer any questions you have. Then give it a try. It may work fabulously for you and your family.

Cook Once a Week

Prepare your main course dishes once a week and you'll be saving both time and money. If the cooking-one-day-a-month strategy sounds too intense for you, but you like the overall concept, perhaps this one will be the right fit.

Set aside a morning or afternoon for your meal preparation. You'll eat some of the meals this week and perhaps some in later weeks, so plan ahead. For example, if you make two pans of lasagna, you may have four meals for your family. To avoid taste boredom, you could serve one meal this week and freeze the rest. Then reheat and serve each of the remaining meals over the next three weeks.

Shop for groceries a day or two prior to your cooking day. Purchase those ingredients you'll need for your menus, and base your menus on this week's sales on roasts, hams, and chicken. Also look for special prices on vegetables, either fresh or frozen, and fruit.

The advantages of cooking for the week are the same as those for cooking once a month and also include the following:

♦ It usually takes only 4 to 6 hours.

♦ It's less tiring than cooking for a whole month at once.

♦ The freezer space in your kitchen refrigerator is probably large enough without needing a second refrigerator or freezer.

♦ It saves time on days when you're too busy to cook.

♦ You optimize savings on grocery store sales by purchasing in quantity.

♦ You always have food on hand for family members who aren't available to eat at meal times.

 Kitchen Wise

Most often, you'll be eating fruit fresh, raw and uncooked. Purchase only the amount you'll eat that week. If you're canning fruit or making pies and cobblers, purchase enough on sale or during harvest season for your longer-term eating needs.

Cooking ahead in large quantities makes sense if you have the inclination, time, and organizational abilities. If you don't, don't worry. You can still save money by cooking dinners on a mostly daily basis.

Cook Almost Daily

If you use your weekly menu plan, cooking almost daily will still save you money. Most days you'll cook; other days you'll be creative with leftovers or reheat frozen meals that you prepared earlier.

For one dinner, you could prepare a ham and bean soup. Make enough for at least two meals, possibly three. Serve the soup for dinner along with a tossed green salad. Freeze the rest in meal-sized packages. You can also store some of the soup in the refrigerator for lunches and possibly breakfasts later that week.

For each week, figure out which days you have time to cook and which ones you don't. When you're cooking a recipe that lends itself to many servings, such as enchiladas, stews, soups, lasagna, and casseroles, you can make two full recipes and freeze one for later use.

On the days when you don't have time to cook, defrost and/or reheat a precooked entrée. Add a side salad or vegetable and you have dinner.

Breakfast cooking on weekdays is usually simple. We've found that cooking an egg takes 2 to 3 minutes, about as much time as it takes to prepare a cold breakfast of cereal with yogurt or milk. By using the microwave to cook bacon or ham, they can be served alongside eggs in mere minutes. Add a piece of fruit, and you have a breakfast that will hold a person well until lunchtime.

Kitchen Wise

Most home-prepared foods will store safely in the refrigerator for 3 to 5 days. If you won't eat the food within that timeframe, cover it tightly and freeze it. Food in the freezer will keep for 3 to 6 months. After that, expect freezer burn and loss of taste and flavor.

Another breakfast favorite you can cook quickly in the morning is steel-cut oats. Soak dry oats overnight by adding them to the recommended amount of boiling water. Remove from heat, stir, and cover. In the morning, reheat the needed number of servings either on the stove or in the microwave. Add cheese or an egg along with fresh or dried fruit, and you have a super-nutritious and cost-saving meal.

Your preparation of lunches varies based on each person's needs and schedule. How many of your family members eat lunch at home? How many eat at work or school? Here are some money-saving ideas:

♦ Pack sack lunches for those who work or attend school. Make sandwiches or salads and add sliced cheese, fruit, sliced carrots or celery, or a cookie.

♦ For eat-at-home lunches, eat the same as a sack lunch or heat soup, small portions of dinner entrées, leftovers, or eat simple fare such as cheese and vegetables or meat and cheese rollups.

♦ Keep ground beef patties frozen separately in the freezer. For weekend lunches, grill hamburgers.

♦ Bean soup is high in nutrition and easy to heat and serve. Ditto for chicken noodle soup.

Midday snacks are here to stay. Going for 5 or 6 hours between meals without eating isn't programmed into human biology. People usually get hungry 3 or 4 hours after a regular meal. In the recipe section of this book, check out the snacks, appetizers, side dishes, and lunches for suggestions. Snacks are designed to satisfy hunger for just a couple of hours until the next regular meal.

Money Matters _____

Foods high in nutritional value aren't necessarily costly. Many soups are high in protein and fiber, are flavorful and satisfying, and are very economical.

Baking

So far, we've discussed meals but ignored desserts and sweet treats. They belong in a special category. A person doesn't need to eat baked goods and sweet treats to eat well. However, we suspect that folks with a sweet tooth would disagree.

If you or members of your family need to feed a sweet tooth, you or they can include baking in food preparation. However, before you do, price store-bought baked goods and compare them to homemade treats. You may or may not save money by baking at home.

If you want to make homemade cookies, cakes, pies, candy, and desserts, set aside time once or twice a week to bake.

We've included a chapter on desserts in this book to give you ideas for delicious cookies and other baked goods so you can save money on treats.

Kitchen Wise _____

Usually you'll save money by purchasing bread at the grocery store. Baking bread at home can be time consuming, especially if you don't own an automatic bread baker. If you love homemade bread then go for it, but don't expect to save enough money to make it financially worthwhile.

Neighborhood Cooking Co-Ops

Have you thought about participating in a neighborhood cooking co-op? Most include five families. Each member cooks one workday night a week for everyone in the co-op. He or she then delivers the hot meal to each family in time for dinner on the designated evening. Co-ops can be an ideal way to save time and money, but there are some pros and cons.

Pros:

♦ Your only obligation is to prepare one dinner meal every week.

♦ You receive or eat dinner meals the other four workdays of the week. Some co-ops deliver the meals to your home, while for others you'll need to pick them up. In some co-ops, the families eat together at a different home for 4 days during the week.

♦ You save preparation time.

♦ You don't need to even think about what to serve for three dinners each week.

Cons:

♦ You need to enjoy the other members' cooking.

♦ You'll need to attend organizational meetings and deal with problems that arise.

♦ It may not be suitable for families with members who have food allergies or picky eaters.

♦ You'll need about 10 to 12 delicious, easy-to-prepare, and easy-to-serve entrées, including side dishes, salads, and desserts.

These are the basic requirements for organizing a neighborhood food co-op:

♦ Every member should live within a couple blocks of each other for ease of delivery.

♦ You need to make provisions for vacations, illness, holidays, blizzards, and business travel obligations.

♦ You must define the content of meals—does the co-op expect meat or meatless meals, fresh produce, bread, sides, dessert?

♦ Make an agreement for how to drop out without hard feelings if the co-op doesn't work for you.

To learn more, research neighborhood cooking co-ops on the Internet and talk with some friends who may already participate in one. You may find that a co-op suits your needs perfectly.

Wise Use of Food

Some ways of eating and handling food can be very expensive. If you recognize some bad habits in yourself or in family members, plan to make serious changes. Don't let yourself lose money with bad food habits.

If you hate leftovers and refuse to eat them, try this solution: Never cook more food than you and your family can eat at one meal. Figure 3 to 4 ounces of meat per person and moderate portions of salads and side dishes. If you're throwing out food after every meal, it's time to prepare less food, and it's time to reassess your attitudes about food, eating, and saving money.

 Money Matters _____

No one would toss money into the trash or shove it in the garbage disposal and grind it to a pulp. But that's exactly what happens when a person throws out leftovers! Leftovers are literally savings in your refrigerator.

On the other hand, don't polish off every last morsel of food left on other people's plates. Once you've eaten enough food to feel satisfied, stop eating.

To save money, don't serve "family style," in which you put bowls of food on the table for everyone to serve themselves. Instead, serve small to moderate amounts of food on individual plates at the stove prior to sitting down to eat. The family can go back for seconds if they need more.

Don't serve everyone too much food, hoping they'll eat it all to avoid waste. And don't let yourself become the family garbage disposal. It's fattening.

When you have leftovers in the pot, refrigerate them for snacks or lunch the next day.

"I'm hungry for something, but I don't know what it is." This sounds like an excuse to run to the store for a costly treat. Resist the urge. Instead, pause and drink a glass of water. Then assess your true hunger feelings and, if needed, eat a small snack of a salty, sweet, or meaty food.

Economize when unwrapping food. One friend usually has three loaves of the same kind of bread opened at the same time. The loaves dry out and need to be discarded before her family of three can eat them all. Instead, don't open the second loaf until you've eaten the first. Be sure to keep extra packages of food such as bread, cereal, and jam out of sight in the cupboard or pantry so family members don't accidentally open the second package before the first one is eaten.

Kitchen Wise _____

Store unopened loaves of bread in the freezer to preserve freshness. Storing in the refrigerator makes bread go stale faster. For opened loaves, store wrapped at room temperature.

Food That Expires Slowly

We sometimes find a lonely wilted and moldy bag of something that was once green at the bottom of our vegetable crisper in the refrigerator. Perhaps it was cilantro? Parsley? Lettuce? An onion? It's hard to say. All we know is that it died a slow death because we forgot to eat it.

Fresh is great for herbs, but if you can't eat the bunch before they expire, use dried herbs instead. The shelf life of dried herbs and spices can last a year or so, but after a while, they lose their flavor. To extend flavor and shelf life, store in a dark and cool location with the bottles closed tightly.

Moldy or spoiled fruit is always sad. It would have tasted so good if only we'd seen it in time. Bread goes moldy in some climates. In the desert air where we live, it usually curls up and dehydrates unless we take care to wrap it.

Good kitchen management can prevent these kinds of money-wasting carelessness. Even if a person only wasted 50¢ on that expired cilantro, it's still 50¢ thrown in the trash.

Every time you cook veggies and restock your vegetable bin, check the bottom for produce you may have forgotten. Rotate the fruit in your bins by eating the oldest first so you don't waste food. Freeze refrigerated meats if you can't cook them within two days. Ditto fish. You absolutely don't want to smell old fish, let alone eat it.

Store food as directed on the label. Fresh ground peanut butter needs to be refrigerated or it turns rancid. The same goes for fresh nuts and seeds.

Think of expired food as lost money. Food eaten in its prime is money spent wisely.

The Least You Need to Know

◆ Cook family meals once a month, once a week, or daily for money savings.

◆ Neighborhood meal co-ops can be a great choice for busy working parents.

◆ Reduce food waste by planning, serving, and cooking carefully.

◆ Price store-bought baked items to determine whether you'll save money by baking at home.

Part 2

Shopping for Groceries and Saving on Food

Read the ads, be on the alert for food coupons, and pay attention to unadvertised specials at the grocery store. It's time to go shopping.

Use our grocery shopping form to make a concise and orderly list, review your weekly menus, and shop when you aren't already hungry. You'll be saving money every step of the way.

To save money when eating out, use coupons, share meals, and consult your "eating-out" budget before you order. With mindful ordering and complete gustatory enjoyment, you can eat out and save money, too.

And don't forget to enjoy the fruits of gardening and preserving food. Not only will you save money, you'll also enjoy the satisfactions of these "hands-on" projects.

Chapter 6

The Shopping List

In This Chapter

- ◆ Putting your list in store order
- ◆ Researching grocery store sales
- ◆ Stocking food staples in your pantry
- ◆ Cooking equipment needs

Writing a clear and organized grocery-shopping list will save you money. If you wander into the store looking for something delicious to eat for dinner, chances are good you'll be lured by the wonderful smells wafting from the hot foods section of the deli. Purchasing ready-to-eat succulent prime rib, fried chicken, or lasagna with meatballs will blow your budget.

In fact, if you are known to break down and buy takeout when it's not in the budget, you may need to go shopping early in the day before such food is available or later in the evening after the deli foods are either sold out or the deli is put to bed for the night.

In this chapter, we show you how to write your shopping list and make the best use of your weekly menu plan.

The First Ingredient List

The first time you write your weekly ingredient list, set aside an hour. You'll need this much time to think through how much food you'll need to purchase for each meal. This depends on the size of your family.

To start your list, use these categories:

Fruit	Vegetables
Canned Goods	Frozen Foods
Meat and Fish	Dairy
Baking	Oils and Sauces
Condiments	Snacks
Breads	Cereal/Grains/Pasta

For these examples, we'll be referring to the weekly menu from Chapter 4 titled **Sample Week 1.**

The first item of the week is Sunday brunch of Savory Spinach and Bacon Bake, sliced apples and bananas, and toast. For a family of four, you'll need only one half of the following recipe. You can also prepare the full recipe and save half for breakfasts later in the week.

6 slices turkey bacon (about $^1/_4$ lb.)

2 cups fresh spinach, washed and dried

8 large eggs

$^1/_4$ cup milk

$^1/_4$ tsp. ground black pepper

$^1/_4$ tsp. garlic powder

$^1/_4$ tsp. dried parsley

1 cup chopped tomatoes

$^1/_3$ cup grated Parmesan cheese

On your weekly ingredient list, you would put the following:

Produce—2 cups spinach

　　2 tomatoes

　　2 apples

　　2 bananas

Meat—$^1/_4$ lb. turkey bacon

Dairy—8 large eggs

　　$^1/_4$ cup milk

　　$^1/_3$ cup grated Parmesan cheese

Bread—4 slices bread

Condiments—black pepper

　　garlic powder

　　dried parsley

Beverages—coffee, tea

　　Dinner that day is pot roast, red potatoes, carrots, ice cream, chocolate sauce. Add these ingredients to the preceding list. Now your list looks like this:

Produce—2 cups spinach

　　2 tomatoes

　　2 apples

　　2 bananas

　　8 red potatoes

　　8 carrots

Meat—$^1/_4$ lb. turkey bacon

　　1 to $1^1/_4$ lb. pot roast

Dairy—8 large eggs

　　$^1/_4$ cup milk

　　$^1/_3$ cup grated Parmesan cheese

Frozen foods—ice cream

Bread—4 slices bread

Sauces—chocolate sauce

Condiments—black pepper

  garlic powder

  dried parsley

Beverages—coffee, tea

Add to the list the ingredients for your daily snack of hummus with crackers and celery sticks. The following recipe serves 8, so you'll have enough left over to use for another snack or as a sandwich spread later in the week.

  1 (15-oz.) can garbanzo beans

  2 TB. tahini or sesame seed paste

  2 TB. lemon juice

  1 tsp. minced garlic

  2 TB. olive oil

  2 tsp. dried cumin

  1 tsp. dried coriander

So now your list should look like this:

Produce—2 cups spinach

  2 tomatoes

  2 apples

  2 bananas

  8 red potatoes

  8 carrots

  8 celery stalks

Meat—$1/4$ lb. turkey bacon

  1 to $1^{1}/_{4}$ lb. pot roast

Dairy—8 eggs

$^1/_4$ cup milk

$^1/_3$ cup grated Parmesan cheese

Canned goods—1 (15-oz.) can garbanzo beans

Frozen foods—ice cream

Bread—4 slices bread

Sauces—$^1/_2$ cup chocolate sauce

2 TB. lemon juice

Baking and pantry—2 TB. olive oil

Snacks—2 cups crackers

Spices and condiments—black pepper

garlic powder

dried parsley

tahini

minced garlic

cumin

coriander

Beverages—coffee, tea

Kitchen Wise

We've left out the quantities in the condiments section because you won't be purchasing these items often. Before you go to the store, check your spice and condiment supply to determine if you're running low on any of the items. If so, add that item to your list.

Continue this process for every meal planned for the upcoming week. Just keep adding the amount of food you need to purchase to the preceding list.

After you have completed the list, total the ingredients by type. If your meal plan calls for a total of 24 eggs for the week, then you need to purchase 2 dozen.

This sounds like a lot of work, and it will be the first time you do it. However, as you continue to plan weekly menus and write lists, you'll develop an instinctive feel for the process, and eventually it will take far less time.

Money Matters _____

Make a note on your weekly calendar if you can serve two meals from one recipe. In the preceding example, the Sunday brunch menu of Savory Spinach and Bacon Bake serves eight, so you have four additional servings for the week that can be eaten for snacks, breakfast, or lunch. Do the same for the hummus snack.

Make a Shopping List

First you need a form. The best forms follow the flow of the grocery store, so you can proceed down each aisle in an orderly fashion. This saves you time and actually saves money. When you don't need to wander around looking for a specific item, you'll be less likely to become sidetracked with yet one more opportunity for an impulse purchase.

Here's our favorite list. If it doesn't follow the flow of your grocery store aisles, you may want to change it to meet your needs or find one that does.

With this blank sheet in hand, transfer your ingredients to the list. The form doesn't provide for quantities, so add them to the left of each item. If you need more space in some categories, put them on the back of the list. For example, you may need two types of beef: a chuck roast and a skirt steak. If you can't squeeze all the details on the front, use the back.

Money Matters _____

You'll find plenty of clever, innovative, and expensive nonfood items such as disposable plastic food storage containers and fancy sticky plastic wrap. Don't buy them. Instead, use the effective, simpler, and cost-saving supplies.

This shopping list includes nonfood items such as batteries and dishwasher soap. We haven't included them in your food budget. Still, you may need to purchase them, so go ahead and add the items you need to the list to save time with a single shopping trip.

Keep nonfood items separate from the food items in your budget accounting. That way, you'll have accurate information when you reconcile your budget to actual expenditures at the end of the month.

Fruit

- ☐ Apples
- ☐ Bananas
- ☐ Grapes
- ☐ Lemons/limes
- ☐ Oranges
- ☐ Pears

Vegetables

- ☐ Broccoli
- ☐ Carrots
- ☐ Cauliflower
- ☐ Celery
- ☐ Cucumbers
- ☐ Mushrooms
- ☐ Onions
- ☐ Peppers
- ☐ Potatoes
- ☐ Tomatoes

Canned Goods

- ☐ Beans/legumes
- ☐ Chiles, diced
- ☐ Clams
- ☐ Corn
- ☐ Olives
- ☐ Salmon
- ☐ Spaghetti sauce
- ☐ Tomatoes
- ☐ Tuna fish

Frozen Foods

- ☐ Corn
- ☐ Green beans
- ☐ Ice cream
- ☐ Peas
- ☐ Pie crust
- ☐ Spinach

Meat and Fish

- ☐ Bacon
- ☐ Beef
- ☐ Chicken
- ☐ Fish
- ☐ Ground beef
- ☐ Pork
- ☐ Sausage
- ☐ Turkey

Dairy

- ☐ Butter
- ☐ Eggs
- ☐ Cheese
- ☐ Cottage cheese
- ☐ Cream cheese
- ☐ Milk
- ☐ Sour cream
- ☐ Yogurt

Baking

- ☐ Baking powder
- ☐ Baking soda
- ☐ Cocoa
- ☐ Flour
- ☐ Nuts
- ☐ Spices
- ☐ Sugar
- ☐ Vanilla

Oils and Sauces

- ☐ BBQ sauce
- ☐ Honey
- ☐ Olive oil
- ☐ Salad dressing
- ☐ Soy sauce
- ☐ Vinegar

Condiments

- ☐ Jelly/preserves
- ☐ Ketchup
- ☐ Mayonnaise
- ☐ Mustard
- ☐ Olives
- ☐ Peanut butter
- ☐ Pickles

Snacks

- ☐ Candy
- ☐ Chips
- ☐ Cookies
- ☐ Crackers
- ☐ Dried fruit
- ☐ Raisins
- ☐ Salted nuts
- ☐ Snack bars

Breads

- ☐ Pitas
- ☐ Sourdough
- ☐ Stone-ground
- ☐ Tortillas

Cereals/Grains/Pasta

- ☐ Barley
- ☐ Macaroni
- ☐ Rice
- ☐ Spaghetti
- ☐ Steel-cut oats

Nonfood Items

- ☐ Conditioner
- ☐ Contacts cleaner
- ☐ Deodorant
- ☐ Floss
- ☐ Lotion
- ☐ Pain reliever
- ☐ Razors
- ☐ Shampoo
- ☐ Shaving cream
- ☐ Soap
- ☐ Toothpaste

Paper Products

- ☐ Aluminum foil
- ☐ Facial tissues
- ☐ Paper towels
- ☐ Plastic bags
- ☐ Plastic wrap
- ☐ Toilet paper

For the House

- ☐ Batteries
- ☐ Bleach
- ☐ Dishwashing soap
- ☐ Garbage bags
- ☐ Household cleaners
- ☐ Laundry soap
- ☐ Light bulbs
- ☐ Softener

Other

Grocery shopping list.

Budget-Wise, High-Nutrition Foods

As you refine your shopping list, choose from this list of economically priced healthy foods. They offer reliably good value for the price, season after season, in most areas of the country:

Fresh produce: Carrots, celery, iceberg lettuce, onions, sweet potatoes, broccoli, spinach.

Fresh fruit: Apples, oranges, bananas, pears.

Canned foods: Tomatoes (whole or diced), tuna, beans, spaghetti sauce, soups, pineapple.

Dairy: Butter, milk, powdered milk, eggs, bulk cheese, cottage cheese, plain yogurt, large containers of shredded cheese.

Frozen foods: Vegetables such as peas, corn, green beans, broccoli.

Meat: Bacon, chicken, ground beef, chuck roast, pork roasts, turkey.

Seafood: Fresh seafood varies widely by location and time of year.

Baked goods: Sliced stone-ground bread, sourdough bread.

Purchase other foods in season or when they go on special. Fresh vegetables and fruit grown in the United States are plentiful in the summer and early autumn. The rest of the year, most fresh produce is flown in from other countries like South America and Mexico. Because of this, you can find bargains on produce at other times of the year, too.

Money Matters

Stay flexible when you shop. Use your list rigorously unless you find well-priced specials or in-season produce when you get to the store.

You'll regularly find specials on meats and fish, both advertised and unadvertised. At our local store, Sunday evening is a great time to find unadvertised meat and fish specials. Even living in the land-locked Rocky Mountain states, we can find specials on fresh fish every couple of weeks.

Staples for Your Pantry and Refrigerator

Keep these foods on hand as a rule. When you get close to running out of a specific item, replenish it. That way you won't need to include these items in your weekly ingredient list. These keep for a long time when stored properly, and you'll always have them on hand when a recipe calls for a specific ingredient.

Black pepper	Butter
Flour	Garlic, fresh, crushed in jar
Honey	Jam or jelly
Ketchup	Lemon juice, bottled
Mayonnaise	Mustard
Olive oil	Peanut butter
Pickles	Salt
Soy sauce	Sugar

Vinegar, either red wine or cider for salad dressings

Add others, such as barbecue sauce or bottled salad dressings, if you use them frequently.

Spices

Spices are key ingredients in many meals, but luckily a small investment at the store will last for many months. Since you'll be purchasing spices infrequently, it's a good idea to keep these on hand. Replenish only when you're about to run out.

Basil	Bay leaf
Celery salt	Celery seed
Chili powder	Cilantro
Cinnamon	Coriander
Cumin	Curry powder
Fennel seed	Garlic, minced, in a jar—refrigerate
Garlic powder	Ginger
Lemon pepper	Mustard, ground
Oregano	Paprika

Parsley	Pepper, black, ground
Red pepper flakes	Rosemary
Sage	Salt
Tarragon	Thyme

Tasty Tidbits _____

We used a wide variety of spices in this book's recipes to enhance the taste of your food and to keep your taste buds from getting bored with the "same old" tastes day after day.

The preceding list contains the basics. Add your favorites to the list.

Ingredients Used in This Book

The following is a list of the ingredients used in this cookbook. We've used only those ingredients that let you eat well and meet your budget goals.

Fresh vegetables:

Asparagus	Beets
Bell peppers	Broccoli
Carrots	Cauliflower
Celery	Cilantro
Cucumbers	Lettuce
Mushrooms	Onions
Parsley	Parsnips
Radishes	Red potatoes
Spinach	Squash
Sweet potatoes	Tomatoes
Turnips	Zucchini

Frozen vegetables:

Corn

Peas

Green beans

Spinach

Fresh fruit:

Apples

Bananas

Cantaloupe

Grapes

Melons

Peaches

Plums

Avocado

Berries

Cherries

Lemons/limes

Oranges

Pears

Pomegranate

Canned foods:

Corn

Legumes

Pasta sauce

Rotel

Tomatoes

Green chiles

Olives

Pickles

Salmon

Tuna

Sauces:

Hot sauce

Salsa

Worcestershire sauce

Pancake syrup

Soy sauce

Other groceries:

Barley

Jelly/preserves

Lemon/lime juice

Honey

Ketchup

Mayonnaise

Oatmeal, steel cut

Peanut butter

Rice

Tofu

Pasta

Prepared mustard

Tahini (sesame paste)

Oils/vinegars:

Balsamic vinegar

Olive oil

Rice vinegar

Cider vinegar

Red wine vinegar

 Kitchen Wise _____

If you only purchase one type of vinegar, make it cider vinegar. You can substitute this for other vinegars. The taste won't be quite the same, but the food will always be delicious. Balsamic and wine vinegars cost more, so decide if you can afford these specialty vinegars on your budget.

Dairy:

Butter

Cottage cheese

Eggs

Ice cream

Monterrey Jack cheese

Sour cream

Cheddar cheese

Cream cheese

Heavy cream

Milk

Parmesan cheese

Yogurt

Meat:

Bacon, both turkey and regular

Chicken

Ground turkey

Pork

Turkey

Beef

Ground beef

Ham

Sausage

Seafood:

Catfish

Salmon

Tuna

Halibut

Shrimp

Baked goods:

Corn tortillas

Sourdough bread

Wheat tortillas

Other breads

Crackers

Stone-ground bread

Whole-wheat pita bread

Baking:

Baking powder

Brown sugar

Cocoa

Pie shell

Sugar

Yeast

Baking soda

Chocolate chips

Flour

Powdered sugar

Vanilla flavoring or extract

Snacks:

Corn chips

Potato chips

Nuts

Seeds

Other supplies:

Aluminum foil

Plastic food storage bags

Parchment paper

Alcohol:

Stout beer, either alcoholic or nonalcoholic versions

These basic ingredients offer plenty of variety and nutritional value. The price point is low to moderate.

Basic Cooking Equipment You Need

You can cook or prepare all the recipes in this book with simple cooking equipment. Here's what we suggest you have:

Small, medium, and large saucepans

Medium-size skillet

Roasting pan with lid

Oven casserole baking dish, 9×13-inch

Broiler pan or cookie sheet suitable for broiling

Cake pans, 9-inch diameter

Pie pan, 9-inch diameter

Cookie sheets

Aluminum foil

Knives—paring, medium, and a chef knife with wide cutting blade

Large spoon

Fork

Tongs are nice but optional

Large bowl for tossing salads

Serving bowls

Potholders or a kitchen towel

Electric blender

Slow cooker

Outdoor grill, optional

If you don't own all of these items, you can use fewer and still cook up a terrific meal.

If you need to go shopping, you may be able to find serviceable pots and pans at thrift shops and dollar stores.

Kitchen Wise

If you don't own a slow cooker, you can use the oven. Place the ingredients in a roasting pan, cover with a lid, and cook at a very low oven temperature—about 225°F to 250°F. Cook for as many hours as the recipe states. For safety reasons, you may want to do this only if you can be at home when the oven is on.

Food Storage Containers

You have plenty of options for storing food in the refrigerator and freezer:

- **Heat-resistant and freezer-safe Pyrex glass containers with plastic lids.** They preserve the taste of the food well without adding a plastic flavor. They are reusable and can do double duty as serving dishes. Wash in the dishwasher. They are safe to use for microwaving and reheating.

- **Plastic containers with lids.** Not heat resistant but good for storing in the refrigerator or freezer. They are reusable and dishwasher friendly. However, they can pick up food smells and colors, and sometimes they alter the taste of foods. Avoid microwaving or reheating food in these containers because the toxins in the plastic can get into your food.

- **Disposable plastic food containers.** They cost more than plastic bags and are only good for a couple uses. They won't hold up well in the dishwasher. Overall, they are not a money-wise purchase. Never reheat food in these containers as the toxic plastic can leach into your food.

- **Plastic bags.** Good for one use, they work well in the refrigerator and freezer. Use these to pack lunches and to store food in the freezer.

Saving Money on Household Supplies

You can save money on household supplies with these substitutions:

- Clean and maintain drains in sinks and showers regularly with basic kitchen supplies. Every month, put a half cup of baking soda down the drain. Add a half cup of white vinegar and quickly cover the drain. You'll hear lots of foaming going on. In a half hour, remove the cover and run clear water for 30 seconds. You'll maintain fresh-smelling drains and loosen clogs so that you don't need to phone the plumber later.

♦ You never need to purchase fabric softener again if you use dryer balls. They're widely available at discount stores or home-item specialty stores. They cost about $10 to $15 and last for years. Simply put the two balls in the dryer and dry as you normally would. The balls fluff the clothes and eliminate static electricity. Because of the fluffing, your clothes dry faster, saving electricity.

♦ Keep a plastic spray bottle filled with half white vinegar and half water. Use this solution to clean dirt from walls, door jambs, counters, sinks, bathtubs, and floors. This is way less costly than expensive spray cleaners and works quite well.

♦ Skip shower gel and use bar soap. It lasts longer and costs less.

♦ Instead of bath salts, use baking soda or Epsom salts in your bath water. Both are great for your skin and soothe sore muscles.

Search online for more information about saving on household cleaners and products. You can also find books with savings tips on household products.

The Least You Need to Know

♦ Use your weekly menu plan to create your grocery shopping list.

♦ Save money by purchasing only the items on your list.

♦ Keep your pantry stocked with spices and staples.

♦ You can use basic, inexpensive cookware to prepare the recipes in this book.

The Well-Informed Shopper

In This Chapter

- ◆ Saving money while you shop
- ◆ Managing coupons and special offers
- ◆ Avoiding expensive impulse purchases
- ◆ Choosing your regular grocery store

Grocery store designers and managers understand your innate need for visual and taste stimulation. The stores are designed in a way that encourages you to make impulse purchases of the highest profit items in the store. Seldom, if ever, will those high-priced items be on your shopping list.

Think of shopping as a game. The store entices; you resist and stick to your budget. Like a video game, the challenges await you at every corner and in every aisle.

In this chapter, we show you how to navigate your way through the maze of culinary temptations so you stay within your budget. You'll conquer the grocery store maze rather than have it get the best of you and ruin your efforts.

Shop First at Home

With shopping list in hand, take a trip through your provisions. Go through the fruit bowl, pantry, refrigerator, and freezer. Your mission is twofold:

1. Toss out any food that has rotted, molded, or shriveled up. Also toss any food that looks so unappetizing that no one will eat it. Make a note: You may not want to prepare certain recipes again and should adjust your shopping accordingly.

   While you're doing this, evaluate why the food didn't get eaten. Did you forget about it? Did you purchase too much? Or have you avoided clearing out the kitchen in a while? Plan to make future adjustments to avoid throwing out food.

2. Look for foods you have on hand that you can eat in the next week. You may find frozen meat buried under other foods. Ditto frozen vegetables, tortillas, or ice cream. Your pantry may already hold a jar of spaghetti sauce you can use for dinner that week.

Make a note on your shopping list that you already have those items and check them off your list.

Do the same for nonfood home items such as dishwasher soap, toothpaste, white vinegar, and aluminum foil.

 Kitchen Wise _____

> We love white vinegar. It's great for cleaning when added to water in a spray bottle. Paired with baking soda, it can clean and clear drains. Baking soda is super for light scouring. Add $^1/_2$ cup baking soda to your bath water and have a superb and soothing soak for just pennies. You'll find it more effective for relaxation and soothing sore muscles than fancy and pricey bath salts.

Shopping the Sales

Sales can save you money. They can also cost you money, depending on how you shop. This is a tricky concept, so we'll explain. Here's an example: if you don't need a new pair of jeans but you purchase some because they're on sale, you have spent money you didn't need to spend. You didn't really save money, you spent money—you just spent less on an item you didn't need.

However, if you needed a pair of jeans—maybe your current pair is worn out, has holes, or doesn't fit—and you purchased new jeans on sale and saved $15, then you saved money.

 Money Matters _____

> This concept of saving or wasting money on sales is subtle, and it can take years to break yourself of the impulse to buy. If you stay focused, you'll learn to ignore sales if you aren't already planning to purchase an item. Only take advantage of the sales for items you're planning to purchase already, whether it's food, clothing, travel, or household furnishings. Soon you'll be rewarded for good choices by seeing real savings in money.

The same is true for food. If you purchase a food item on sale that you don't usually eat, it's probably an impulse purchase. Food processing companies run frequent sales on high-profit and costlier products to gain customer loyalty, so decide if you really want to participate. Determine if you think the food would offer nutrient-dense healthy food. It may turn out to be a treat food that you would only eat occasionally.

The best budget-wise foods to purchase on sale are the basics: meats, fish, cheese, dairy, eggs, vegetables, fruit, nuts, honey, butter, and olive oil.

When you can find sales on pantry staples, purchase them because they seldom go on sale. These include spaghetti sauce, spices, cocoa, condiments, olives, and sugar.

Looking for Sales

Specials on food change weekly, so you'll need to check out the specials at least once a week. However, it's best if you keep an eye out for them daily. Clip the information and put it in a weekly shopping folder, or save the entire flier for your favorite grocery store.

Newspapers are a superb source for finding out about advertised specials. You'll find ad inserts on the day your local paper carries food columns. Usually that's Wednesday. You'll also find fliers on other days, so be sure to read or save all the ad inserts in the paper.

Check your mailbox on Tuesdays. Typically, the same fliers are sent to your home or apartment. Our local ads this week include $1.99 per pound for sirloin tip roast, chicken breast, and chuck roast. Eggs are 99¢ per dozen. Watermelon is 29¢ per pound. Not only that, they're advertising a BOGO on London broil. (That's store jargon for "buy one, get one" free.) This means London broil is half price on Friday, Saturday, and Sunday. Other discounted protein foods are baby back ribs, rib eye steak, whole chickens, lobster, and crab.

The mention of all this food may be making you feel hungry. That's exactly the point of the ads. These fliers can help you decide what you're interested in eating. So don't just toss those advertising packets in the trash. Instead, use them to help plan your meals and shopping.

You can plan your weekly menus by reading the fliers. If chicken is on sale, add chicken to the menu. Ditto any fresh vegetables that you would normally eat. Look for seasonal specials on fruit, too. You could save money. Apples, oranges, and pears store well in the crisper section of the refrigerator for up to a month.

In-Store Unadvertised Specials

On specific days, you'll find good sales once you get to the store. Here in Utah, Sunday night is a great time to shop for meat. The store is mostly empty, few customers are shopping, and the markdowns on meat and fish are terrific. We've purchased ground beef for 99¢ per pound.

Kitchen Wise _____

All produce has a "sell-by" date. The produce staff needs to remove outdated products daily. If you love to eat the freshest produce, be sure to purchase well before the "sell-by" date.

The fresh produce may look a bit tired, though. If you can shop two days a week, look for the freshest produce midmorning on Monday. Or ask the produce staff which days they receive and stock fresh shipments and then shop on those days.

Coupons

Coupons work for saving money even when the specific product isn't on sale. Saving, using, finding, and trading coupons is so popular that these activities now go under the name "couponing."

As you collect coupons, remember that if you purchase an item you wouldn't normally purchase or an item that you don't need or have on your shopping list, then you're not saving money. You're spending more money. If the coupon is for an item that you need or are planning to purchase anyway, only then do you save money.

Don't get so caught up in using your coupons that you overspend your budget on stuff you don't need. Food processors and manufacturers offer coupons as a way to promote their products and as a way to get people to purchase the products. This is great—if you actually use the product.

You'll find coupons in/on the following:

Money Matters _____

You can find coupons online for groceries and virtually anything else. You'll even find shopping cart coupon codes for websites that sell clothing, books, and arts and craft supplies.

- Grocery store shelves

- Grocery store checkout tapes

- Newspapers and mailers

- Magazines

- Coupon websites

As you gather coupons, you'll need a way to manage them so you can use them before their expiration date. Here's a simple way to do this.

Purchase some business-size envelopes. Label them by week to correspond to your weekly grocery-shopping trip. Each time you receive a new food-item or household-item coupon, file it in the correct envelope. Make sure the envelope date is prior to the expiration date.

Money Matters _____

You can request e-mail news-letters from some Internet coupon sites. They'll arrive in your inbox weekly to keep you up-to-date on new coupon offerings.

Before your weekly shopping trip, sort through the coupons so you know what you have. Take them to the store and redeem them at the checkout lane.

Choosing the Grocery Store

You probably already have a grocery store that you use regularly. Most likely it's close to your home, it's convenient, and best of all, you know where everything is. Keep it as your "go-to" favorite if you feel the prices are low or reasonable.

However, you have plenty of choices for where to shop. In this list, we review the pros and cons of your many options.

- **Major grocery store chains.** Easy to shop, send regular sale fliers, good service, have a pharmacy, fresh produce, some gourmet items, deli, bakery, fresh meat, and seafood.

- **Independent grocers.** Prices may be high, produce not so fresh, limited selection. Usually cater to small city neighborhoods.

- **Discount store grocery stores.** Target, Wal-Mart, and Kmart now sell groceries. The prices are good. Some don't have full-service meat counters, some do. Some don't stock a wide variety of brand names, some do. We love the fresh produce and scrumptious bakery items at the one closest to us. But we pass on the prepackaged meat in the freezer.

- **Health food grocers.** Offer organic produce and meats and high-quality "green" household products and personal care items. Prices are high. Seldom carry lightbulbs, batteries, and similar household items. Great takeout bakery and deli. May have a salad bar and eating area.

- **Warehouse grocery stores.** Annual membership fee. Good prices, but you need to purchase big quantities. Prices lower than or equal to major grocery store chains. Good for large families. Great if you have adequate freezer space. May need to repack foods in serving-size portions before storing. Great prices for household items like laundry detergent and paper products.

- **Ethnic markets.** Quality is uneven—some are great; others are dusty and dismal. Some have great prices. Use occasionally but not for your regular weekly shopping.

- **Farmers' markets.** Offer locally grown produce but not always. Check those out-of-season strawberries. They may have come from South America. Bring cash. May or may not be organic. Bring more cash.

- **Cheese shops.** Don't be tempted if you're on a budget.

- **Specialty food shops.** You may find some bargains at times, but overall, the prices are higher, and you can find similar tastes and similar brands in a regular grocery store at lower prices. These include bakeries, meat shops, olive oil stores, nut and fruit shops, and others.

- **Butcher shops.** You can find good prices and high prices. Shop the posted specials.

- **Online.** Order online and have your local grocery store deliver for a $10 fee. A great choice if you order what's on sale and shop conservatively. Eliminates impulse purchases.

◆ **Internet grocery stores.** Shop for canned goods, food in jars, and other staples at Internet sites such as Amazon.com. Great selection, average prices. A superb option if you live out in the wilderness, miles from the nearest grocery store. Yes, we know people who live 45 minutes from a grocery store.

 Money Matters

Some national grocery store chains and warehouse stores also sell gas. You can fill up with a discount based on the dollar volume of your recent purchases or simply by being a member. The convenience and extra savings are terrific.

Your Weekly Shopping Trip

Your challenge is to navigate through the maze of temptations, kiosks, and end caps to arrive at the checkout lane with only the items you have on your list. We've all seen or been the shopper who asks the person bagging our groceries to put the fresh donuts on the top of the bag. Once in our car, we open that bag and eat the donuts before we drive home.

Hey, if you need your treat and it's in the budget (and you prefer to eat in your parked car in front of the store), go for it. Otherwise, you can hide it when you get home. Then save your treat for a quiet moment—provided your treat is allocated for in the budget.

If it sounds like the budget is controlling your life, well, it is controlling some of your life. But not all of it. Not walks in the park, or free concerts, or baby hugs. The budget is just a part of your life.

As you walk through the store, notice the layout. The specialty foods and treats are often at the front, lining your path to the food you need. You may find the fresh potato chip station, the gourmet cheeses, fresh artisan breads, prepared deli foods, and the coffee shop. Ignore these. Move on valiantly toward the perimeter of the store where you'll find vegetables, produce, meats, and fish. Purchase those. Then move on to the dairy section for eggs, milk, cheeses, and butter.

Then—and only then—start down the aisles for canned goods, crackers, coffee, frozen foods, and baking supplies. Proceed to the household products section for detergent, plastic bags, lightbulbs, paper products, and the like. End with personal care items like soap, aspirin, and toothpaste.

Create your regular personalized path through the aisles, always starting with shopping the perimeter and then weaving through the aisles to end at the checkout lane. This will leave you less space in your cart for the items you don't need.

In-Store Tactics

How you shop will determine your success at eating well on a budget. Well-informed shoppers know the ropes. We want you to know them, too. Follow these guidelines:

- Don't shop when you're hungry. The worst times to shop are right before dinner or right before lunch. Your hunger will prompt you to blow the budget. Impulse buys will feel irresistible, so only shop after eating.

- Eliminate distractions. If possible, shop by yourself so you can focus and concentrate. Leave the children at home or shop when they're in school. Like children everywhere, they'll beg for treat foods, run up and down the aisles, or somehow be distracting. We know. We've shopped with our children. Sometimes you'll need to take them with you, but as a rule you'll stick to your plan better if you shop alone. Spouses can also be disruptive, so bring them along with discretion.

- Give yourself time to shop. Rushing through the store isn't fun and could be tough on your budget.

- Take a list and a pen or pencil. Check off items as you purchase them. Be disciplined about this.

- Be goal oriented. You are on a mission. You are in control. You are staying within your budget.

- Shop at the best overall store that meets your savings needs. If you have time, you can shop other stores for sales later.

- With your calculator or mobile phone, keep a running total as you shop. This will definitely keep you in the money.

Money Matters

Years and years ago, mom would count items as the cashier rang them up at the checkout lane. She'd multiply by 50¢ and be right on the money for the total bill. If she purchased 50 items, her bill would be about $25. Mom's math works today if you figure a dollar an item. In some parts of the country, you may need to figure $1.25 or $1.50 per item.

- Calculate the per-unit cost as you choose what quantity to purchase. Don't assume the larger package offers the best cost per unit. Sometimes the larger packages of paper products or spaghetti sauce cost more per unit than the smaller sizes.

- Purchase the basics first. This includes produce, meats, eggs, and dairy. Then shop for other items.

Shop with the confidence that comes from being prepared and knowing that you're doing a good job for yourself and your family. Avoid feeling sorry for yourself when you have to pass up impulse buys. That can actually lead you to give in and make those buys. Think of yourself as a smart shopper and a smart money manager while you shop.

Purchasing Guidelines

To receive the most value for your money, only purchase the most appealing foods. We've all unpacked groceries and wondered how we could have ever selected that specific cucumber. It's soft in spots and withered in others. Rats. We've wasted money because only part of the cucumber is edible and appealing.

Here are some things to check when shopping to get the most value for your dollar:

- Choose meat that looks fresh and hasn't turned brown around the edges. If you can smell it, make sure it smells fresh.

- Fish should have a fresh, briny smell. Older fish gets a pallor on the skin and can smell unappealingly fishy. If shopping for fresh fish, make sure the eyes aren't milky.

- Check bags of fruit and vegetables to make sure that none of them is moldy or soft. If so, choose another bag or ask the produce staff to make you up a fresh bag. Don't purchase fruit in paper bags unless you have checked the items at the bottom of the bag for freshness. This goes for packaged fresh vegetables, too.

- Packaged berries are often moldy, and the mold is hard to detect. Most berries are packaged so you can't see the ones at the bottom. If in doubt, ask the produce manager if you can return them if moldy or don't purchase them.

Kitchen Wise _____

Don't purchase vegetables and fruit at the front of the bins. Instead, select those at the back of the bins. Usually those are the most recently stocked items and are fresher.

◆ Check store "sell-by" dates on vegetables and produce. Ask the produce staff how to determine that date. Purchase items that will last the longest.

◆ Check each egg in the carton to make sure it isn't cracked or sticking to the container. Eggs stay fresh a long time in the refrigerator.

◆ If you aren't skilled at selecting fresh melons or pineapples, ask the produce staff to select one for you and learn the process for yourself.

Purchasing well can actually save you money, so take your time and don't rush. You'll be saving money and preventing waste if you take shopping seriously.

Prepared Foods

Purchasing some prepared foods can save you money. Check out the price per serving of the large baked chickens at the warehouse grocers or the fried chicken combos and the fish and chips at the grocery store. Sometimes you can't prepare the food at home for less money.

In that case, go ahead and purchase takeout. At home, prepare a fresh vegetable or fruit salad, add a side vegetable, and you have an easy meal.

Warehouse grocery stores offer prepared meals that aren't in any way reminiscent of the old-fashioned TV dinners. They're balanced, delicious, and prepared without mystery ingredients like preservatives and artificial flavors and colorings. Not to mention the price is usually right. If the price fits into your budget, enjoy them when you need a takeout meal.

The Least You Need to Know

◆ Shop sales and clip coupons to save money.

◆ Choose a grocery store that meets your needs and offers good sales.

◆ Shop with a list, and shop prepared to meet your budget goals.

◆ Select food carefully for freshness and long refrigerator life.

Chapter 8

Eating Out on a Budget

In This Chapter

◆ Eating out wisely

◆ Managing school lunch costs

◆ Eating for less at restaurants

◆ Entertaining on a budget

Eating out is fun. Someone else prepares the food. You don't need to cook. Often someone else serves you. You feel treated. The menu offers lots of choices, some of which you don't cook at home. You can satisfy your hankering for new tastes while others in your family can satisfy theirs.

Eating out is fun, too, because you can eat with others. It becomes a form of entertainment. The downside is that eating out costs money, and now that you're on a budget, you'll need to consider the cost as part of your food budget.

In this chapter, we discuss eating out for pleasure and convenience. We'll also discuss how to evaluate whether you and your children should buy lunch at school or work, or if packing a sack lunch makes more "cents."

Essential Meals Out

Unless you and your spouse both work at home and you home school your children, you'll need to figure school lunches and work lunches into your food budget. Your choices are simple: either purchase from a school or work cafeteria, go out to eat, or carry along a sack lunch.

How you make that decision can be complex. Some factors to consider are convenience, cost, quality of food—especially at school—and social factors. If your teenager finds it really uncool to pack a lunch, you may need to hone your negotiation and/or parenting skills. In the following sections, we give you information and guidelines for making these choices.

School Lunches

Your children can often eat a good meal at school, depending on the school district. Some cafeterias offer sandwiches, salads, and hot meals, many of which are nutritionally balanced and satisfying. There's plenty of variety, so each day even a picky eater can find something good to eat. The cost is low to moderate. Students pay for the foods they put on their trays, so the cost of each meal can vary based on the price of the entrée and the number of side dishes and add-ons the student chooses.

If your school district doesn't offer healthy foods, you may want to get involved with other parents to request changes to the lunch menu for fresh foods, lower sodium, and lower fat content.

At the time of this writing, a student can eat modestly for about $2 to $2.50 per day at the school cafeteria. Here's how you pay: You'll write a check to deposit money into the child's lunch account. At the checkout lane, rather than pay cash, the student's account is debited. When funds in the lunch account get low, you'll be asked to add more money to the account. If the account has a positive cash balance at the end of the school year, or if your child changes schools, you'll receive a refund for the balance.

Money Matters

The School Nutrition Association works to ensure that all children have access to healthful school meals and nutrition education. You can visit its website at www.schoolnutrition. org to learn more about how it represents the nutritional interests of children.

Your child may qualify for a reduced-fee or free lunch based on your household income, even temporarily. If you think your family might qualify, check with the school. The child may also qualify to receive free breakfast.

If you choose to have your children purchase lunch from the school cafeteria, you can teach them to budget and manage their lunch money. Give them a daily amount that they can spend for food from their account. They'll learn to avoid purchasing the pricier add-ons and side dishes, such as ice cream and yogurt beverages, while choosing the prepared meals or salad bar.

Some junior high and high school students don't like to eat in the cafeteria for social reasons and instead prefer to go off campus for lunch. This costs more than eating in the cafeteria. If your children want to eat off campus, you can give them a budget for off-campus meals or ask them to pay for those lunches with their own money.

It may seem hard on your children to give them food and eating budgets when eating at school, but it's not. Think of it as a life lesson. Budgeting is an important skill for managing life, one that's not taught in high school and seldom taught in college. You are supplementing their education by teaching them to budget and be responsible for spending money.

Even though the cost of school cafeteria lunches can be low and the selection nutritious, you can save money by packing school lunches for your children. Your initial objection may be that it takes too much time for you to pack lunches every morning. It does take some time to get the mechanics figured out, but after that you can prepare nutritious lunches in minutes. You can also prepare the sack lunches the night before.

 Money Matters _____

If you usually pack a school lunch and you can afford it, try letting your children eat one or two meals a week at the school cafeteria. They can choose which day and what entrée and have some freedom and variety.

For starters, purchase lunchboxes or use paper bags. You may want to purchase insulated lunch boxes that keep meals cold and fresh until lunchtime. You'll need paper napkins, sandwich bags, and food containers if you want to get fancy. Here are some sample school lunchbox menus:

- The old standby: peanut butter and jelly sandwich, a couple of carrot sticks, an apple, and a cookie or two

- Cheese and/or meat sandwich, celery sticks, pear, and a small muffin

- Cold chicken tenders or Bottom-of-the-Bag Chicken (from Chapter 11) with a green salad, grapes, and a cupcake

- Salad with meat, seafood, or cheese in a food container with dressing, a banana, and a small granola bar

- ◆ Cold pasta salad with cheese and legumes, sliced green bell pepper and cucumber, and a slice of cake

- ◆ Soup or stew in a wide-mouth thermos, crackers or chips, celery and carrot sticks, and trail mix

For beverages, you can pack a serving size container of 100 percent juice and a small carton of milk. Keep the meals simple. Your children don't need hand-rolled sushi or fettuccini alfredo. They only need a nutritious lunch.

Plan the weekly lunchbox menu when you plan dinner menus for the week. That way, you'll be able to coordinate family meals with lunchbox offerings. For example, you can bake extra chicken for an evening meal and add the drumsticks or chicken tenders to a lunchbox sometime that week. The same is true for sliced roast beef served with a salad in a lunchbox.

Each morning, set up your kitchen workspace so that you can quickly pack lunches and have them ready when the children leave for school. Have a cutting board, knife, food storage bags, food containers, and napkins nearby. Prewash lettuce and cut up vegetables, such as carrot sticks and celery, the night before when you prepare dinner.

If you're preparing several lunches, label each bag with the child's name. Set up an assembly line at the kitchen counter. You can have lunches packed in 5 to 10 minutes.

For students, there can be a stigma attached to eating a sack lunch. The attitude varies so much, though. Some students prefer home meals to cafeteria food; others think of sack lunches as high status. Others couldn't care less. Talk with your children about sack lunches. Find out what foods and treats they want and provide them when possible. If one child loves bologna and mustard sandwiches on white bread and another prefers peanut butter and honey on whole wheat, prepare what they like as best you can. It would be great if you could upgrade the "bologna on white" to "ham on stone ground" for nutritional reasons, but if you can't, prepare a lunch that your child will eat.

Kitchen Wise _____

If your child has access to a microwave to heat up lunch, then you can pack foods that taste better heated, like enchiladas and toasted cheese sandwiches.

Lunches at Work

Packing a lunch is your most economical choice for lunch at work. Unlike school lunches, eating out every day can be quite costly, even if you eat at the least expensive restaurants—usually fast-food joints.

As you consider your eating choices, think about what a lunch break means for you. How do you use your lunch break? As a time …

♦ To physically take a break, get away from the office, and relax. If you pack a lunch, you may want to avoid the lunchroom and instead eat outdoors if weather permits. On colder days, you may not be able to find an indoor location to eat your meals away from the office. You could try the shopping mall. You may want to mix packing a lunch with eating out.

♦ To see friends and socialize. If your friends also pack a lunch, the lunchroom may suit you perfectly. If all your friends eat out, join them only occasionally or bring your packed lunch with you if the situation permits.

♦ To eat, read, and unwind. A quiet spot outside or the lunchroom may be perfect for you.

♦ For exercise and movement. After your time at the gym or running outside, enjoy a sack lunch in the lunchroom or perhaps at your desk.

♦ To run errands. A sack lunch can work perfectly for you as a quick meal on the go.

Money Matters

Many fast-food restaurants offer dollar menus. You can purchase a double cheeseburger, small fries, side salad, and soda for a dollar each—that's $4 plus change. Certainly, that's economical. But eating that diet every day may not be eating well. You decide.

Don't Get Burned

Eating a sack lunch at your desk may not meet your personal lunch break needs. Over time, your space can feel claustrophobic if you sit there all day.

All of these choices work for packing a lunch. You can also pack a lunch several days a week and then eat out with friends one or two days. Be sure that you plan all the costs in your budget regardless and then order your meals out based on your budget allowance.

When it comes time to pay the bill, you can request separate checks. If anyone seems put off, let the person know you're on a food budget and need to be more accountable for a while. Most people understand.

Money Matters _____

> One businessperson relishes the break of eating out midday but also lives on a budget. His goal is to eat for $5 or less every day. He's found restaurants that serve small chef salads or hearty soups for under $5. He eats well because he's ferreted out the best nutritional lunch buys in his work neighborhood.

Pack your lunch with the foods you enjoy. They can be food you cooked for dinner earlier in the week. Here are a couple choices, assuming you have access to a microwave.

- Omelets or scrambled eggs

- Any kind of salad: vegetable, fruit, chef's

- Soups, stews

- Quesadillas, enchiladas, and burritos

- Lasagna, meatballs, pasta

- Fried chicken

- Hot or cold sandwiches

- Vegetables with dips or salsa

Money Matters _____

If you take clients or customers to lunch, be sure that those expenses are reimbursed by the company.

Pack your lunch in a container that can keep foods cold, especially if the lunchroom doesn't offer adequate refrigerator space.

Eating Out for Fun

Eating out is an important part of most people's social life. Virtually anywhere you go for entertainment, food is plentiful and abundant. Think of ballparks, sporting events, movie theaters, and concerts. Even shopping malls have indoor food courts and restaurants sprinkled throughout the parking lots.

People like to eat out. It's fun, easy, relaxing, and usually delicious. It offers different, perhaps even exotic, tastes and taste-bud experiences. Someone else serves you and cleans the dishes after you leave.

We also eat out to celebrate special occasions—wedding anniversaries, Valentine's Day, and other special personal events.

As you're living on a food budget, you may be able to eat out based on your budget numbers. However, it's easy to overspend when you eat out, so in this section we'll give you suggestions for enjoying yourself and purchasing carefully.

Restaurant Choices

To help you decide where to spend the "eat-out" portion of your food budget, we've listed types of restaurants with pros and cons.

The coffee shop. This is a great environment for chatting with friends, but the cost of the coffee is high. The same is true with the snacks. If you go, order plain coffee or tea and hold off on the lattes and cappuccinos. Take a pass on snacks, bottled juices, and water.

Sporting events. Most venues don't allow you to bring in food, and the price of the food is high. After all, you're a captive audience. Eat before you go and/or eat after you go. Plan ahead of time how much money you can spend. Take that amount in cash, and when the money's gone, stop purchasing.

Fast food. The food is inexpensive and nutritious if you choose carefully. Check out the bargain meals—usually a dollar each for a hamburger, fries, and side salad. Avoid the supersize and elaborate offerings—they cost more but don't deliver more nutritional value, just more calories and fat. The lack of ambience and uncomfortable seating encourage you to eat quickly and leave.

Moderately priced sit-down restaurants. The prices aren't low but perhaps are lower than at a fine-dining restaurant. They are often part of a restaurant chain. Because of this, the food is usually high quality with fresh ingredients, freshly baked breads, and time-tested entrées. Even though these restaurants are moderately priced, the add-ons (such as appetizers and side dishes) can make your total bill quite high. You'll spend less money if you eat the same foods at home. Be sure to be realistic when you budget to eat at these restaurants. Some of these restaurants offer coupons and early-bird specials.

Money Matters _____

One local moderately priced restaurant offered an early-bird special on Mondays of lobster for $15.95. We went often and shared the meal. Our cost, including coffee or iced tea, tip, and taxes, was about $25 for a terrific meal. Unfortunately, they no longer offer this treat. But you may be able to find similar deals where you live. Some restaurants now charge a split-entrée fee, so ask before you order.

High-end eateries. These restaurants are expensive and offer ambience and some sort of prestige. They can be where the "in-crowd" gathers or where businesspeople with generous expense accounts entertain clients. Some specialize in romantic settings for special occasion meals. Plan to spend money. The entrées are expensive, and even the sparkling water can cost upwards of $12 a bottle. Eat here only if your budget allows or someone else is buying. These restaurants seldom offer coupons or specials.

Money-Saving Ways to Eat Out

You can save money when eating out. Yes, you'll need to use some restraint, but that may be worth a night out. Be sure to enjoy every bite.

- Split the entrée with your spouse or friend. You won't go hungry at all. Most restaurant portions are huge and more than enough for two people. Even if the restaurant you choose has a split-entrée fee, you'll still eat for about half. That's terrific for your budget.

- Avoid eating at buffets, including brunch buffets. You can't split a meal because each person who eats is charged the cost of the meal.

- Avoid ordering the add-ons. These are often the high-markup items such as appetizers and desserts.

- Order an appetizer and small salad if the cost is less than a full entrée. You may even choose to split an appetizer and salad with a friend and still get plenty to eat.

- Pass on the cocktails, beer, and wine. These are high-markup items. Figure that a bottle of wine costs as much as an entrée, so your bill will be as high as if you had one additional person join you for dinner.

Money Matters _____

Most restaurant servers are fine if you split a meal. Lots of people do. One time in Great Britain, the pub owner wouldn't let us split a meal—he refused to give us a second fork. So we shared a fork. Then, for dessert, he gladly gave us two forks. Go figure. And the entrée was so huge it could have fed four people.

- Pass on beverages except tap water. The cost of tea, bottled water, coffee, and sodas is high, and you don't need them in order to enjoy your dinner.

- Consider dessert carefully. If you order dessert and four forks for four eaters, it may be affordable. But restaurant desserts are an unnecessary expense when you're eating out on a budget.

- Use restaurant coupons. You can find them in the newspaper, coupon mailings, and online.

- Take advantage of early-bird specials. The cutoff time can be 6 or 6:30 P.M. Beat the crowd and save money.

- Ask for a take-home container for food you don't eat. Reheat and eat it for lunch or breakfast the next day.

- If you're eating by yourself or if you're unable to share an entrée, order a full entrée, eat half, and put the other half in a take-home container.

- Before you order the daily special, ask how much it costs. It is often more expensive than regular entrées.

When eating out with others, it's fine to ask for separate checks. If everyone ate about the same amount of food, then split the bill. Don't be shy—you don't need to help pay for someone's bottle of wine that you didn't help drink or someone's enormous sushi habit.

Figure the cost of a 15 percent tip for your server into your budget. Don't skimp on tips, for all the obvious reasons. It's mean, and we're sure it brings bad luck.

Entertaining

Go ahead and invite friends over for dinner or game night. You can if you plan well on your budget. The easiest way for you and your guests is to ask them to bring a dish. You all get to have a great time and the expense is lower for you. Then, of course, you'll reciprocate when you go to their houses.

Many of the recipes in this book work well as your contribution to potlucks at church or for book club. They also are delicious for dinner parties. What you serve doesn't need to be elaborate, just cooked with love.

If the guys have a monthly poker night and absolutely have to eat takeout ribs or barbecue, go with it. And budget the cost of the meal. And any winnings or losses.

The Least You Need to Know

◆ School lunches may be an economical way to eat, or you may want to pack your children's lunches.

◆ Pack a lunch for work to save money, and budget for lunches at the cafeteria or restaurant.

◆ Save money when eating out by using cost-saving tips.

◆ Use potluck dinners for entertaining to save money and still have friends over.

Chapter 9

More Ways to Save on Food

In This Chapter

- Learning how to cook
- Growing and enjoying fresh herbs
- Keeping a vegetable garden
- Preserving, canning, and freezing foods
- Stocking the deep freeze

Saving money on food can be fun, relaxing, and inspiring. "Huh?" you may be thinking. Yes, there's work to it. And if you love numbers and accounting spreadsheets, you could find fun and comfort in that detail work. But even if you don't care for math, there are other ways of finding pleasure in a food budget.

If you love being outdoors and feeling close to the earth, gardening could be peaceful and rewarding—both to your spirit and your food budget. Preserving foods you grow or purchase can also be fun, and it's a project that you can do solo or turn into family time.

The process of cooking can be soothing and enjoyable while expressing love and care. That is, if you already know how to cook or want to learn.

In this chapter, we give you information on how to incorporate fun and pleasurable activities that are healthful for you and your family—and healthy for your food budget.

Your Cooking Skills

Most of us could stand to hone our cooking skills. If you're already a superb cook, you may want to keep up-to-date with the latest innovations and trends. Even if you don't think you have any culinary skills, after taking a class or two, you might discover a chef deep inside waiting to emerge.

Learning how to cook is important for saving money on food. Even the least expensive takeout and frozen dinner selections cost more than preparing foods at home. Sure, a person can sustain life on takeout and frozen entrées, but you can't eat well in the long run and usually not even in the short run.

Don't Get Burned _____

A steady diet of takeout and prepared foods means ingesting food preservatives and too much salt or sodium. What isn't included are enough vegetables and fruit. To eat well, you need at least five (and preferably more) of these important foods every day. Before you purchase prepared foods, read the label carefully to make sure you are supporting your health and not eating lots of "mystery" ingredients.

Cooking can be an art form or a necessity or both. For many people, their approach varies based on time and urgency constraints. But if cooking is drudgery for you, you may need to make some changes. Here are some free or inexpensive suggestions:

◆ Watch the cooking shows on television. You'll learn the step-by-step approach to easy cooking. If you want to hone your skills, tune in to more challenging techniques and celebrated chefs. Just remember that watching isn't the same as doing. You've got to practice it yourself.

◆ Attend free cooking classes at a local grocery store or community center.

◆ Take a moderately priced cooking class at a community school, extension service, or cooking store.

◆ Cook with friends to learn their practical ways of cooking for a family.

◆ Check out books from the library on how to cook.

If you know how to cook but don't like to cook, you may need to tweak your point of view as well—especially if you're the only person in the household who can do the family cooking. You'll find some of these suggestions throughout this book, but we've compiled them for you here in one place:

- ◆ Teach your children to cook and have them prepare a meal or two every week.

- ◆ Join a neighborhood cooking co-op in order to trade out cooking responsibilities with other families several times a week.

- ◆ Cook with your spouse or partner, sharing responsibilities for slicing, sautéing, baking, presentation, and cleanup.

- ◆ Cook enough food for a week once a week, or for a month once a month, to lighten daily cooking chores.

- ◆ Find ways to make cooking fun. Tune in to your favorite music on your music player, cook along with a television chef, sing, or watch your favorite television show or videos.

- ◆ Enlist other family members to set the table, load the dishwasher, and clean up.

Tasty Tidbits _____

Getting motivated to love cooking or to learn to cook may seem impossible. For some people, it's challenging. So face it and accept the challenge. You'll figure out a way.

Get yourself motivated, even if it's hard to do. If saving money and having more money left over every month isn't enough motivation, find your motivation somewhere else. Talk with friends, read cooking magazines, do more exercise, or say positive affirmations.

More Flavorful Foods

Most of our recipes call for dried herbs. They are inexpensive, and a little goes a long way. Usually a teaspoon or less adds distinctive flavor to the recipe and enhances the taste of your food.

Our recipes don't call for fresh herbs because they're costly when you purchase them in the store, and they don't stay fresh for long. Ours have rotted in the food crisper of the refrigerator more than once. While fresh herbs purchased from the store provide great taste for one recipe, they were ultimately a waste of money unless we used them all at once.

The good news is that when you grow your own herbs, you are growing a renewable food source that barely costs pennies per serving. In fact, fresh herbs are free once you pay for the seeds, pot, soil, and water.

The advantage of using fresh herbs is that they make delicious foods taste fabulous. To validate this, I prepared two Greek salads in the past week. In one, I used dried oregano; in the other, I used fresh oregano from the herb pot on the front porch. There was a big difference. Both salads were yummy, but the one with the fresh Italian oregano tasted better. The fragrant flavor sparkled. It had more expression, as if it formed exclamation points in my mouth with each bite.

Fresh herbs can add a taste of elegance and authenticity to ordinary budget fare. Plain old spaghetti prepared with fresh basil, rosemary, or oregano and sprigs of fresh parsley won't taste like it's on a budget. You'll feel pampered and like you're eating gourmet while saving money.

Here's how to put together an herb pot, with estimated prices:

♦ Buy one already planted at the garden shop (about $30 or more). You may find some better prices later in the growing season.

♦ Purchase the herbs as bedding plants and plant them in a large pot (about $20 or more). You'll need to purchase a pot, bedding plants, and potting soil.

♦ Purchase seeds and plant them in an herb pot (about $10 for seeds, pot, and soil).

You can keep the herb pot outdoors in the warm months. In the winter, bring it indoors and place it in a sunny window. You'll enjoy the taste of fresh herbs all year round.

Here are some herbs you can plant and care for easily:

♦ Oregano

♦ Thyme

♦ Rosemary

♦ Tarragon

♦ Chives

♦ Parsley

♦ Sage

♦ Basil

♦ Cilantro

♦ Dill

♦ Mint

To harvest the herbs, simply pinch off or cut off the amount you need for your recipe. This stimulates new growth in the plant, so you're actually keeping the plant vibrant and healthy. Use fertilizer that's safe for vegetables and water as directed.

You'll become a believer in the power of fresh herbs after a couple of meals. They are a great addition to eating well and saving money.

Fresh from the Garden

Growing vegetables in your backyard is a wise way to save money and eat well on a budget. If you already enjoy the bounty of your vegetable patch, you know the benefits.

Homegrown produce tastes better than store bought. Working in the yard is relaxing and rewarding. You can make good use of any extra food by canning it or freezing it. Later in the year, during the cold months, you'll have "free" food in your pantry or freezer ready to eat. You save money twice—once by eating it fresh from the garden and again by eating the excess stored food later in the year when produce typically costs more.

If you don't garden, consider getting started this year. You need a patch of land or some large containers for your porch or patio. Cultivate the soil with good topsoil. Do some research on the Internet or at your local county extension office. Talk with the master gardener at the garden shop. Find out which vegetables grow well in your climate zone.

Unless you have experience or supreme confidence, start small. Plant a couple of easy-to-grow vegetables and learn how to manage your garden. This means how to control bugs, how to fertilize, how to harvest, and how to save the seeds for next year's crop.

Be careful that you use safe products for pest control and fertilizer. After all, you're going to eat what's in the garden. Check out what commercial products to use for an organic garden. Often an organic garden is no more work on a small scale than growing regular produce.

Don't Get Burned

Heirloom varieties of vegetables are luscious and delicious but may not be easy to grow. The same is true of "specialty" vegetables. When starting out, plant the varieties that are easy to grow. There's plenty of time for planting fancy produce after you gain experience.

The most economical way to plant your vegetable garden is with seeds. You can plant them in a shallow tray on a sunny windowsill in early spring and then transplant them after the last frost date. Check with your garden store or the Internet to find the last frost date in your climate. Here in Utah and Colorado, it's the first weekend after Mother's Day, or officially May 15.

You could purchase bedding plants of vegetables, but they cost more than seeds. By starting your seeds in a windowsill planter, you're growing your own bedding plants and saving money.

Learn more about vegetable gardening on television or from books at the library. The Internet is also a superb source of information on gardening.

 Money Matters

> Keep your seeds from last year's crop. Remove some from the vegetables you grew and dry them on paper towels. Store them in small plastic bags and label them. Use them for your next year's crop. Some specialty vegetables can't be grown from seeds that you save. If you want to grow from seeds, make sure the vegetables you plant are open-pollinated or heirloom varieties. Do some research for your growing area so you know which plants to grow for seeds.

Stocking Your Pantry with Preserved Food

When you're blessed with a bumper crop of vegetables, or when you happen upon a terrific sale of bulk fresh produce, make good use of it. Since you can't eat it all while it's still fresh, preserve it and enjoy it later. Here's an overview of how to preserve different types of food.

Freezing

You'll need adequate freezer space—perhaps a second refrigerator or a deep freezer. For supplies, you'll need freezer storage bags or containers and an indelible marking pen.

Freezing vegetables, fruit, and meat is easy. But some vegetables don't freeze well. Don't bother freezing cucumbers, lettuce, radishes, celery, whole tomatoes, and new potatoes.

To freeze vegetables, wash or rinse them well. Blanch them in boiling water to preserve their freshness. To learn the specifics on how to blanch different vegetables and prepare them for freezing, go to www.helpwithcooking.com/food-storage/freezing-vegetables.html.

For instructions on freezing specific fruit, go to www.helpwithcooking.com/food-storage/prepare-freeze-fruit.html. You can find additional websites with good information on freezing as well as books on the subject at the library.

Place prepared produce in freezer-safe packaging such as freezer-safe glass or plastic jars, plastic freezer bags, vacuum packages, freezer foil, or freezer-paper freezer bags in serving-size amounts. Label with the date frozen. Fruit and vegetables will stay good in a freezer stored at 0°F for 12 months. Citrus fruit will only freeze well for 3 to 4 months.

Meats can be frozen right from the store without additional preparation. Seal in freezer-safe packaging. Generally speaking, frozen meat should be eaten within 6 months of freezing to preserve freshness and prevent freezer burn.

 Money Matters

Consider purchasing a side of beef or lamb if you have a deep freezer. The cost is less per pound than at the grocery store, and you have the convenience of always having meat on hand for meals. With some suppliers, you can specify which cuts of meat you prefer.

Canning

Putting up food by canning was popular years and years ago before the invention of the freezer. Freezing foods is easier and takes less time. Canning is more technical and precise and more labor intensive.

However, canning is wonderful if you want to make specialty condiments such as sweet and sour pickles, dilled green beans, chutney, spiced peaches, or jams and jellies. You can also can fruit and vegetables so that later in the winter you can savor the wonderful tastes of your harvest.

The process of canning is technical, and you must follow directions precisely to be successful and stay healthy. If you do it incorrectly, you could grow botulism and other poisons in the jars. Don't let this warning discourage you, however. Folks have been canning for centuries. For an authoritative source for canning and recipes, see Appendix B.

Canning requires heavy-sided glass jars, called Mason Jars, with sealable lids. You can purchase these from the grocery store in harvest season. After you prepare and cook the produce, fill the clean jars. Put on the two-part lids and place the jar in a boiling water bath. The water must cover the top of the jar. The heat from the water makes the lids seal and kills any bacteria or organisms that can spoil the food. The airtight seal preserves the product for years, although you'll probably wind up eating it sooner.

Have you ever noticed that when you open a jar of salsa or jelly that the top of the lid pops and you hear a whooshing sound? That's because you're breaking the "canning" seal on the jar.

Canning can be a fun family project with everyone working together. It makes the eating more memorable and satisfying.

Drying

Drying food is a preservation process that takes the moisture from food. Dehydrated food is great for mountain climbers but seldom is eaten in homes for family meals. The single exception is meat—beef, turkey, or buffalo—jerky.

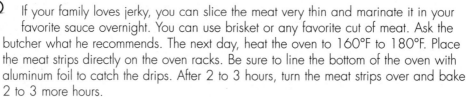

Kitchen Wise _____

If your family loves jerky, you can slice the meat very thin and marinate it in your favorite sauce overnight. You can use brisket or any favorite cut of meat. Ask the butcher what he recommends. The next day, heat the oven to 160°F to 180°F. Place the meat strips directly on the oven racks. Be sure to line the bottom of the oven with aluminum foil to catch the drips. After 2 to 3 hours, turn the meat strips over and bake 2 to 3 more hours.

You won't save money by drying food—unless your family consumes huge amounts of jerky.

The Least You Need to Know

◆ Cooking meals at home is healthy for your budget and saves money.

◆ Keep a pot of fresh herbs on your windowsill or patio to flavor your cost-saving meals with their aromatic tastes.

◆ Grow some of your own vegetables to save money.

◆ Preserve foods by freezing or canning.

Part 3

Recipes for Eating Well

You can save money every time you prepare a meal with these recipes. You'll find recipes for breakfasts, snacks, both meat-based and vegetarian entrées, a plethora of vegetable and grain side dishes, and sweet and lively desserts.

Many of our recipes are prepared so that you have leftovers to use later in the week for lunches, snacks, and dinner ingredients. To keep your taste buds satisfied, the recipes offer varied tastes—some ethnic, some regional, some totally new. Most recipes suggest variations so you can substitute ingredients you already have on hand.

The recipes also invite you to add your own personalized touch with seasonings, choices of cheese, produce, and other optional ingredients.

Enjoy!

10

Breakfasts

In This Chapter

- ◆ Preparing well-balanced breakfasts
- ◆ Recipes for both quick and leisurely cooking
- ◆ Enjoying varying tastes and ingredients
- ◆ Pleasing any finicky eaters in your family

Breakfast is so important—it's your most important meal of the day. That's why we've devoted an entire recipe chapter to breakfasts. Research studies show that people who eat breakfast consume more vitamins and minerals and eat less fat throughout the day than people who skip breakfast. Breakfast eaters also weigh less and have lower cholesterol. Women who eat one to two eggs for breakfast eat less food during the day and weigh less than women who don't. Eating a nutritious and balanced breakfast improves productivity, endurance, and concentration in adults and children.

Your children need a healthy breakfast to jump-start their day at school or play; you need breakfast to jump-start your metabolism and enhance your work life.

The good news is that eating a simple breakfast fits well into your food budget. Try simple, balanced meals such as an egg and fruit, yogurt and oatmeal, or cereal, milk (2 percent), and fruit. These are quick and inexpensive yet tasty and wholesome. Make time for this meal and a place for it in your budget.

Kitchen Wise _____

To fry an egg, use a cast-iron skillet that you season only for cooking eggs. Heat the skillet over medium-low heat and then add a small pat of butter. When it melts, add an egg. Cook as desired. Never wash the pan with soap and water. It will rust. Instead, wipe it with a paper towel or wash it only with water and dry well. Your pan will cook up the best eggs ever, and they won't stick.

In this chapter, you'll find recipes for everything from hand-held, grab-and-go weekday breakfasts to beautiful weekend brunches.

Chile Egg Puff

A zesty morning twist on chile rellenos. This reliable favorite coaxes even the slowest risers out of bed.

½ tsp. olive oil

1 (4-oz.) can whole green chiles

1 cup Monterey Jack cheese, shredded

5 eggs

¼ cup flour

2 tsp. baking powder

¼ tsp. ground black pepper

1 cup cottage cheese

1 TB. 2 percent milk

Yield: 1 9×13-inch casserole
Prep time: 10 minutes
Cook time: 35 minutes
Serves: 8
Serving size: 1 slice
Each serving has:
182 calories
8.7 g fat
4.1 g saturated fat
244 mg sodium
14.9 g carbohydrates
4.2 g dietary fiber
12.8 g protein

1. Preheat oven to 400°F. Coat a 9×13-inch baking dish lightly in olive oil. Drain chiles and remove any seeds. Stuff each chile with Monterey Jack cheese and place into the baking dish.

2. In a large mixing bowl, combine eggs, flour, baking powder, pepper, cottage cheese, and milk. Pour egg mixture on top of chiles.

3. Bake 35 minutes until eggs are set and pulling away from the sides of the dish. Remove from the oven when top is golden. Cool 10 minutes before slicing and serving.

Kitchen Wise

The chiles at the bottom make this a beautiful dish, and the texture provided by cottage cheese always earns rave reviews. This dish tastes great cold and holds up very well in the refrigerator, making it a perfect alternative to donuts for morning meetings.

Savory Spinach and Bacon Bake

The pungent flavors of spinach and smoked bacon brighten any morning. The red tomatoes and crisped cheese topping catch the eye and tempt the palate.

Yield: 1 pie
Prep time: 20 minutes
Cook time: 35 minutes
Serves: 8
Serving size: ⅛ pie
Each serving has:
117 calories
6.9 g fat
2.4 g saturated fat
276 mg sodium
8 g carbohydrates
3 g dietary fiber
11.4 g protein

6 (about ¼-pound) slices turkey bacon

2 cups fresh spinach, washed and dried

8 eggs

¼ cup 2 percent milk

¼ tsp. ground black pepper

¼ tsp. garlic powder

¼ tsp. dried parsley

½ tsp. olive oil

1 cup chopped tomatoes

⅓ cup grated Parmesan cheese

1. Cook bacon until crisp, crumble, and set aside.

2. Remove stems from spinach and tear leaves into small pieces.

3. In a large mixing bowl, combine eggs, milk, pepper, garlic, and parsley. Stir vigorously. Add spinach and bacon, stirring gently to combine. Pour egg mixture into a 9×13-inch baking dish lightly coated with olive oil.

4. Spread chopped tomatoes on top of mixture and bake 25 minutes in a 375°F oven. Remove from the oven and sprinkle with Parmesan cheese. Return to the oven and bake another 10 minutes until edges are dry and center does not jiggle when touched. Allow to cool before cutting and serving.

 Tasty Tidbits

In summer, grow some tomatoes of your own. Nothing beats the flavor—and the price—of homegrown tomatoes. Experiment with colorful heirloom varieties for a season full of delicious discoveries. Try sweet red Zebra Stripe or tangy Big Rainbow.

Poached Eggs on Turkey

With a slice of turkey, a poached egg, and a sprinkle of parsley, you have a quick and easy breakfast.

4 eggs

4 (1-oz.) slices turkey

½ tsp. olive oil

Ground black pepper

1 tsp. dried parsley

Yield: 4 eggs
Prep time: 10 minutes
Cook time: 8 minutes
Serves: 4
Serving size: 1 egg
Each serving has:
111 calories
5.8 g fat
1.8 g saturated fat
82 mg sodium
0.4 g carbohydrates
0 g dietary fiber
13.9 g protein

1. In a large saucepan, bring 3 cups of water to a boil, then reduce heat to medium. Allow water to cool slightly, until it is lightly simmering. Crack each egg into a small bowl, then gently ease the egg into the water. Cook 4 minutes, or 3 minutes if you like runny yolks. Use a slotted spoon to remove poached eggs and set aside on a paper towel to absorb excess water.

2. In a lightly oiled skillet, warm turkey slices over medium-high heat for 3 minutes on each side. Place each slice on a plate and top with a poached egg.

3. Sprinkle each egg with pepper to taste and parsley for color. Serve immediately.

 Tasty Tidbits _____

Jazz up this simple dish for brunch by adding apple slices to the skillet and sautéing them with the turkey. Serve alongside the eggs.

Just Right Cheese Omelet

Tasty eggs cooked to perfection with creamy mild cheese.

Yield: 1 omelet
Prep time: 5 minutes
Cook time: 5 minutes
Serves: 2
Serving size: ½ omelet
Each serving has:
165 calories
12.3 g fat
5.1 g saturated fat
174 mg sodium
1.3 g carbohydrates
0 g dietary fiber
12.3 g protein

½ tsp. olive oil

3 eggs

2 TB. 2 percent milk

¼ tsp. ground black pepper

⅛ tsp. salt

¼ cup shredded Monterey Jack cheese

1. Lightly coat a medium skillet with olive oil. Preheat over medium-low heat.

2. In a medium bowl, combine eggs, milk, pepper, and salt. Whisk briskly.

3. Pour egg mixture into the skillet. Lift the skillet slightly from the burner and swirl egg mixture around in the skillet to coat the sides and spread mixture evenly. Return the skillet to the burner. Cook undisturbed for 2 minutes until eggs begin to set up. Lift the skillet again and swirl mixture to move any remaining liquid to the sides of the skillet. Return the skillet to the burner.

4. When omelet edges begin to crisp and pull away from the sides of the skillet, sprinkle cheese on half the omelet. Run a fork or spatula under the half without cheese and fold it over the cheese. Cook folded omelet another minute to allow cheese to melt. Remove from heat and serve immediately.

Variation: You can use other types of cheese such as Cheddar or Swiss. You can also add diced cooked meats, like ham or turkey, or diced vegetables such as tomatoes, bell peppers, celery, onions, or black olives.

Kitchen Wise

Swirling the egg mixture in the skillet is the key to a perfectly cooked omelet.

Zesty Breakfast Burritos

The flavor of the green chiles with the black beans makes this dish delicious.

1 (15-oz.) can black beans	**¼ tsp. cayenne pepper**
½ cup diced green chiles	**¼ tsp. garlic powder**
½ cup chopped tomato	**6 whole-wheat tortillas**
¼ cup diced green bell pepper	**6 TB. shredded cheese (use whatever kind your family likes)**

Yield: 6 burritos
Prep time: 10 minutes
Cook time: 5 minutes
Serves: 6
Serving size: 1 burrito
Each serving has:
423 calories
6.6 g fat
1.8 g saturated fat
221 mg sodium
69.1 g carbohydrates
13.9 g dietary fiber
21.5 g protein

1. Drain and rinse black beans. In a large skillet over medium-high heat, combine beans, chiles, tomatoes, bell pepper, cayenne pepper, and garlic powder. Cook 5 minutes, stirring frequently, until bell pepper begins to soften.

2. Spoon mixture into tortillas, sprinkle with cheese, and roll burritos up tightly. Enjoy immediately.

Tasty Tidbits

You can make these burritos spicier or milder. Adjust the heat by increasing or decreasing cayenne pepper. If limes are in season, add a squeeze of fresh lime juice to the beans for an authentic touch.

Baked Scotch Eggs

Pub food for breakfast? With a few healthy modifications, why not? Just skip the pint and enjoy a piping hot cup of tea.

Yield: 4 eggs
Prep time: 20 minutes
Cook time: 50 minutes
Serves: 4
Serving size: 1 egg
Each serving has:
343 calories
21.6 g fat
6.8 g saturated fat
662 mg sodium
15 g carbohydrates
0.9 g dietary fiber
21.1 g protein

4 eggs

8 oz. ground turkey sausage

2 egg whites

¾ cup sourdough bread-crumbs

1. To hard boil eggs, place eggs gently into a medium saucepan. Cover eggs with enough water to fill half the pan. Bring to a boil, turn off heat, and leave eggs in hot water, covered with lid, 15 minutes. Remove and drain, rinsing eggs with cool running water for a minute to stop cooking. Crack eggs gently and remove shells, and set eggs aside.

2. Preheat oven to 350°F. Divide sausage into quarters. With each quarter, form a patty in your hand, place a hard-boiled egg in the center of each patty, and wrap around the egg. Make sure to seal the edges.

3. In a small bowl, whisk the 2 egg whites. Dip each sausage-wrapped egg into the egg whites, dredge each ball in bread-crumbs, and place on a cookie sheet lined with parchment paper.

4. Bake 35 minutes until golden brown and crispy outside. Allow eggs to cool slightly, slice each egg in half, and serve.

 Tasty Tidbits

If you prepare these eggs the night before and refrigerate until morning, you'll have a scrumptious surprise. They taste even better cold! Take one with you for breakfast on the run.

Banana Honey Oatmeal

The nutty flavor and light crunch of steel-cut oats compliments the creamy sweetness of ripe bananas. You'll never settle for instant oatmeal again.

1 cup steel-cut oats	**1 tsp. vanilla**
4 cups water	**2 bananas, sliced**
¼ tsp. salt	**½ cup 2 percent milk**
1 tsp. butter	**2 TB. honey**

1. In a medium saucepan, combine oats, water, salt, and butter. Bring to a boil and then reduce heat to medium. Simmer oats 25 minutes, stirring occasionally.

2. Add vanilla. Simmer for 10 minutes, stirring frequently as oatmeal thickens.

3. Remove oats from heat and divide into 4 bowls. Top each with half a sliced banana, 2 tablespoons milk, and ½ tablespoon honey, and enjoy.

Yield: 4 bowls
Prep time: 5 minutes
Cook time: 40 minutes
Serves: 4
Serving size: 1 bowl
Each serving has:
189 calories
3.1 g fat
1.3 g saturated fat
174 mg sodium
37.5 g carbohydrates
3.6 g dietary fiber
4.4 g protein

Kitchen Wise

Steel-cut oats are sometimes called pinhead, Irish, or Scotch oats. They take longer to cook than instant or rolled oats, but for taste and health benefits, they are well worth the extra effort.

Baked Cranberry Apple Oatmeal

This delicious oatmeal casserole is nutty, sweet, tart, and creamy. The oats soak overnight, so prepare before going to bed.

Yield: 4 bowls
Prep time: 25 minutes
Cook time: 12 minutes
Serves: 4
Serving size: 1 bowl
Each serving has:
252 calories
2.4 g fat
0.8 g saturated fat
55 mg sodium
54.7 g carbohydrates
4.3 g dietary fiber
6.2 g protein

4 cups water

1 cup steel-cut oats

½ tsp. olive oil

1½ cups applesauce

⅓ cup honey

1 cup frozen cranberries, thawed

1 cup low-fat plain yogurt

1. Bring water to a boil in a saucepan with a tight-fitting lid. Add oats, stir, turn off heat, and cover. Leave overnight or at least 6 hours. Drain.

2. Preheat oven to 400°F. Lightly coat a 9×13-inch baking dish with olive oil. In a large mixing bowl, combine oats, applesauce, honey, and cranberries. Pour mixture into the baking dish and bake 12 minutes, or 15 minutes if you prefer softer oatmeal.

3. Remove from oven and allow oatmeal to cool slightly. Serve in individual bowls with ¼ cup yogurt.

Variation: For a special treat for brunch, add ½ cup diced orange-colored fruit like peaches or apricots before baking. You can also sprinkle a bit of cinnamon or nutmeg on top before serving.

Kitchen Wise

Steel-cut oats, also called oat groats, are a coarsely cut whole grain. The coarse cutting preserves oatmeal's natural nutty flavor.

Baked French Toast with Honey Walnut Syrup

The bread soaks in the cinnamon batter overnight and then is baked with a honey walnut syrup before serving.

4 eggs

½ cup 2 percent milk

½ tsp. cinnamon

1 tsp. vanilla

8 slices day-old crusty French bread

¼ cup butter, melted

¼ cup honey

¼ cup maple syrup or pancake syrup

½ cup chopped walnuts

Yield: 8 slices
Prep time: 30 minutes
Cook time: 40 minutes
Serves: 8
Serving size: 1 slice
Each serving has:
222 calories
13.2 g fat
4.8 g saturated fat
141 mg sodium
21.7 g carbohydrates
0.8 g dietary fiber
5.9 g protein

1. In a mixing bowl, combine eggs, milk, cinnamon, and vanilla. Place bread slices in a 9×13-inch baking dish and pour egg mixture over bread. Cover the dish and refrigerate overnight.

2. Preheat the oven to 350°F.

3. In another 9×13-inch baking dish, stir together butter, honey, maple syrup, and walnuts. Place soaked bread slices on top of the syrup and nuts. Bake 40 minutes or until the slices puff up and turn golden brown.

4. Remove slices from the baking dish with a spatula and place a slice on each of 8 plates with syrup side up. Evenly divide the nutty syrup among the 8 dishes. Serve immediately.

Variation: Add ½ cup chopped pecans, almonds, or cashews in place of the walnuts.

Tasty Tidbits

Using stale bread makes the toast hold up well to soaking and baking. Fresh bread could crumble or seemingly melt into the batter.

Cottage Cheese and Fruit

Cottage cheese and peanut butter are topped with fruit for a delicious and energizing breakfast.

Yield: 6 cups
Prep time: 5 minutes
Cook time: None
Serves: 4
Serving size: 1½ cups
Each serving has:
367 calories
18.6 g fat
4.8 g saturated fat
608 mg sodium
30.6 g carbohydrates
3.6 g dietary fiber
24.1 g protein

4 large crisp lettuce leaves

2 cups low-fat cottage cheese

½ cup peanut butter

1 apple, chopped

1 sliced banana

2 TB. honey

1. Arrange 4 lettuce leaves on separate plates. Place ½ cup cottage cheese and 2 tablespoons peanut butter onto each lettuce leaf.

2. Divide chopped apple and sliced banana and place on top of cottage cheese.

3. Drizzle each serving with ½ tablespoon honey and serve.

 Tasty Tidbits

The combination of cottage cheese and peanut butter may sound a little weird, but it's surprisingly good. Sliced strawberries in season make a tasty addition.

Fresh Fruit with Tangy Yogurt Sauce

The combination of textures and sweet and tart fruits wake up the senses and start the day off right.

½ cup frozen cranberries, thawed

½ cup orange juice

¼ cup honey

2 cups low-fat plain yogurt

2 apples, sliced

2 bananas, sliced

⅓ cup chopped walnuts

Yield: 8 cups
Prep time: 15 minutes
Cook time: 10 minutes
Serves: 4
Serving size: 2 cups
Each serving has:
314 calories
8.4 g fat
1.7 g saturated fat
89 mg sodium
54.8 g carbohydrates
4.5 g dietary fiber
10.1 g protein

1. In a medium saucepan over medium heat, combine cranberries and orange juice. Cook 5 minutes, add honey, and continue simmering for 5 more minutes. Stir often. Remove from heat and cool slightly.

2. In a medium bowl, combine cooled cranberry sauce with yogurt and stir until well blended.

3. In a large mixing bowl, combine apples, bananas, and walnuts. Divide fruit mixture between two bowls. Drizzle yogurt sauce generously over fruit and serve immediately.

Variation: Replace the apples and bananas with seasonal fruit such as oranges, kiwis, and peaches.

Kitchen Wise

Save time in the morning by preparing the cranberry sauce and yogurt mixture the night before. Store it in the refrigerator overnight. In the morning, slice the fruit and enjoy.

Nutty Fruit Parfait

This creamy, crunchy, layered delight makes a perfect breakfast for hectic mornings.

Yield: 2¼ cups
Prep time: 10 minutes
Cook time: None
Serves: 2
Serving size: 1⅛ cups
Each serving has:
335 calories
20.4 g fat
2.3 g saturated fat
87 mg sodium
28.7 g carbohydrates
3.6 g dietary fiber
14.2 g protein

1 cup low-fat plain yogurt

½ cup chopped walnuts

1 TB. honey

¼ cup frozen mixed berries, thawed

¼ cup diced apple

¼ cup sliced banana

In a glass or bowl, layer ½ cup yogurt, ¼ cup chopped walnuts, and ½ tablespoon honey. Do not mix. Cover nuts and honey with berries. Top with remaining yogurt. Add apples and bananas to the glass. On top, add rest of walnuts and ½ tablespoon honey.

Variation: Substitute almonds or cashews for the walnuts.

 Tasty Tidbits _____

Add a little more crunch to this treat by mixing in ¼ cup healthy breakfast cereal as a layer of its own.

Lunches

In This Chapter

- ◆ Packing a budget-conscious and healthy to-go lunch
- ◆ Preparing hearty lunches to eat at home
- ◆ Enjoying comfort foods
- ◆ Making gourmet meals

Whether you brown bag it or enjoy your midday meal at home, we've chosen recipes packed with flavor and the nutrition you and your family need to finish the afternoon strong.

Lunch is a perfect time to enjoy lighter foods and smaller amounts of food than you may prefer to eat for dinner. Pair smaller portions of these recipes with a bowl of soup (see Chapter 12) or a salad (see Chapter 14) to make lunchtime eating more interesting.

Lunch offers a good opportunity to use up leftovers and stretch your food budget. Save your leftover meats, soups, and vegetables. Check the refrigerator before you prepare lunch and enjoy the rewards of cooking that you've already done while saving money.

Mediterranean Veggie Pockets

A zesty way to enjoy the bright, nutritious flavors of the Mediterranean, with creamy garbanzo beans, garlic, and lemon tucked into pita bread.

Yield: 6 pockets
Prep time: 15 minutes
Serves: 6
Serving size: 1 pocket
Each serving has:
261 calories
7 g fat
1.5 g saturated fat
161 mg sodium
30.3 g carbohydrates
6.3 g dietary fiber
19.4 g protein

1 cup garbanzo beans

3 TB. bottled salad dressing (use your family's favorite)

3 pitas

8 oz. roast beef in 6 slices

½ cup shredded lettuce

¼ cup diced tomatoes

¼ cup shredded cucumber

1. Combine garbanzo beans and salad dressing in a blender and purée until semi smooth.

2. Slice each pita in half. Spoon $\frac{1}{6}$ of bean mixture into each pocket and spread all the way to bottom and sides with the back of the spoon. Add 1 slice roast beef to each pita. Fill each pocket with equal amounts of lettuce, tomato, and cucumber. Serve.

Bottom-of-the-Bag Chicken

Stop throwing away the crumbs at the bottom of a bag of whole-grain chips or crackers. Turn them into a crunchy coating for oven-baked chicken strips. Store crumbs in an airtight container until ready to use so they do not become stale.

1 lb. chicken breasts

½ cup crushed whole-grain chips or crackers

1 egg, beaten

Yield: 16 chicken strips
Prep time: 15 minutes
Cook time: 15 minutes
Serves: 8
Serving size: 2 strips
Each serving has:
135 calories
5.7 g fat
1.5 g saturated fat
89 mg sodium
2.4 g carbohydrates
0 g dietary fiber
17.4 g protein

1. Preheat oven to 400°F. Rinse chicken breasts and cut into long 1-inch-wide strips. Set aside.

2. In a large bowl, crush chips or crackers. In a small bowl, beat egg. Dip each chicken strip into egg and then into chip mixture. Coat each piece well and place on a cookie sheet covered with parchment paper.

3. Bake 15 minutes until crispy. Cool slightly before serving.

Variation: Use white fish or salmon in place of the chicken. Different chips and crackers produce amazingly different tastes. Try flavors such as real Cheddar, sea salt and vinegar, coarse stone-ground wheat, or crunchy corn.

Tasty Tidbits

Serve chicken fingers with several different sauces to add variety to your meals. Try honey mustard, salsa, or for a buffalo wing flavor, serve with sour cream and hot sauce.

Tuna Salad with Vegetables

An open-faced tuna melt with a touch of dill and the tangy bite of sharp Cheddar.

Yield: 3 melts
Prep time: 5 minutes
Cook time: 7 minutes
Serves: 6
Serving size: ½ sandwich
Each serving has:
214 calories
11.3 g fat
4.1 g saturated fat
282 mg sodium
12.3 g carbohydrates
0.5 g dietary fiber
15.6 g protein

8 oz. canned tuna, drained

¼ cup diced red bell pepper

⅛ cup celery, diced

¼ cup mayonnaise

1 tsp. dill

3 slices sourdough bread

3 slices sharp Cheddar cheese

1. Preheat oven to 350°F. In a large bowl, combine tuna, bell pepper, celery, mayonnaise, and dill. Spread tuna mixture on sourdough slices. Cover each piece with a slice of Cheddar.

2. Place sandwiches on a baking sheet and warm in oven 10 minutes until cheese is bubbly. Cut each slice in half. Serve.

 Kitchen Wise _____

Prepare the tuna salad the night before serving to strengthen the taste of the dill. Cover well and refrigerate.

Chili-Stuffed Potato Skins

Zesty homemade chili and Cheddar cheese tops baked red potatoes.

4 small new red potatoes, baked	**½ cup shredded Cheddar cheese**
1 cup chili (see Chapter 12)	**2 TB. sour cream**

1. Preheat oven to 425°F. Wash potatoes. Bake for half an hour. You can take a shortcut and microwave potatoes. Wash and then poke each with a fork several times. Place on a dish in the microwave and cook on high for 15 minutes. Remove and cool.

2. Cut each potato in half and carefully scoop out insides with a spoon. Place scooped-out halves on a cookie sheet lined with parchment paper or aluminum foil.

3. Spoon chili into each potato skin, sprinkle with 1 tablespoon cheese, and bake at 425°F for 10 minutes or until cheese is bubbling. Remove and top each with ¾ teaspoon sour cream. Serve immediately.

Variation: Top each potato skin with 1 tablespoon of salsa before topping with sour cream.

Yield: 8 potato skins
Prep time: 15 minutes, after potatoes bake
Cook time: 10 minutes, after potatoes bake
Serves: 4
Serving size: 2 skins
Each serving has:
259 calories
9.6 g fat
5.3 g saturated fat
435 mg sodium
34.8 g carbohydrates
6.9 g dietary fiber
10.2 g protein

Kitchen Wise

Stretch your food budget farther by using leftover chili for lunch and saving the insides of the potatoes to use to thicken a hearty soup.

Grown-Up Peanut Butter and Jelly

Enhance the flavor of this old standard with bananas and berries and enjoy with icy lemonade.

Yield: 2 sandwiches
Prep time: 10 minutes
Cook time: None
Serves: 4
Serving size: ½ sandwich
Each serving has:
276 calories
16.6 g fat
3.5 g saturated fat
210 mg sodium
27.3 g carbohydrates
3.3 g dietary fiber
9.1 g protein

4 slices stone-ground bread

8 TB. peanut butter

1 banana, sliced

¼ cup frozen mixed berries, thawed

2 TB. honey

1. Toast bread. Spread 2 tablespoons peanut butter on each slice. Cover two slices evenly with banana.

2. In a small bowl, crush mixed berries with the back of a spoon. Add honey to the bowl and warm in the microwave on high for 15 seconds. Stir well.

3. Spoon berry sauce on the two bread slices without bananas. Put a banana side together with a berry side, cut in half, and serve.

Kitchen Wise

Children love these sandwiches as much as adults do. In place of bananas and berries, try pineapple with shredded coconut, peaches, Granny Smith apple slices, or raisins with jam.

Rarebit and Turkey Sandwich

This English favorite, heated cheese sauce on toast, is enriched with turkey and seasoned with cayenne.

2 TB. prepared stone-ground mustard

½ cup shredded Cheddar cheese

1 TB. olive oil

¼ tsp. ground black pepper

4 (1-oz.) slices turkey

4 slices stone-ground bread

⅛ tsp. cayenne pepper

Yield: 4 slices	
Prep time: 5 minutes	
Cook time: 10 minutes	
Serves: 4	
Serving size: 1 slice	
Each serving has:	
227 calories	
10.1 g fat	
4.1 g saturated fat	
316 mg sodium	
18.2 g carbohydrates	
0.8 g dietary fiber	
15.6 g protein	

1. Preheat broiler on low.

2. In a medium bowl, combine mustard, Cheddar, olive oil, and pepper.

3. Place two slices of turkey on each slice of bread. Spoon cheese mixture over turkey and bake on a cookie sheet under broiler until golden and bubbling.

4. Sprinkle slices with cayenne pepper. Serve immediately.

Tasty Tidbits

Stone-ground mustard tastes best in this dish. It gives rarebit a tangy, pungent flavor of coarse mustard mingling with Cheddar cheese.

Turkey and Cranberry Wrap

Smoked turkey and tangy cranberries are wrapped with crunchy walnuts and apples for a colorful and hearty lunch.

Yield: 4 wraps
Prep time: 10 minutes
Cook time: 20 seconds
Serves: 4
Serving size: 1 wrap
Each serving has:
309 calories
6.3 g fat
0 g saturated fat
753 mg sodium
47.8 g carbohydrates
3.9 g dietary fiber
15 g protein

¼ **cup frozen cranberries, thawed**

¼ **cup honey**

2 TB. chopped walnuts

4 whole-wheat tortillas

8 oz. cooked turkey breast, chopped

1 cup fresh spinach, torn in small pieces

1 apple, unpeeled and diced

1. In a small bowl, combine cranberries and honey. Microwave on high for 20 seconds. Stir in walnuts and set aside.

2. In the center of each tortilla, arrange turkey, spinach, and apples. Spoon cranberry mixture over top.

3. Wrap each tortilla by folding up the bottom and then folding both sides toward the center. Eat with a fork or carefully with your hands.

Variation: When pears are in season, slice one or two for this wrap, add with the apples, and enjoy a refreshing twist on the standard turkey sandwich.

 Kitchen Wise

When cranberries are in season, and on sale, buy them fresh and enjoy the tangy crunch only fresh cranberries have. You can freeze whatever you don't use right away.

Cheese Wraps with Vegetables and Herbs

With cream and cottage cheeses and crunchy vegetables lightly flavored with garlic and cayenne pepper, this wrap makes a perfect on-the-go lunch.

¼ cup cottage cheese

2 oz. cream cheese

1 tsp. garlic powder

½ tsp. parsley

¼ tsp. cayenne pepper

3 TB. bottled salad dressing of your choice

4 whole-wheat tortillas

1 cup spinach, torn in small pieces

¼ cup shredded carrots

¼ cup chopped celery

Yield: 4 wraps
Prep time: 15 minutes
Cook time: None
Serves: 4
Serving size: 1 wrap
Each serving has:
251 calories
12 g fat
3.8 g saturated fat
365 mg sodium
26.7 g carbohydrates
2.5 g dietary fiber
7.4 g protein

1. In a small bowl, mix together cottage cheese, cream cheese, garlic, parsley, and cayenne pepper. Spread ¼ of cheese mixture on each tortilla.

2. Top evenly with spinach, carrots, and celery. Wrap each tortilla by folding up the bottom and then folding both sides toward the center.

 Tasty Tidbits _____

Add mashed legumes or shredded Parmesan to these vegetarian wraps.

Baked South-Of-The-Border Tortillas

The classic combination of beans, green chiles, and tomatoes baked to crispy perfection.

1 (16-oz.) can refried beans

$\frac{1}{2}$ cup tomatoes, chopped

1 (4-oz.) can diced green chiles

$\frac{1}{4}$ tsp. chili powder

$\frac{1}{4}$ cup Cheddar cheese, shredded

8 corn tortillas

$\frac{1}{4}$ cup Monterey Jack cheese, shredded

4 TB. taco sauce or salsa

1. Preheat oven to 375°F.

2. In a medium saucepan over medium heat, combine beans, tomatoes, chiles, chili powder, and Cheddar cheese. Stir until smooth and cheese melts.

3. Build four stacked sandwiches, starting with 4 baked tortillas. Spread $\frac{1}{4}$ of bean mixture over each tortilla, sprinkle with $\frac{1}{2}$ tablespoon Monterey Jack cheese, and drizzle with taco sauce. Top with another tortilla. Drizzle more taco sauce and sprinkle with remaining cheese.

4. Place tortilla sandwiches on a cookie sheet and bake 10 minutes or until cheese is bubbling. Cut sandwiches in two and serve immediately.

 Don't Get Burned

Make sure you have plenty of napkins for this cheesy delight, and you probably shouldn't be wearing a white shirt. Eat slowly and savor every bite.

Creamy Chicken and Raisin Salad

Golden raisins sweeten this refreshing dish for a light lunch.

8 oz. cooked chicken breast, chopped

½ cup low-fat plain yogurt

⅛ cup golden raisins

⅛ cup walnuts, chopped

½ cup chopped celery

2 TB. honey

1 tsp. curry powder

1 tsp. chili powder

4 crisp lettuce leaves

Yield: 4 salads
Prep time: 5 minutes
Cook time: None
Serves: 4
Serving size: 1 salad (about ½ cup)
Each serving has:
189 calories
5 g fat
1 g saturated fat
83 mg sodium
15.9 g carbohydrates
1.1 g dietary fiber
20.6 g protein

1. In a large bowl, combine chicken, yogurt, raisins, walnuts, celery, honey, curry powder, and chili powder. Stir well.

2. Spoon salad onto lettuce leaves and serve.

Variation: If you are lactose intolerant, substitute mayonnaise for the yogurt in this recipe.

Tasty Tidbits

Pack this salad to go by wrapping it in a whole-wheat tortilla. When grapes are in season, add ¼ cup sliced green grapes to the salad for a refreshing, sweet crunch.

Baked Salmon and Asian Cabbage Salad

Pineapple-glazed salmon fillets perfectly compliment this sweet and sour cabbage salad.

Yield: 6 salads
Prep time: 20 minutes
Cook time: 25 minutes
Serves: 6
Serving size: 1 salmon fillet and ½ cup salad
Each serving has:
232 calories
13.9 g fat
2.5 g saturated fat
366 mg sodium
6.9 g carbohydrates
1.5 g dietary fiber
17.7 g protein

6 (18-oz.) salmon fillets

½ cup canned pineapple juice

2 TB. soy sauce

¼ cup rice wine vinegar

2 TB. olive oil

3 cups cabbage, shredded

1 cup carrots, shredded

1. Preheat oven to 350°F.

2. In a large bowl, soak salmon in pineapple juice for 15 minutes. After marinating, place salmon fillets into a 9×13-inch baking dish lined with oiled aluminum foil. Top each fillet with a spoonful of pineapple juice and bake covered for 15 minutes. Remove cover and bake an additional 10 minutes.

3. In a small bowl, combine soy sauce, rice wine vinegar, and olive oil. Whisk thoroughly. Mix cabbage and carrots in a large bowl, add dressing, and toss. Spoon ½ cup cabbage salad onto 6 plates. Top with salmon while still warm. Serve immediately.

Tasty Tidbits _____

Give this salad a refreshing crunch by adding chopped water chestnuts and sliced green onions. If you don't have rice wine vinegar on hand, use cider vinegar, which blends delectably with soy sauce.

Garbanzo and Cottage Cheese Salad with Pita Chips

A quick and savory cottage cheese salad with a Mediterranean flavor.

3 pieces pita bread, cut into triangles

1 cup drained cooked or canned garbanzo beans

1 cup low-fat cottage cheese

½ cup shredded carrots

½ cup chopped green bell pepper

¼ tsp. ground black pepper

¼ tsp. cumin

¼ tsp. dried cilantro

2 TB. cider vinegar

2 TB. olive oil

Yield: 3¼ cups salad
Prep time: 10 minutes
Cook time: 12 minutes
Serves: 6
Serving size: About ½ cup salad
Each serving has:
285 calories
7.7 g fat
1.3 g saturated fat
329 mg sodium
39.8 g carbohydrates
6.9 g dietary fiber
14.5 g protein

1. Toast pita bread and cut into 6 wedges each.

2. In a medium bowl, mix beans, cottage cheese, carrots, bell pepper, pepper, cumin, cilantro, vinegar, and olive oil. Stir well. Divide mixture onto 6 serving plates.

3. Tuck pita chips into bean and cheese salad on each plate. Serve immediately.

Tasty Tidbits _____

This hearty luncheon salad supplies plenty of energy and high-quality protein to take you through even the longest afternoon without fatigue.

Egg Salad with Red Pepper and Walnuts

Egg salad is flavored with red pepper flakes and sweet pickles and made crunchy with celery and chopped nuts.

Yield: 4 salads
Prep time: 10 minutes
Cook time: 10 minutes
Serves: 4
Serving size: 1 salad
Each serving has:
210 calories
14.7 g fat
3.6 g saturated fat
311 mg sodium
5.9 g carbohydrates
1.2 g dietary fiber
14.6 g protein

8 hard-boiled eggs, chopped

¾ cup low-fat plain yogurt

2 TB. chopped sweet pickles

½ cup celery, diced

¼ cup chopped walnuts or pecans

2 TB. prepared brown mustard

½ TB. celery seed

¼ tsp. crushed red pepper flakes

1. In a large bowl, combine eggs, yogurt, pickles, celery, nuts, mustard, celery seed, and red pepper. Stir gently until well mixed.

2. Spoon egg salad onto 4 plates. Serve with whole grain crackers, on a bed of lettuce, or spread on toast.

Variation: In place of the eggs, use flaked tuna or chopped ham.

 Tasty Tidbits

This egg salad travels well wrapped up in a whole-wheat tortilla, and you can take tomato soup in a coffee mug with a lid.

Hawaiian Ham Rollups

Ham and tangy pineapple make this ultra-quick lunch a family favorite.

1 tsp. olive oil	**½ cup crushed pineapple**
4 whole-wheat tortillas	**2 TB. Parmesan cheese**
8 (1-oz.) slices ham	**¼ cup bottled poppy seed salad dressing**

1. Heat olive oil on low heat in a large skillet. Sauté each tortilla until slightly crisp. Then lightly sauté ham slices.

2. On each tortilla, arrange 2 slices ham and 2 tablespoons crushed pineapple. Sprinkle with Parmesan cheese and roll up. Serve with salad dressing in small side bowl for dipping.

Yield: 4 rollups
Prep time: 5 minutes
Cook time: 5 minutes
Serves: 4
Serving size: 1 rollup
Each serving has:
277 calories
12.4 g fat
2.2 g saturated fat
692 mg sodium
29.3 g carbohydrates
2.6 g dietary fiber
10.1 g protein

Chapter 12

Soups and Stews

In This Chapter

- ◆ Blending nutritious ingredients and flavors
- ◆ Hot and hearty meals for cool weather
- ◆ Enjoying the simplicity of one-pot meals
- ◆ Making plenty to freeze for upcoming quick meals

A hot bowl of homemade soup or hearty stew is perfect for chilly days and cold nights. It provides a thoughtful and comforting meal for family and friends. Pair with fresh bread, cheese slices, or a light salad and you have a wholesome and healthy meal.

These soup and stew recipes may appear to have lots of ingredients, but you'll stay on budget by using ingredients you can buy in bulk like carrots, potatoes, mushrooms, onions, and legumes. Store soups and stews in airtight containers in the refrigerator. You can also freeze them in meal-size portions. Defrost and reheat when you need to whip up—or, in this case, defrost—a quick dinner.

Kitchen Wise _____

If you have a sunny windowsill, you can grow fresh thyme, parsley, basil, oregano, and cilantro to use fresh herbs in soups and stews in place of dried ones.

In this chapter, we've included some of our favorite recipes with flavors of the Southwest and Rocky Mountains, where we both live. However, you'll also find recipes with flavors from across the country and around the world.

Nine Vegetable Soup

This recipe provides the natural sweetness of a rainbow of vegetables with a hint of heat. Serve with slices of sharp Cheddar cheese and crusty sourdough bread.

¼ **cup diced onions**

¼ **cup diced celery**

¼ **cup diced green or red bell pepper**

¼ **cup chopped mushrooms**

¼ **cup shredded carrots**

3 TB. olive oil

1 cup chopped green beans, fresh or frozen

1 cup frozen corn, thawed

2 cups diced sweet potatoes

1 (15-oz.) can diced tomatoes

⅛ **tsp. garlic powder**

⅛ **tsp. dried parsley**

1 bay leaf

⅛ **tsp. salt**

⅛ **tsp. ground black pepper**

⅛ **tsp. crushed red pepper flakes**

4 cups water

Yield: About 10 cups
Prep time: 15 minutes
Cook time: 35 minutes
Serves: 8
Serving size: 1¼ cups
Each serving has:
125 calories
5.4 g fat
0.8 g saturated fat
158 mg sodium
18.6 g carbohydrates
3.7 g dietary fiber
2.1 g protein

1. In a large stockpot over medium heat, sauté onion, celery, bell pepper, mushrooms, and carrots in olive oil until soft.

2. Add green beans, corn, sweet potatoes, tomatoes, garlic powder, parsley, bay leaf, salt, pepper, red pepper, and water.

3. Bring to a boil, reduce heat, and simmer 25 minutes. Remove bay leaf. Serve immediately or cool before freezing.

Tasty Tidbits

Any vegetable you and your family enjoy works well in this soup. You can add broccoli, water chestnuts, tomatillos, radishes, or parsnips. Let your children choose and prep veggies—they'll be more excited about eating veggies if they help to prepare them.

Chicken Noodle Soup with Vegetables

This is a delicious blend of vegetables and herbs simmered with tender chicken and whole-wheat spaghetti.

Yield: About 8 cups
Prep time: 10 minutes
Cook time: 35 minutes
Serves: 8
Serving size: 1 cup
Each serving has:
174 calories
5.6 g fat
1.1 g saturated fat
90 mg sodium
10.9 g carbohydrates
2.1 g dietary fiber
19.9 g protein

1 lb. chicken breast, cut into small cubes

¼ cup diced onions

2 TB. olive oil

¼ cup shredded carrots

¼ cup diced green or red bell pepper

⅛ tsp. garlic powder

1 bay leaf

⅛ tsp. dried thyme

⅛ tsp. salt

⅛ tsp. ground black pepper

3 cups water

2 cups whole-wheat spaghetti, broken

1 cup broccoli florets

1. In a stockpot over medium-high heat, sauté chicken and onions in olive oil for 10 minutes. Add carrots, bell pepper, garlic powder, bay leaf, thyme, salt, and pepper. Stir 2 minutes and add water.

2. Bring to a boil. Reduce heat to medium. Add noodles and broccoli and simmer 8 to 10 minutes until pasta is al dente.

3. Remove bay leaf and serve immediately.

 Tasty Tidbits

If you prefer, cook the noodles separately according to the package's directions. Add a portion to each bowl and then add the soup. This helps keep noodles from getting mushy and over-cooked if the soup is not served immediately.

Ham and White Bean Soup

Smoky ham simmered with creamy white beans is finished with a dash of hot sauce.

2 TB. olive oil

¼ cup finely diced onions

¼ cup finely diced celery

¼ cup diced carrots

½ tsp. crushed garlic

1 cup cooked, chopped ham

1 cup canned navy beans, drained and rinsed

3 cups water

⅛ tsp. salt

⅛ tsp. ground black pepper

½ tsp. dried thyme

1 TB. bottled hot sauce, optional

Yield: About 6 cups	
Prep time: 10 minutes	
Cook time: 30 minutes	
Serves: 6	
Serving size: 1 cup	
Each serving has:	
199 calories	
7 g fat	
1.3 g saturated fat	
370 mg sodium	
23.1 g carbohydrates	
9.1 g dietary fiber	
11.6 g protein	

1. Heat olive oil in a large stockpot over medium heat. Add onions, celery, carrots, and garlic. Stir often for 3 minutes. Add ham and cook just until ham begins to brown.

2. Add beans and water. Bring to a boil. Reduce heat to medium. Simmer 15 minutes covered. Add salt, pepper, and thyme. Stir well and cook 10 additional minutes uncovered.

3. Ladle into individual bowls and serve with a dash of hot sauce, if you prefer.

Tasty Tidbits

You can use any white bean (or combination of white beans) for this soup, such as cannellini, garbanzo beans, or white kidney beans.

Lentil Soup

A kaleidoscope of vegetables and lentils is finished with tangy red wine vinegar.

Yield: About 6 cups	
Prep time: 10 minutes	
Cook time: 40 minutes	
Serves: 6	
Serving size: 1 cup	
Each serving has:	
124 calories	
0.4 g fat	
0 g saturated fat	
115 mg sodium	
21.5 g carbohydrates	
10.5 g dietary fiber	
8.7 g protein	

¼ cup finely chopped onions

¼ cup finely chopped celery

½ cup diced green or red bell pepper

½ tsp. olive oil

½ tsp. crushed garlic

¼ tsp. dried parsley

¼ tsp. salt

1 cup dried lentils, rinsed

3 cups water

½ cup shredded zucchini

½ cup shredded carrots

¼ cup chopped spinach, fresh or frozen

1 TB. red wine vinegar

1. In a stockpot over medium heat, sauté onion, celery, and bell pepper in olive oil until soft. Add garlic, parsley, salt, lentils, and water. Bring to a boil, reduce heat, and simmer 20 minutes.

2. Add zucchini and carrots and simmer for 10 minutes. After simmering, add spinach and red wine vinegar. Stir well and simmer for 3 additional minutes. Serve immediately.

Tasty Tidbits

If you don't have red wine vinegar, use cider vinegar. It has a different flavor, but the result is still scrumptious.

Creamy Clam Chowder

This New England–style chowder has tender clams and potatoes, a touch of herbs, and a little cream.

2 slices turkey bacon, chopped

½ cup diced celery

4 medium-size new potatoes, cut into 1-inch cubes

¼ tsp. dried parsley

¼ tsp. dried thyme

4 cups water

2 (10-oz.) cans minced clams, with their juice

⅛ tsp. ground black pepper

1 cup heavy cream

1 cup sourdough croutons

Yield: About 9 cups
Prep time: 10 minutes
Cook time: 35 minutes
Serves: 9
Serving size: 1 cup
Each serving has:
157 calories
5.5 g fat
3.1 g saturated fat
742 mg sodium
12.1 g carbohydrates
1.4 g dietary fiber
7.4 g protein

1. In a large stockpot, combine bacon, celery, and potatoes. Stir over medium heat for 5 minutes. Add parsley and thyme. Cook 5 more minutes until bacon crisps.

2. Add water and bring to a boil. Reduce heat to medium. Add clams. Simmer covered for 20 minutes.

3. Add pepper and cream. Stir well and heat through 5 minutes. Serve with sourdough croutons.

Tasty Tidbits

Garnish this rich, elegant soup with fresh chopped chives or parsley.

Chicken Tortilla Soup

Mild green chiles and spicy cayenne pepper give this soup depth, while fresh cilantro and lime round out the medley of flavors.

Yield: About 9 cups
Prep time: 10 minutes
Cook time: 15 minutes
Serves: 8
Serving size: 1 cup
Each serving has:
343 calories
3.8 g fat
0 g saturated fat
125 mg sodium
57.3 g carbohydrates
14.1 g dietary fiber
20.9 g protein

1 cup chopped, cooked chicken breast

1 (12-oz.) can diced tomatoes

¼ cup finely diced onions

1 (15-oz.) can pinto beans, drained and rinsed

¼ cup diced green or red bell pepper

¼ cup frozen corn

1 (4-oz.) can diced green chiles

¼ tsp. garlic powder

¼ tsp. chili powder

¼ tsp. cayenne pepper

9 cups water

4 whole-wheat tortillas

2 TB. finely chopped fresh cilantro or 1 tsp. dried cilantro

2 limes, cut into wedges

1. In a stockpot over medium heat, combine chicken, tomatoes, onions, beans, bell pepper, corn, green chiles, garlic powder, chili powder, cayenne pepper, and water. Stir well and bring to a boil. Reduce heat and simmer 15 minutes, stirring occasionally.

2. Preheat oven to 350°F. Cut tortillas into long, thin strips. Arrange in a single layer on a cookie sheet and bake 10 minutes until crispy.

3. Serve soup in individual bowls and sprinkled with cilantro, a lime wedge, and topped with crispy tortilla strips.

Tasty Tidbits

Dress this soup up with avocado slices or sour cream for a creamier taste. Turn up the heat with hot sauce.

Southwestern Corn Chowder

Sweet corn and peppers simmered with cumin are finished with the light touch of creamy yogurt.

¼ cup finely diced celery

1 cup frozen corn, thawed

¼ cup diced green or red bell pepper

2 cups diced sweet potatoes

½ tsp. ground cumin

⅛ tsp. cayenne pepper

½ cup frozen green peas

2 cups 2 percent milk

2 cups water

¼ tsp. dried oregano

⅛ tsp. salt

⅛ tsp. ground black pepper

4 TB. low-fat plain yogurt

Yield: About 8 cups
Prep time: 10 minutes
Cook time: 45 minutes
Serves: 8
Serving size: 1 cup
Each serving has:
106 calories
1.7 g fat
0.9 g saturated fat
79 mg sodium
19.2 g carbohydrates
2.7 g dietary fiber
4.2 g protein

1. In a large stockpot, combine celery, corn, bell pepper, and sweet potatoes. Cook over medium heat for 5 minutes. Stir and add cumin and cayenne pepper. Heat 5 more minutes until corn darkens.

2. Add peas, milk, and water. Bring to a boil and then reduce heat to medium. Simmer covered for 25 minutes. Season with oregano, salt, and pepper. Simmer 10 more minutes uncovered. Serve in individual bowls with ½ tablespoon yogurt.

Tasty Tidbits _____

Serve this delectable soup with Fiesta Salad (see Chapter 14) for a complete southwestern feast.

Stout Potato Cheese Soup

This hearty, beer-based potato soup is finished with cream and cheese.

Yield: About 8 cups
Prep time: 10 minutes
Cook time: 30 minutes
Serves: 8
Serving size: 1 cup
Each serving has:
135 calories
8.6 g fat
3.7 g saturated fat
64 mg sodium
9.2 g carbohydrates
1.6 g dietary fiber
3.3 g protein

2 TB. olive oil

¼ cup chopped celery

2 cups diced new potatoes

2 cups chopped cauliflower

½ tsp. dried parsley

¼ tsp. dried rosemary

3 cups water

1 (12-oz.) bottle stout beer

½ cup heavy cream

½ cup shredded cheese (Cheddar, Swiss, American)

1. Heat olive oil in a stockpot over medium heat. Add celery and potatoes. Stir gently to coat potatoes and cook 8 minutes.

2. Place cauliflower in a microwave-safe bowl with 2 tablespoons of water, cover, and microwave on high for 4 minutes. Mash cauliflower with the back of a spoon and set aside.

3. Add parsley and rosemary to the stockpot with potatoes. Stir well to coat potatoes. Add water and bring to a boil. Reduce heat to medium.

4. Add cauliflower and beer. Simmer 20 minutes over medium heat, stirring occasionally.

5. Increase heat to medium-high, slowly add cream and cheese, and stir continuously until cheese melts and soup heats through again. Serve immediately.

Variation: We can't think of a cheese that doesn't taste great in this soup—try Gouda or Colby for delicious differences. Feel free to use more than one kind.

 Tasty Tidbits _____

Beer deepens the flavors, giving this dish its robust character. Buy a single bottle if you can to keep your meal costs down. Any stout beer will do, alcoholic or nonalcoholic.

Split Pea Soup

This is a light and colorful vegetable soup with a touch of ham.

¼ cup diced onions

¼ cup diced celery

¼ cup diced carrots

½ tsp. olive oil

⅛ tsp. crushed garlic

⅛ tsp. dried parsley

1 bay leaf

1 cup dried split green peas, rinsed

3 cups water

¼ cup cooked diced ham

Yield: About 5 cups
Prep time: 10 minutes
Cook time: 30 minutes
Serves: 4
Serving size: 1¼ cups
Each serving has:
189 calories
1.3 g fat
0 g saturated fat
134 mg sodium
31.6 g carbohydrates
13.1 g dietary fiber
13.7 g protein

1. In a stockpot over medium heat, sauté onion, celery, and carrots in olive oil until soft. Add garlic, parsley, bay leaf, peas, and water. Bring to a boil, reduce heat, and simmer for 20 minutes.

2. Add ham and simmer 10 more minutes. Remove bay leaf. Serve immediately or cool before freezing.

Tasty Tidbits

Toss in any vegetables left over from other meals, like zucchini, corn, tomatoes, or bell peppers. You will make a colorful soup and make room in your refrigerator.

Tomato Soup

This classic soup is smooth and savory and goes well with most lunch or dinner entrées.

Yield: About 6 cups
Prep time: 10 minutes
Cook time: 40 minutes
Serves: 6
Serving size: 1 cup
Each serving has:
279 calories
1.1 g fat
0 g saturated fat
68 mg sodium
53.2 g carbohydrates
16.2 g dietary fiber
16.9 g protein

2 (15-oz.) cans skinned and seeded stewed tomatoes

1 (15-oz.) can great northern beans, drained and rinsed

½ cup chopped red bell pepper

¼ tsp. garlic powder

⅛ tsp. dried parsley

⅛ tsp. salt

⅛ tsp. ground black pepper

⅛ tsp. crushed red pepper flakes

1 TB. honey

2 cups water

1. In a large stockpot, combine tomatoes, beans, bell pepper, garlic powder, parsley, salt, pepper, red pepper, and honey. Cook over medium heat for 10 minutes. Stir often.

2. Add water and bring to a boil. Reduce heat to medium and simmer 15 minutes. Stir often.

3. Remove from heat and allow to cool slightly. Carefully pour soup into a blender in batches; do not fill the blender more than halfway. Hold lid down with a folded towel to avoid splashing the hot soup. Purée 1 minute until smooth. Return to the stockpot. Heat through for 10 minutes over medium heat. Serve immediately or cool before freezing.

Tasty Tidbits

You'll enjoy this soup when it's not puréed, too.

Miso Soup

This light, slightly salty soup makes the perfect start to any Asian-themed meal.

4 cups water

1 cup thinly sliced mushrooms

½ cup thinly sliced carrots

¼ cup thinly sliced celery

4 TB. miso paste

1 TB. soy sauce

¼ cup diced firm tofu

2 TB. diced green onions

Yield: About 6 cups
Prep time: 5 minutes
Cook time: 15 minutes
Serves: 6
Serving size: 1 cup
Each serving has:
39 calories
1.2 g fat
0 g saturated fat
595 mg sodium
5 g carbohydrates
1.2 g dietary fiber
2.9 g protein

1. In a large stockpot, combine water, mushrooms, carrots, and celery. Bring to a boil and then reduce heat. Simmer 10 minutes.

2. Whisk in miso and soy sauce. Stir in tofu. Top with green onions. Serve immediately.

Kitchen Wise

Store leftover tofu in fresh water in the refrigerator and cover tightly to preserve freshness.

Beef Stew

This is slow-cooked, savory beef with hearty vegetables, a hint of red wine, and rosemary.

Yield: 10 cups
Prep time: 20 minutes
Cook time: 8 hours
Serves: 8
Serving size: About 1¼ cups
Each serving has:
241 calories
7.1 g fat
1.9 g saturated fat
56 mg sodium
19.7 g carbohydrates
2.2 g dietary fiber
18.8 g protein

2 TB. olive oil

1 lb. stewing beef, cut in small cubes

¼ cup flour

1 cup red wine

2 cups water

1 TB. minced garlic

¼ cup diced onion

2 cups cubed sweet potatoes

1 cup sliced carrots

1 cup green beans

1 cup sliced mushrooms

2 TB. apricot jam

½ tsp. dried rosemary

1. In a large skillet over medium heat, warm olive oil. Dredge beef cubes in flour and brown for 8 minutes. Transfer to slow cooker.

2. In a slow cooker, combine red wine, water, garlic, onion, sweet potatoes, carrots, green beans, mushrooms, and apricot jam.

3. Set the slow cooker to low. Cook 8 hours. During last 15 minutes of cooking, add rosemary. Serve hot.

Variation: Put any of your favorite vegetables, and even some fruits, in this beef stew. Try butternut squash, parsnips, dried apricots, or apples. You can also use plum, quince, or even cherry jam.

 Tasty Tidbits

Slow cooking makes even tough cuts of meat tender and delicious. Stewing meat is often less expensive than more premium cuts. Start the slow cooker in the morning to give the meat plenty of time to cook. Dinner will be ready on time.

Red Chili

This chili is slow cooked to bring out all the fantastic flavors of this classic favorite.

1 lb. lean ground beef

1 (15-oz.) can red kidney beans, drained and rinsed

1 (15-oz.) can pinto beans, drained and rinsed

3 cups water

¼ cup minced onions

1½ cups diced green or red bell pepper

1½ cups diced celery

1½ cups frozen corn

1 TB. minced garlic

2 tsp. ground cumin

2 tsp. chili powder

1 tsp. ground black pepper

Yield: About 16 cups
Prep time: 10 minutes
Cook time: 6 hours
Serves: 16
Serving size: About 1 cup
Each serving has:
250 calories
2.6 g fat
0.8 g saturated fat
38 mg sodium
36 g carbohydrates
8.9 g dietary fiber
20.9 g protein

1. Brown ground beef in a large skillet over medium heat. Drain off grease and place in a slow cooker.

2. Add beans, water, tomatoes, onions, bell pepper, celery, corn, garlic, cumin, chili powder, and pepper.

3. Set the slow cooker to low, cover, and cook 6 hours. Serve hot.

Variation: Increase the heat of this chili by adding bottled hot sauce, cayenne pepper, or fresh hot chili peppers such as habaneros or pequins. Add your favorite vegetables to this chili. Try eggplant, zucchini, green beans, or sweet potatoes for a little variety.

Tasty Tidbits _____

Don't have a slow cooker? It's worth the investment. They are inexpensive and time saving. You'll find yourself using it to make delicious dishes all week long, not just on busy weekdays.

White Chili

Made with chicken or turkey, this chili offers mild Southwestern flavors of garlic, low-heat chiles, and cilantro.

Yield: About 12 cups
Prep time: 10 minutes
Cook time: 6 hours
Serves: 12
Serving size: About 1 cup
Each serving has:
284 calories
4.2 g fat
0.9 g saturated fat
39 mg sodium
41.2 g carbohydrates
13.4 g dietary fiber
21.6 g protein

2 TB. olive oil

1 lb. ground turkey (or chicken)

2 cups water

1 (15-oz.) can white kidney beans, drained and rinsed

1 (15-oz.) can pinto beans, drained and rinsed

1 cup diced new potatoes

1 (4-oz.) can diced mild green chiles

1 cup frozen corn

1 cup diced green bell pepper

1 tsp. minced garlic

1 tsp. cumin

1 tsp. ground coriander

1 TB. chopped fresh cilantro

1. Heat olive oil over medium heat in a large skillet. Add turkey (or chicken) and brown. Spoon meat into a slow cooker.

2. To the slow cooker add water, beans, potatoes, chiles, corn, bell pepper, garlic, cumin, and coriander.

3. Set the slow cooker to low, cover, and cook 6 hours. In the last 15 minutes of cooking, add cilantro. Serve hot.

 Tasty Tidbits

Serve this mild chili with a tossed green salad or fresh fruit.

Chapter 13

Snacks and Appetizers

In This Chapter

- ◆ Snacking that's easy on your budget
- ◆ Offering superb nutrition between meals
- ◆ Snacks that are great for easy and casual entertaining

Snacks are an important part of our eating. They get us through an energy lull in the late afternoon and satisfy growling stomachs if lunch is delayed. After-school snacks are a wonderful way to shift gears from school to either playtime or homework.

In this chapter, we selected great tasting mini-meals prepared in healthy ways. You can save money and improve your nutrition by preparing home-made snacks. Most commercial and processed snacks and appetizers are full of too much sugar and fat, yet offer little to no nutritional value.

Enjoy spicy hot drumsticks, baked sweet potato chips, and savory vegetable and chip dips. All of these recipes can be served for company, barbecues, and potlucks.

Baked Hot Drumsticks

These are like hot wings—except not fried and not made from wings. A healthier take on this sweet and spicy, messy favorite, these are served with crunchy veggies.

Yield: 6 drumsticks
Prep time: Overnight and 10 minutes
Cook time: 45 minutes
Serves: 6
Serving size: 1 drumstick
Each serving has:
151 calories
8.1 g fat
1.7 g saturated fat
207 mg sodium
5.5 g carbohydrates
0.9 g dietary fiber
13.5 g protein

¼ cup apple juice

¼ cup cider vinegar

1 tsp. minced garlic

6 chicken drumsticks

1 TB. bottled barbecue sauce

¼ cup blue cheese dressing

1 cup celery sticks

1 cup carrot sticks

1. In a large bowl, combine apple juice, cider vinegar, and garlic. Add drumsticks, cover, and marinate overnight in the refrigerator.

2. Preheat oven to 400°F. Line a cookie sheet with aluminum foil. Place a wire rack on the cookie sheet. Arrange drumsticks in a single layer on the rack.

3. Place barbecue sauce in a small bowl. Brush over chicken and bake 45 minutes, turning and basting several times. Serve drumsticks hot with blue cheese dressing, celery, and carrot sticks.

Variation: If you prefer a milder taste, use soy sauce, rice wine vinegar, and honey as a marinade for the drumsticks.

 Tasty Tidbits

Serve Baked Hot Drumsticks as a halftime snack during football season.

Asian Chicken Appetizers

Drumsticks are cooked in a sauce of onions, soy sauce, aniseed, and cloves to lend an oriental flavor.

4 chicken drumsticks

1 green onion, cut into 1-inch lengths

2 TB. soy sauce

1 cup water

1 tsp. aniseed or fennel seed

2 whole cloves

2 TB. honey

Yield: 4 drumsticks	
Prep time: 10 minutes	
Cook time: 45 minutes	
Serves: 4	
Serving size: 1 drumstick	
Each serving has:	
117 calories	
2.7 g fat	
0.7 g saturated fat	
491 mg sodium	
9.8 g carbohydrates	
0 g dietary fiber	
13.3 g protein	

1. Place drumsticks in a medium saucepan. Add green onion, soy sauce, water, aniseed or fennel seed, cloves, and honey. Cover.

2. Over medium-high heat, bring to a boil and simmer 30 minutes. Uncover and cook 15 minutes, basting drumsticks as they cook. Serve hot or chilled.

Tasty Tidbits _____

Make these a meal by serving with rice and vegetable stir-fry.

Hummus

Creamy and smooth garbanzo beans are puréed with lemon juice and sesame paste. This spread is delicious served with pita bread or as a vegetable dip.

Yield: About 2 cups
Prep time: 10 minutes
Cook time: None
Serves: 8
Serving size: About ¼ cup
Each serving has:
249 calories
8.7 g fat
1.1 g saturated fat
18 mg sodium
33.7 g carbohydrates
9.7 g dietary fiber
11 g protein

1 (15-oz.) can garbanzo beans, drained

2 TB. tahini or sesame seed paste

2 TB. lemon juice

1 tsp. minced garlic

2 TB. olive oil

2 tsp. ground cumin

1 tsp. ground coriander

1. In a blender, purée garbanzo beans, tahini, lemon juice, garlic, olive oil, cumin, and coriander. Pulse until smooth.

2. Transfer to a serving dish and serve.

Variation: Blend roasted red bell peppers into hummus to add color and bright flavor.

 Tasty Tidbits

Hummus is a delicious and hearty Middle Eastern and Mediterranean dip. Serve as a dip or spread on sandwiches for a substantial snack.

Crunchy Jicama Snack

This crisp white vegetable is seasoned with parsley, chili powder, and lime for a fresh crunchy taste.

1 jicama root, peeled and cut into sticks or slices

1 tsp. salt

⅛ tsp. cayenne pepper

1 TB. chopped fresh parsley or 1 tsp. dried parsley

1 TB. lime juice

Yield: About 4 cups
Prep time: 10 minutes
Cook time: None
Serves: 8
Serving size: About ½ cup
Each serving has:
23 calories
0.1 g fat
0 g saturated fat
149 mg sodium
5.3 g carbohydrates
3 g dietary fiber
0.4 g protein

1. Place jicama into a medium bowl. Sprinkle with salt, cayenne, and parsley. Toss with lime juice.

2. Serve as finger food or on small plates.

Variation: Substitute cilantro for the parsley.

Tasty Tidbits

Jicama is a large root vegetable grown in Central America. It's crunchy and vaguely tastes like water chestnuts.

Guacamole

This is a delicious, easy-to-make version of the classic buttery avocado, tomato, and chiles dip.

Yield: About 2 cups
Prep time: 10 minutes
Cook time: None
Serves: 8
Serving size: About ¼ cup
Each serving has:
88 calories
7.4 g fat
1.1 g saturated fat
5 mg sodium
6 g carbohydrates
3.8 g dietary fiber
1.3 g protein

2 large avocados

2 TB. lemon juice (or lime juice)

1 (10-oz.) can Rotel

1. Slice avocados in half lengthwise and twist gently to separate. Scoop out flesh into a medium bowl. Pour lemon juice over avocado and mash gently with the back of a spoon.

2. Add Rotel. Stir gently until well combined but not smooth. Serve immediately.

Variation: If you like spicy guacamole, add 1 teaspoon of your favorite bottled hot sauce.

 Tasty Tidbits

Rotel is a brand name for a perfect combination of canned tomatoes and chiles. It's also inexpensive and a perfect accompaniment to grilled chicken, cottage cheese, rice, or vegetables. Look for it with the canned vegetables or in the Latino section of your grocery store. If you cannot find Rotel, mix a can of diced tomatoes, diced chiles, and a sprinkle of garlic powder.

Deviled Eggs

These picnic and barbecue favorites have a hint of tarragon.

12 hard-boiled eggs

¼ cup mayonnaise

1 tsp. dry ground mustard

1 TB. dried tarragon

1 tsp. paprika

Yield: 24 egg halves
Prep time: 15 minutes
Cook time: None
Serves: 12
Serving size: 2 egg halves
Each serving has:
92 calories
6.6 g fat
1.6 g saturated fat
97 mg sodium
2.4 g carbohydrates
0 g dietary fiber
6.1 g protein

1. Carefully cut each hard-boiled egg in half lengthwise. Gently remove yolks and place in a large bowl. Place empty whites aside on a cookie sheet lined with foil.

2. To the bowl with yolks, add mayonnaise, mustard, and tarragon. Use the back of a spoon to crush the yolks and stir until well combined. Spoon yolk mixture into egg whites.

3. Refrigerate 1 hour covered. Sprinkle with paprika before serving.

Variation: Try Parmesan cheese with a sprinkle of cayenne pepper in the yolk mixture.

Kitchen Wise

Add your favorite spices and condiments, such as chutney or diced sweet pickles, to the yolk mixture to dress these classic favorites up for a special occasion.

Oven-Baked Potato Chips

Skip the frying, these potato chips are deliciously crisp and peppery.

Yield: About 4 cups
Prep time: 5 minutes
Cook time: 25 minutes
Serves: 4
Serving size: About 1 cup
Each serving has:
134 calories
6.9 g fat
1 g saturated fat
152 mg sodium
17.1 g carbohydrates
2.7 g dietary fiber
1.8 g protein

2 new potatoes, sliced very thin

2 TB. olive oil

¼ tsp. salt

1 tsp. ground black pepper

1. Preheat oven to 420°F.

2. In a large bowl, gently combine potatoes and olive oil.

3. Arrange potato slices in a single layer on a cookie sheet lined with parchment paper or aluminum foil. Sprinkle with salt and pepper. Bake 20 minutes until crispy. Serve immediately.

Variation: Sweet potatoes taste great baked this way, as do beets and carrots. Just be sure to slice them as thin as you can.

 Don't Get Burned _____

Watch your potatoes carefully as they near the end of baking so you can take them from the oven when they reach your preferred toasted color.

Avocado Kraut Cups

Buttery avocado and tangy sauerkraut in a crisp tortilla cup offer a surprisingly delicious combination.

3 whole-wheat tortillas

1 cup sauerkraut

1 tsp. dry ground mustard

½ tsp. ground black pepper

1 avocado, cut into small cubes

Yield: 12 cups
Prep time: 15 minutes
Cook time: 10 minutes
Serves: 4
Serving size: 3 cups
Each serving has:
262 calories
13.2 g fat
1.5 g saturated fat
488 mg sodium
30.4 g carbohydrates
8.1 g dietary fiber
6.1 g protein

1. Preheat oven to 375°F.

2. Cut tortillas into small circles with a biscuit cutter, or use an inverted drinking glass as a guide. Tuck each round into a mini muffin tin. Bake for 10 minutes at 375°F until crisp. Set aside to cool.

3. In a medium bowl, combine sauerkraut, dry ground mustard, and pepper. Mix well. Gently fold in avocado cubes. Spoon mixture into tortilla cups. Serve immediately.

Tasty Tidbits _____

Bring these to a potluck or a barbecue for an inexpensive but very popular contribution.

Hot Spinach and Artichoke Dip

Three cheeses blend with garlic and herbs, delicate artichoke hearts, and tangy spinach in this veggie dip your family will love.

Yield: 1½-quart dish
Prep time: 10 minutes
Cook time: 40 minutes
Serves: 8
Serving size: ¼ cup
Each serving has:
209 calories
17.4 g fat
10.8 g saturated fat
252 mg sodium
7.7 g carbohydrates
3.2 g dietary fiber
7.6 g protein

1 (12-oz.) package light cream cheese, softened

1 tsp. cayenne pepper

2 tsp. minced garlic

1 tsp. ground black pepper

1 TB. dried oregano

1 (14-oz.) can artichoke hearts, chopped

2 cups fresh spinach, torn into small pieces

⅓ cup shredded Monterey Jack cheese

¼ cup shredded Parmesan cheese

1. Preheat oven to 375°F.

2. In a large bowl, combine cream cheese, cayenne pepper, garlic, pepper, and oregano. Stir until cream cheese is almost smooth. Add artichoke hearts, spinach, and Monterey Jack cheese. Stir to combine.

3. Transfer mixture to 1½-quart baking dish. Sprinkle top with Parmesan cheese and bake 40 minutes. Serve immediately.

 Tasty Tidbits

This dip is great with crunchy vegetables and fruits like broccoli, celery, carrots, jicama, and apples. If your children are picky eaters, this scrumptious dip could change they way feel about vegetables. Offer vegetables and sweet potato chips for dipping.

Warm Onion and Mushroom Dip

Warm, earthy mushrooms and sweet onions are mixed into cool cream cheese for a delicious, quick dip your family and company will love.

1 (12-oz.) package light cream cheese, softened

1 tsp. dried parsley

2 TB. olive oil

2 cups sliced mushrooms

½ cup diced red onions

2 tsp. ground black pepper

Yield: About 3 cups
Prep time: 10 minutes
Cook time: 8 minutes
Serves: 12
Serving size: ¼ cup
Each serving has:
124 calories
12.2 g fat
6.5 g saturated fat
85 mg sodium
1.8 g carbohydrates
0 g dietary fiber
2.6 g protein

1. In a medium bowl, combine cream cheese and parsley. Stir gently to combine. Set aside.

2. In a medium skillet over medium heat, warm olive oil. Add mushrooms, onions, and pepper. Cook 7 minutes until soft. Stir often.

3. Pour hot mushroom mixture over cream cheese. Fold mushrooms into cream cheese gently until well combined. Serve immediately.

Tasty Tidbits

Serve this dip with Oven-Baked Potato Chips and a bowl of celery and carrot sticks for family game night. Or dress it up for parties by serving topped with chopped tomatoes and bacon, with veggies cut into wedges for dipping.

Cool Dill Dip

Crunchy water chestnuts add texture to this creamy dill dip that goes perfectly with all your favorite fresh vegetables.

Yield: About 2½ cups
Prep time: 10 minutes
Cook time: None
Serves: 10
Serving size: About ¼ cup
Each serving has:
73 calories
1 g fat
0.5 g saturated fat
113 mg sodium
11.1 g carbohydrates
2 g dietary fiber
5 g protein

1 cup cottage cheese

1 cup low-fat plain yogurt

2 TB. finely minced red onions

1 (8-oz.) can sliced water chestnuts, drained and roughly chopped

1 TB. dried dill

2 tsp. lemon pepper

1 tsp. dried parsley

1. In a large bowl, combine cottage cheese, yogurt, onion, water chestnuts, dill, lemon pepper, and parsley. Stir well.

2. Cover and chill 1 hour before serving.

 Tasty Tidbits

Dill's bright flavor is a great compliment to softer veggies like cherry tomatoes, asparagus, and bell peppers.

Quick Fruit Salsa

This spicy and sweet salsa mixes soft chiles and tomatoes with crunchy apples and bell peppers.

1 (10-oz.) can Rotel

1 apple, unpeeled and diced

¼ cup dried apricots, chopped

¼ cup diced red or green bell pepper

In a medium bowl, combine Rotel, apples, apricots, and bell pepper. Cover and chill 2 hours to blend flavors before serving.

Variation: Try frozen black cherries in this salsa. Thaw them in the microwave and chop coarsely. You can also use dried, fresh, or frozen fruit such as strawberries, mangoes, pears, pomegranates, and bananas.

 Kitchen Wise

Serve Quick Fruit Salsa as a side with roasted and grilled meats or cooked vegetables or as a dip with corn chips.

Yield: About 2 cups
Prep time: 10 minutes
Cook time: None
Serves: 8
Serving size: About ¼ cup
Each serving has:
19 calories
0.1 g fat
0 g saturated fat
71 mg sodium
4.8 g carbohydrates
1.1 g dietary fiber
0.4 g protein

Chapter 14

Salads

In This Chapter

- Eating plenty of vegetables on a limited budget
- Preparing "gourmet-type" salad dressings
- Spicing up salads for enticing tastes

Don't forget the fresh vegetables. Researchers have found that the first food people cut out when they need to eat on a budget is fresh produce. Don't do it. Your body needs it. So do your children, no matter what they think to the contrary.

You may need to eat less of the more expensive types of produce such as berries and avocados. But check out sales and stock up on large bags of carrots, celery, onions, and lettuce. The same goes for green beans and broccoli.

As you read through these recipes, you may find some ingredients that seem a bit out of your budgetary reach. Don't worry. Instead, substitute with produce you have on hand or with produce that's in season and thus less expensive.

That way, you'll try new vegetables and flavor combinations based on what's on sale at the store. Encourage your children to choose some of the produce for salads and enlist their assistance in the preparation. They'll be excited (fingers crossed) to eat their creations.

Use small to moderate amounts of salad dressing so you can enjoy the natural flavors of the ingredients. You can prepare the dressings in this chapter or use your own bottled favorites. Don't drown your salads in salad dressings, avoid the extra calories and the waste of money.

Kitchen Wise _____

Create a quick and unusual salad dressing by mixing together 2 teaspoons of fruit jam, 1 teaspoon of hot sauce, and ¼ cup of olive oil.

To further save on calories, don't add salad dressing to the salad. Instead, pour some dressing into a small container. When eating, dip your fork into the dressing, then spear some salad and eat it. You'll still enjoy the flavor but consume far fewer calories.

These crisp, crunchy salads are perfect as side dishes. Add meat or cheese to the salads and they'll work as a main course.

Spring Salad

This crisp, nourishing salad showcases the freshest—and best priced—produce spring has to offer, including sweet peas and peppery radishes.

3 cups lettuce, torn in 1½-inch pieces

¼ cup sliced radishes

¼ cup peas, fresh or frozen

½ cup diced celery

½ cup broccoli florets

1 cup cherry tomatoes

2 TB. olive oil

2 TB. cider vinegar

¼ tsp. minced garlic

2 TB. lemon juice

1 tsp. dried parsley or 1 TB. chopped fresh parsley

Yield: About 6 cups	
Prep time: 15 minutes	
Cook time: None	
Serves: 4	
Serving size: About 1½ cups	
Each serving has:	
91 calories	
7 g fat	
1 g saturated fat	
26 mg sodium	
6.2 g carbohydrates	
2.1 g dietary fiber	
1.7 g protein	

1. In a large bowl, combine lettuce, radishes, peas, celery, broccoli, and tomatoes.

2. In a medium bowl, combine olive oil, vinegar, garlic, lemon juice, and parsley. Whisk well. Pour over vegetables and toss gently until vegetables are coated with dressing. Serve immediately.

Variation: Try kohlrabi in this spring salad—it tastes a little like sweet cabbage. Or try Swiss chard.

Tasty Tidbits _____

Eating vegetables that are in season and locally produced keeps costs down. You'll find that everything tastes better, too!

Summer Salad

This delicious salad has almost as many fruits as vegetables, with a tangy and sweet strawberry poppy seed dressing.

Yield: About 8 cups
Prep time: 15 minutes
Cook time: None
Serves: 4
Serving size: About 2 cups
Each serving has:
105 calories
3.8 g fat
0.5 g saturated fat
74 mg sodium
17.3 g carbohydrates
3.2 g dietary fiber
2.2 g protein

3 cups fresh spinach, stems removed, torn in 1½-inch pieces

1 cup grapefruit slices

½ cup diced cucumber

½ cup diced jicama

1 medium tomato, chopped

1 cup red or green grapes

1 TB. poppy seeds

½ cup crushed strawberries, juices reserved

2 TB. mayonnaise

2 TB. vinegar

1 TB. honey

1. In a large bowl, combine spinach, grapefruit, cucumber, jicama, tomato, and grapes.

2. In a medium bowl, combine poppy seeds, strawberries, mayonnaise, vinegar, and honey. Whisk well until combined. Pour over vegetables and fruits and toss gently to coat. Serve immediately.

Variation: Try any fruit or vegetable that catches your eye in the summer produce section—especially if it's on sale. Avocado, kiwi, green beans, summer squash, and artichoke hearts taste great in this salad.

 Don't Get Burned _____

Make and follow a plan for the produce you buy or grow. If the fruits and vegetables spoil before you can use them, it doesn't matter how inexpensive they were, the money is still wasted.

Autumn Salad

Earthy, spicy, and fruity flavors mingle in this bountiful seasonal salad.

3 cups romaine lettuce, torn in 2-inch pieces

1 cup shredded red cabbage

½ cup corn, fresh or frozen

1 apple, diced

½ cup dried cranberries

¼ cup chopped walnuts

¼ cup low-fat plain yogurt

¼ cup sour cream

½ TB. dried oregano

½ TB. dried basil

1 tsp. garlic powder

2 TB. red wine vinegar

Yield: About 6 cups
Prep time: 10 minutes
Cook time: None
Serves: 4
Serving size: About 1½ cups
Each serving has:
121 calories
8.2 g fat
2.3 g saturated fat
29 mg sodium
9.8 g carbohydrates
2.5 g dietary fiber
4.4 g protein

1. In a large bowl, combine lettuce, cabbage, corn, apples, dried cranberries, and walnuts.

2. In a medium bowl, combine yogurt, sour cream, oregano, basil, garlic, and vinegar. Whisk until smooth. Pour dressing over salad and toss gently to coat. Serve immediately.

 Tasty Tidbits

Bottled salad dressings can be used in this and almost any other salad. Try Green Goddess and enjoy its tangy flavor with earthy fall vegetables.

Winter Salad

Fresh and pickled root vegetables combine to give this salad its tangy and earthy character.

Yield: About 6 cups
Prep time: 10 minutes
Cook time: None
Serves: 6
Serving size: About 1 cup
Each serving has:
202 calories
9 g fat
1.2 g saturated fat
99 mg sodium
24.7 g carbohydrates
7.3 g dietary fiber
7.3 g protein

2 cups shredded green cabbage

2 cups chopped iceberg lettuce

½ cup shredded carrots

½ cup diced canned pickled beets

1 cup canned garbanzo beans

2 TB. chopped dill pickles

3 TB. olive oil

2 TB. red wine vinegar

1 tsp. Dijon mustard

1. In a large bowl, combine cabbage, lettuce, carrots, beets, garbanzo beans, and pickles.

2. In a medium bowl, whisk together olive oil, red wine vinegar, and mustard. Pour over vegetables and toss gently to combine. Serve immediately.

Variation: Try sweet or spicy cucumber pickles instead of dill for variety.

 Kitchen Wise

Vegetables that make delicious pickles and relishes are carrots, cauliflower, parsnips, jicama, and turnips. These pickles and relishes are easy to make and a great way to save money. Look up recipes on the Internet and experiment in small batches to save money—you will quickly discover new flavors and favorites.

Mexican Vegetable Salad

Black beans and corn mingle with sweet fruit and mild chiles in this colorful salad.

2 medium tomatoes, chopped

1 (15-oz.) can corn, drained and rinsed

1 cup diced papaya

1 (15-oz.) can black beans, drained and rinsed

1 (4-oz.) can diced green chiles

1 TB. lime juice

½ tsp. ground cumin

½ tsp. chili powder

¼ tsp. salt

Yield: About 8 cups
Prep time: 10 minutes
Cook time: None
Serves: 8
Serving size: About 1 cup
Each serving has:
286 calories
2.3 g fat
0 g saturated fat
98 mg sodium
56.2 g carbohydrates
14.3 g dietary fiber
15.1 g protein

1. In a large bowl, combine tomatoes, corn, papaya, beans, chiles, lime juice, cumin, chili powder, and salt. Stir gently to mix.

2. Chill 15 minutes or overnight to combine flavors. Serve chilled.

Variation: In place of the papaya, substitute peaches, grapes, or an apple.

Tasty Tidbits

You can use any type of bean you have on hand in this salad. Double the recipe for a potluck or an outdoor party to accompany hamburgers or hot dogs.

Greek Salad

This quick salad exemplifies the light, fresh flavors that define the Mediterranean. Olive oil and red wine vinegar kiss crisp, ripe vegetables.

Yield: About 5 cups
Prep time: 10 minutes
Cook time: None
Serves: 5
Serving size: About 1 cup
Each serving has:
116 calories
9.2 g fat
1.3 g saturated fat
182 mg sodium
8.1 g carbohydrates
2.3 g dietary fiber
1.6 g protein

4 medium tomatoes, cut in ¾-inch cubes

1 medium cucumber, cut in ½-inch pieces

1 green bell pepper, cut in ½-inch pieces

¼ cup kalamata olives

3 TB. olive oil

2 TB. red wine vinegar

1 tsp. dried oregano

½ tsp. salt

2 TB. crumbled feta cheese (optional)

1. In a large bowl, combine tomatoes, cucumber, bell pepper, and olives.

2. In a medium bowl, whisk together olive oil, red wine vinegar, oregano, and salt. Pour over vegetables and toss well.

3. Before serving, sprinkle with feta cheese.

Tasty Tidbits

Serve this crunchy salad with grilled and roasted meats. It's great for summer outdoor meals, too.

Creamy Potato Salad

Tender potatoes are tossed with a creamy, caraway-flavored mustard dressing.

6 new potatoes, washed

½ cup low-fat plain yogurt

2 TB. Dijon mustard

1 tsp. caraway seeds

2 TB. dill pickle relish

¼ tsp. salt

½ tsp. ground black pepper

¼ cup shredded carrots

Yield: About 3 cups
Prep time: 10 minutes
Cook time: 15 minutes
Serves: 6
Serving size: About ½ cup
Each serving has:
171 calories
0.8 g fat
0 g saturated fat
221 mg sodium
37.2 g carbohydrates
5.5 g dietary fiber
5 g protein

1. Boil potatoes in salted water for 15 minutes until tender. Drain but don't cool. Quarter potatoes.

2. In a large bowl, combine yogurt, mustard, caraway seeds, relish, salt, and pepper. Whisk until smooth. Add potatoes and carrots. Toss gently to coat. Chill 1 hour before serving.

Kitchen Wise

Any pickle relish works in this salad. Sweet relish combines delightfully with the mustard and pepper. Spicy relish loses some of its bite with the cool yogurt. Experiment and enjoy!

Crunchy Coleslaw

Two kinds of cabbage, crisp jicama, and sweet pineapple are tossed with a poppy seed dressing.

Yield: About 4½ cups
Prep time: 10 minutes
Cook time: None
Serves: 6
Serving size: About ⅔ cup
Each serving has:
67 calories
3.8 g fat
0.5 g saturated fat
184 mg sodium
8.4 g carbohydrates
2 g dietary fiber
0.9 g protein

2 cups shredded red or green cabbage

1 cup shredded carrots

½ cup jicama sticks, about 2 inches long and 1 inch wide

½ cup red or green bell pepper strips

¼ cup crushed pineapple, drained

¼ cup olive oil

2 TB. lemon juice

2 tsp. poppy seeds

¼ tsp. salt

¼ tsp. ground black pepper

1. In a large bowl, combine cabbage, carrots, jicama, bell pepper strips, and pineapple.

2. In a medium bowl, whisk together olive oil, lemon juice, poppy seeds, salt, and pepper. Pour over cabbage mixture and toss to coat. Chill 30 minutes before serving.

Variation: In the summertime, when they are least costly, add sliced strawberries to this slaw for a sweeter salad.

 Tasty Tidbits

Put a scoop of this creamy slaw on a barbecue pork sandwich or add it to a pita with grilled chicken breast. You will find lots of ways to serve this delicious salad.

Sour Cream Cucumber Salad

Dill and the refreshing, light taste of cucumber flavors this creamy, crunchy side salad.

½ cup sour cream

½ TB. dried dill

½ tsp. salt

1 tsp. ground black pepper

2 cucumbers, sliced

½ cup sliced white or sweet onions, optional

Yield: 4 cups
Prep time: 10 minutes
Cook time: None
Serves: 8
Serving size: About ½ cup
Each serving has:
46 calories
3.1 g fat
1.9 g saturated fat
155 mg sodium
4.2 g carbohydrates
0.6 g dietary fiber
1.1 g protein

1. In a large bowl, combine sour cream, dill, salt, and pepper. Stir well.

2. Add cucumbers and onions. Toss gently to coat. Chill 1 hour before serving. The cucumbers and onions will wilt and become softer the longer you let them marinate in the dressing.

Tasty Tidbits

You can make a delicious cucumber salad without sour cream. Marinate sliced cucumbers in 2 tablespoons cider vinegar, 1 teaspoon dill, and a pinch of salt and pepper for 1 hour in the refrigerator. This is perfect for people who prefer a dressing lower in fat.

Warm or Cold Bean Salad

This colorful and delectable salad blends tangy spinach with garlicky beans.

Yield: About 11 cups
Prep time: 10 minutes
Cook time: 20 minutes
Serves: 10
Serving size: About 1 cup
Each serving has:
342 calories
5.2 g fat
0.8 g saturated fat
22 mg sodium
56.6 g carbohydrates
14.8 g dietary fiber
20 g protein

3 TB. olive oil

1 tsp. minced garlic

1 (15-oz.) can garbanzo beans, drained and rinsed

1 (15-oz.) can black beans, drained and rinsed

1 (15-oz.) can red kidney beans, drained and rinsed

1 (15-oz.) can green beans, drained and rinsed

1 TB. dried parsley

½ tsp. ground black pepper

5 cups torn spinach

2 TB. lemon juice

1. In a large saucepan over medium heat, combine olive oil and garlic. Cook, stirring, for 5 minutes. Add garbanzo beans, black beans, red kidney beans, green beans, parsley, and pepper. Cook 10 minutes until heated through. Remove from heat.

2. Place spinach in a large bowl. Toss with lemon juice. Add warm bean mixture to the middle of the bowl. Serve immediately.

3. To serve cold, refrigerate 4 or more hours before serving.

 Tasty Tidbits _____

This bean salad is perfect for a picnic or barbecue. Just keep the beans warm and the spinach cool and assemble the salad when you arrive. Feel free to bring along a bottle of your favorite hot sauce.

Seven Layer Salad

This salad provides a beautiful combination of colors and textures: crisp cabbage, creamy guacamole and sour cream, and the tanginess of fresh salsa.

2 cups shredded green cabbage

1 (15-oz.) can black beans, drained and rinsed

1 cup corn, canned or frozen

1 avocado, sliced

½ cup sour cream

¼ cup sliced black olives

¼ cup bottled salsa

Yield: About 6 cups
Prep time: 10 minutes
Cook time: None
Serves: 8
Serving size: About ¾ cup

Each serving has:
240 calories
4.5 g fat
2.2 g saturated fat
102 mg sodium
39.2 g carbohydrates
9.3 g dietary fiber
12.9 g protein

1. Spread shredded cabbage on a large plate. Spread black beans in a circle slightly smaller than the cabbage bed. Add corn in a circle smaller than the beans. Top with avocado slices and then with sour cream.

2. Sprinkle olives to the edges of the sour cream layer and top with salsa.

Variation: Add a layer of cooked ground beef to turn this recipe into a main course salad.

Tasty Tidbits _____

Try creamy cannellini beans or mellow pintos. They change the colors and the flavor combinations, making the salad a little different each time.

Curried Fruit and Spinach Salad

A dazzling array of colors brightens this crunchy salad, and the creamy curry dressing enhances the natural sweetness of the fruit.

Yield: About 6 cups
Prep time: 10 minutes
Cook time: None
Serves: 4
Serving size: About 1½ cups
Each serving has:
278 calories
14.2 g fat
3 g saturated fat
72 mg sodium
24.3 g carbohydrates
3.7 g dietary fiber
17.3 g protein

1 cup diced chicken breast

1 apple, diced

½ cup diced celery

½ cup raisins

½ cup chopped walnuts

¼ cup low-fat plain yogurt

¼ cup low-fat sour cream

1 TB. curry powder

2 cups fresh spinach, stems removed, torn into 2-inch pieces

1. In a large bowl, combine chicken, apples, celery, raisins, and walnuts.

2. In a small bowl, combine yogurt, sour cream, and curry powder. Mix until smooth. Spoon over chicken mixture. Toss. Serve immediately on a bed of spinach.

Variation: For different flavors, try green grapes and any nut you like in this salad. Cashews, pecans, almonds, or peanuts taste great with creamy curry.

 Tasty Tidbits

Serve this curry salad in pita bread for a delicious lunchtime treat.

Mint and Melon Salad

Refreshing mint lightly flavors ripe, sweet melons, crisp apples, and tangy oranges.

2 cups diced cantaloupe	**2 TB. chopped fresh mint**
1 cup diced apples	**3 TB. lemon juice**
1 cup orange slices	

1. In a large bowl, combine melon, apples, and oranges.

2. In a medium bowl, whisk together mint and lemon juice. Pour over fruit mixture. Chill 1 hour to blend flavors. Serve cold.

 Tasty Tidbits _____

Mint is easy to grow, so make space in your windowsill for a small mint plant. There are several tasty varieties of mint, including lemon mint and chocolate mint.

Yield: About 4 cups
Prep time: 10 minutes
Cook time: None
Serves: 6
Serving size: About ⅔ cup
Each serving has:
44 calories
0.2 g fat
0 g saturated fat
9 mg sodium
11.1 g carbohydrates
1.8 g dietary fiber
0.9 g protein

Tossed Chef's Salad

Ham, turkey, bacon, and Swiss and Cheddar cheeses lend the classic taste to an all-time favorite salad.

Yield: About 6 cups
Prep time: 10 minutes
Cook time: None
Serves: 4
Serving size: About 1½ cups
Each serving has:
187 calories
12.6 g fat
4.5 g saturated fat
322 mg sodium
7.8 g carbohydrates
1.3 g dietary fiber
11.3 g protein

4 cups chopped lettuce

¼ cup Swiss cheese, sliced in small strips

¼ cup shredded Cheddar cheese

¼ cup chopped ham

¼ cup chopped turkey

¼ cup diced celery

1 cup cherry tomatoes

2 hard-boiled eggs, sliced

½ cup turkey bacon, cooked, cooled, and crumbled

¼ cup bottled salad dressing

1. In a large bowl, combine lettuce, Swiss cheese, Cheddar cheese, ham, turkey, celery, and tomatoes. Toss gently.

2. Place about ¼ salad mixture on individual plates. Top each with egg slices and bacon crumbles. Serve with your favorite bottled dressing.

 Tasty Tidbits

Tossing this salad saves time and money. All of the elements of a traditional chef's salad are here but in much smaller quantities than needed to serve them in the conventional way.

Chef's Choice Salad

This salad makes use of your weekly leftovers—just save them from your main meal and serve them later in this quick-and-easy salad. Each combination offers individual flavors. Experiment to find your favorites. Note: The following values are estimates only. The vegetable side dish you choose may change the values.

2 cups chopped lettuce

2 cups of any combination of the following (recipes in Chapter 20):

Tart and Nutty Green Beans

Basil Broccoli with Cashews

Herbed Roasted Roots

Fruit-Glazed Carrots

Red Cabbage and Zucchini Skillet

¼ cup bottled salad dressing

Yield: About 4 cups
Prep time: 5 minutes
Cook time: 10 minutes
Serves: 4
Serving size: About 1 cup
Each serving has:
187 calories
12.6 g fat
4.5 g saturated fat
322 mg sodium
7.8 g carbohydrates
1.3 g dietary fiber
11.3 g protein

1. Place lettuce in a large bowl.

2. In a large skillet over medium heat, gently warm the leftovers, breaking up any large pieces. When warmed through, spoon on top of lettuce. Serve immediately with bottled salad dressing.

Tasty Tidbits _____

You could find yourself making extra vegetable servings to use in this unique salad. Add chopped cooked meat for a main dish salad.

Chapter 15

Beef and Pork Main Dishes

In This Chapter

- ◆ Turning budget cuts on meat into tempting fare
- ◆ Beef and pork comfort food selections
- ◆ Palate-pleasing marinades and sauces

Enjoy eating meat at budget-conscious prices. Shop sales and weekly specials where you can find reduced prices on expensive cuts of meat. Our recipes also use lower-priced cuts like skirt steak, chuck roast, and flank steak.

Enjoy easy, scrumptious pork chops, tender roast beef, or a comforting casserole. These recipes offer a variety of tastes. You'll find recipes with fruit, herbs, hot spices, and cheese, so choose your favorite for that day. If the recipe sounds too hot or too "herby," make substitutions based on your family's preferences.

Our recipes use creative ways to prepare tender, juicy meat. Quick, pan-seared meats retain their juices. Slow-cooked meats become fall-apart tender. These recipes are family friendly, so you can have a delicious meal that you feel good about eating without breaking your budget.

Orange Spiced London Broil

Mustard, garlic, and orange juice flavor and tenderize the beef.

Yield: About 2 lb.
Prep time: 15 minutes
Cook time: 40 minutes
Serves: 10
Serving size: About 3 oz.
Each serving has:
202 calories
8.5 g fat
3.2 g saturated fat
88 mg sodium
3.2 g carbohydrates
0 g dietary fiber
26.6 g protein

1 cup orange juice

1 TB. minced garlic

2 TB. Dijon mustard

1 tsp. ground black pepper

2 lb. London broil-cut beef

1. The night before you plan to serve, prepare marinade. In a large bowl, combine orange juice, garlic, mustard, and pepper. Whisk well. Place beef in marinade. Cover and refrigerate overnight.

2. Preheat broiler.

3. Place beef on oven broiling pan or preheated grill. Cook 5 to 7 minutes per side. Allow meat to rest 10 minutes after removing from oven, then slice and serve.

Variation: You can use other cuts of beef for this recipe, such as skirt steak or flank steak.

Tasty Tidbits _____

Oranges and other citrus fruits enhance the flavor of beef. Try grapefruit juice instead of orange juice.

Slow-Cooked Pot Roast

Beef roasted with onions and tomatoes at low temperature for a long cook-time make it tender and delicious.

2 TB. olive oil

3 lb. chuck roast

2 medium onions, sliced

2 tsp. minced garlic

1 (15-oz.) can crushed tomatoes

2 carrots, cut in 1-inch pieces

2 TB. red wine vinegar

Yield: 1 pot roast, about 2½ lb.
Prep time: 10 minutes
Cook time: 8 hours
Serves: 10
Serving size: About 4 oz.
Each serving has:
376 calories
15.2 g fat
4.8 g saturated fat
208 mg sodium
8.5 g carbohydrates
2.6 g dietary fiber
48.6 g protein

1. Heat olive oil in a large skillet over medium-high heat. Trim fat from meat. Brown chuck roast on all sides.

2. Place onions, garlic, tomatoes, carrots, and vinegar in slow cooker and stir gently. Place chuck roast on top of vegetables. Cover and cook on low for 8 hours.

3. Remove meat from slow cooker, slice, and serve.

Variation: To cook this chuck roast in a conventional oven, prepare as above but instead preheat the oven to 275°F. Place the meat and vegetables in a covered roasting pan. Roast for 2 to 3 hours until tender.

 **Don't Get Burned**

Add dried herbs, such as tarragon, thyme, rosemary, or basil, in the last half hour of the cooking process. If you add herbs at the start, they may taste bitter after long hours in the slow cooker.

Oven Barbecued Beef

Barbecue sauce and orange marmalade flavor tender shredded beef.

Yield: About 6 cups
Prep time: 5 minutes
Cook time: 8 hours, 30 minutes before serving
Serves: 12
Serving size: About ½ cup
Each serving has:
462 calories
31.6 g fat
12.6 g saturated fat
310 mg sodium
12.6 g carbohydrates
0 g dietary fiber
29.8 g protein

1 red or green bell pepper, thickly sliced

3 lb. beef chuck roast or brisket

1 cup bottled barbecue sauce

¼ cup boiling water

¼ cup orange marmalade

1. Preheat oven to 275°F. Arrange bell pepper slices on bottom of roasting pan. Trim visible fat from meat. Place meat on top of bell pepper slices.

2. In a small bowl, whisk together barbecue sauce, water, and marmalade. Pour mixture over meat. Cover and bake for 3 to 4 hours until meat is tender.

3. Remove meat to a cutting board. Use two forks to shred the meat. Skim fat from sauce in the pan. Stir well. Return shredded meat to the roaster. Cover and bake 30 minutes. Serve hot. Allow it to cool completely before refrigerating.

Variation: Add hot sauce, soy sauce, or cider vinegar if your family likes it a little jazzed up. You can also use pork butt roast.

Don't Get Burned

Using bottled barbecue sauce saves time and money, but read the label. Purchase barbecue sauce with mostly natural ingredients. The ingredients to avoid are high-fructose corn syrup, maltodextrins, and artificial flavorings and preservatives.

Roast Beef

This beef is sprinkled with salt and pepper and open roasted in the oven. Simple and delicious.

3 lb. beef roast

1 tsp. salt

2 tsp. ground black pepper

Yield: About 2³/₄ lb.
Prep time: 5 minutes
Cook time: 3 hours
Serves: 12
Serving size: About 3 oz.
Each serving has:
212 calories
7 g fat
2.7 g saturated fat
269 mg sodium
0.2 g carbohydrates
0 g dietary fiber
34.5 g protein

1. Preheat oven to 500°F. Rinse roast and pat dry. Rub roast with salt and pepper.

2. Place roast in a roasting pan and place the pan in the oven. Reduce heat to 450°F. Cook 30 minutes. Turn the oven off and keep the door closed for 2 hours.

3. Without opening the oven, reheat it to 350°F. Continue roasting 30 minutes. Remove roast from the oven and cool slightly before carving.

Kitchen Wise

Do not open the door of the oven at all while cooking. Keep all that heat inside and enjoy the tasty benefits of a slow, dry-cooked roast.

Pan-Seared Skirt Steak

The steak marinates in grapefruit juice, vinegar, and basil and then cooks quickly in a hot pan to seal in the juices.

Yield: About 1 lb.
Prep time: 5 minutes, 1 hour marinate time
Cook time: 6 minutes
Serves: 4
Serving size: About 4 oz.
Each serving has:
243 calories
11.4 g fat
4.4 g saturated fat
87 mg sodium
2.4 g carbohydrates
0 g dietary fiber
30.4 g protein

½ cup grapefruit juice

2 TB. red wine vinegar

2 tsp. dried basil

1 TB. olive oil

1 lb. skirt steak or hanger steak

1. In a large bowl, whisk together grapefruit juice, red wine vinegar, and basil. Add steak, cover, and marinate in refrigerator 45 minutes.

2. Heat olive oil in a large skillet over medium-high heat. Add steak and cook 3 minutes on each side. Remove from the pan and allow to cool slightly. Slice meat against the grain to make it more tender.

Variation: Customize the marinade with your choice of herbs. Some herbs you can use are rosemary, parsley, cumin, or oregano.

Kitchen Wise

Skirt and hanger steaks are inexpensive and flavorful, just take care not to overcook them. The meat should be slightly pink in the center—remember that the meat will continue to cook slightly after you remove it from the heat.

Quick Beef Fajitas

Use leftovers and enjoy south-of-the-border flavors of garlic, cumin, and salsa in these quick beef fajitas.

2 TB. olive oil

1 TB. minced garlic

1 onion, sliced

1 green or red bell pepper, sliced

2 tsp. ground cumin

½ cup salsa

2 cups sliced or shredded beef

½ cup sour cream

8 whole-wheat tortillas

Yield: 8 fajitas
Prep time: 10 minutes
Cook time: 20 minutes
Serves: 8
Serving size: 1 fajita
Each serving has:
271 calories
11.4 g fat
3 g saturated fat
296 mg sodium
26.4 g carbohydrates
2.9 g dietary fiber
13.8 g protein

1. In a large skillet over medium heat, heat olive oil and sauté garlic, onion, and bell pepper for 5 minutes. Add cumin and salsa. Stir well and cook 5 minutes.

2. Add beef. Cook 10 minutes, stirring occasionally. Wrap beef and vegetables in whole-wheat tortillas. Top each with 1 tablespoon sour cream.

Variation: Add vegetables such as zucchini, broccoli, carrots, or mushrooms to these fajitas. You can use leftover pork in place of the beef.

Kitchen Wise

Using leftovers as substitutions in recipes provides your family with flavor and taste variety, and it gives you an opportunity to save money.

Pork Chops with Rosemary

These pork chops are pan cooked in a rosemary-flavored tomato sauce.

Yield: 4 pork chops
Prep time: 10 minutes
Cook time: 25 minutes
Serves: 4
Serving size: 1 pork chop
Each serving has:
357 calories
26.9 g fat
8.4 g saturated fat
991 mg sodium
9.4 g carbohydrates
2.5 g dietary fiber
19.9 g protein

2 TB. olive oil

4 pork chops (about 1½ lb.)

1 onion, sliced

1 (16-oz.) can tomato sauce (about 2 cups)

1 tsp. dried rosemary

½ tsp. salt

¼ tsp. ground black pepper

½ cup water

1. Trim visible fat from chops. In a large skillet over medium-high heat, brown pork chops in olive oil for 4 minutes on each side. Remove chops from the pan and cover lightly with foil.

2. Add onion to the skillet. Sauté about 5 minutes until onion is softened.

3. Stir in tomato sauce, rosemary, salt, pepper, and water. Bring to a boil, lower heat, add chops, cover, and simmer 10 to 15 minutes. Stir once or twice. Cook until chops are cooked throughout. Serve.

Tasty Tidbits _____

This is one of those dishes that just tastes better with fresh herbs. Rosemary is wonderfully aromatic, and fresh rosemary, picked from your own plant or purchased from the produce section, really makes this dish special.

Mustard-Glazed Ham

Brown sugar and Dijon mustard flavor oven-baked ham.

1 fully cooked ham (about 12 lb.)

1 cup water

1 TB. cider vinegar

¼ cup brown sugar

2 TB. Dijon mustard

1 tsp. ground black pepper

Yield: 1 ham
Prep time: 5 minutes
Cook time: About 4 hours
Serves: 30
Serving size: About 6 oz.
Each serving has:
252 calories
13 g fat
4.4 g saturated fat
1,984 mg sodium
7.1 g carbohydrates
2 g dietary fiber
25.2 g protein

1. Preheat oven to 325°F. Wrap ham in aluminum foil and place in a roasting pan with the fat side up. Bake 20 minutes per pound.

2. In a large saucepan over medium heat, combine water, vinegar, brown sugar, mustard, and pepper. Stir well to dissolve sugar. Simmer for 5 minutes.

3. Remove ham from the oven about 30 minutes before the end of cooking time. Carefully open foil but do not remove. Take off any visible fat. Baste ham with glaze and return to the oven, basting with sauce every 10 minutes until finished cooking. Allow to cool slightly before slicing and serving.

Variation: Try your favorite jam as a quick and delicious glaze for baked ham. Add hot sauce for a spicy taste.

Money Matters

Purchase ham on sale. You can find great bargains occasionally. You'll have plenty of leftovers for sandwiches, omelets, and ham casseroles.

Ham and Noodle Casserole

Creamy and mild Swiss cheese turns baked ham leftovers into a delectable casserole with a comfort-food taste.

Yield: 1 (2-quart) casserole
Prep time: 10 minutes
Cook time: 25 minutes
Serves: 6
Serving size: About 1 cup
Each serving has:
252 calories
10.5 g fat
3.9 g saturated fat
637 mg sodium
23.1 g carbohydrates
2.6 g dietary fiber
16 g protein

1 TB. olive oil

1 (12-oz.) package whole-wheat egg noodles

2 cups cooked ham, chopped

1 cup frozen green peas

1 cup low-fat plain yogurt

½ cup shredded Swiss cheese

1 tsp. ground black pepper

1. Preheat oven to 375°F. Lightly oil a 2-quart casserole dish. Prepare noodles according to package directions. Drain well and place in a casserole dish. Add ham and peas.

2. In a large bowl, combine yogurt, Swiss cheese, and pepper. Stir well. Add to the casserole dish and gently mix in to coat all ingredients. Bake 25 minutes until bubbly. Serve hot.

 Don't Get Burned

Serve this creamy casserole with a fresh green salad, cut up vegetables, or fresh fruit to add important nutrients and fiber to your meal.

Baked Italian Sausage and Peppers with Spaghetti

Bell peppers and carrots compliment the hearty flavors of sausage and tomato sauce.

1 TB. olive oil

1 green or red bell pepper, sliced

1 carrot, sliced

1 (26-oz.) jar pasta sauce

¼ cup water

1 lb. Italian sausage, sweet or hot

1 (1-lb.) package whole-wheat spaghetti

¼ cup shredded Parmesan cheese

Yield: About 8 cups
Prep time: 5 minutes
Cook time: 40 minutes
Serves: 8
Serving size: About 1 cup sauce plus 2 ounces spaghetti
Each serving has:
431 calories
22.2 g fat
6.7 g saturated fat
867 mg sodium
37.7 g carbohydrates
2.9 g dietary fiber
18.9 g protein

1. Preheat oven to 375°F.

2. Lightly oil a 9×9-inch baking dish. Line bottom of the baking dish with bell peppers and carrots.

3. Split sausages in half lengthwise, then cut in half again widthwise. Arrange sliced sausage on top of vegetables.

4. Top sausage with pasta sauce and water. Cover with foil and bake 40 minutes.

5. Prepare spaghetti according to directions, drain, and set aside. Serve sausage and sauce over spaghetti and sprinkle with Parmesan.

 Tasty Tidbits

Make sausage sandwiches with leftovers. Sprinkle Parmesan over sandwich and serve hot.

Chapter 16

Poultry Main Dishes

In This Chapter

- ◆ Poultry recipes that provide plenty of leftovers
- ◆ Enjoying the flavor adaptability of poultry
- ◆ Using savory and sweet ingredients to add variety to poultry dishes

Chicken and turkey are inexpensive, easy to cook, and readily absorb the flavors of fruits, vegetables, herbs, and spices.

Many of these recipes are designed to provide meat for more than one meal. Cook a turkey breast, and you'll have leftovers for two or three meals later in the week, such as tacos or stir-fry. This way, you save money by creatively eating food that's already been cooked.

Baked Chicken with Apples and Sweet Potatoes

The fruity glaze is flavored with Dijon mustard and mild Swiss cheese. Baking brings out the natural sweetness of the apples and sweet potatoes.

Yield: 4 chicken breasts
Prep time: 10 minutes
Cook time: 35 minutes
Serves: 8
Serving size: ½ chicken breast and about ¼ cup apples and sweet potatoes
Each serving has:
248 calories
8.6 g fat
3.5 g saturated fat
172 mg sodium
12.5 g carbohydrates
1.6 g dietary fiber
29.2 g protein

1 TB. olive oil

1 cup apple juice

1 tsp. caraway seeds

¼ cup Dijon mustard

4 (2-lb.) chicken breasts

1 apple, cored and thickly sliced

1 cup peeled and diced sweet potatoes

4 (1-oz.) slices Swiss cheese

1. Preheat oven to 375°F. Lightly oil a 9×13-inch baking dish.

2. In a large bowl, whisk together apple juice, caraway seeds, and Dijon mustard.

3. In the prepared baking dish, arrange chicken, apples, and sweet potatoes in a single layer. Pour apple juice mixture on chicken. Bake 25 minutes.

4. Remove from the oven and cover each chicken breast with a slice of Swiss cheese. Bake 10 additional minutes. Serve while cheese is still bubbly hot.

Variation: Fruit makes a perfect sauce for baked chicken. If your family likes a particular fruit, there is a way to make a sauce for chicken with it. Try apricot jam and your favorite hot sauce, soy sauce with orange marmalade, or raspberry jam, olive oil, and balsamic vinegar.

 Tasty Tidbits

Chicken is terrific for experimenting. Be brave and try something you've never tasted. Peanut butter and cilantro, orange juice and cranberries—you can even try a spicy Mexican chile-chocolate sauce called mole from the Latino section of your grocery store. Mix and match your family's favorite flavors to enjoy chicken many different ways.

Lemon Pecan Stuffed Chicken

The light, nutty filling is flavored with piquant Dijon mustard, and the chicken is baked in individual foil packets.

3 TB. olive oil	¼ cup raisins
4 (2-lb.) chicken breasts	1 tsp. lemon pepper
¼ cup lemon juice	1 small onion, thinly sliced
½ cup chopped pecans	1 carrot, thinly sliced
2 TB. Dijon mustard	

Yield: 4 packets
Prep time: 10 minutes
Cook time: 50 minutes
Serves: 8
Serving size: ½ packet
Each serving has:
200 calories
7.6 g fat
1.1 g saturated fat
102 mg sodium
7.1 g carbohydrates
1.4 g dietary fiber
25.8 g protein

1. Preheat oven to 375°F. Cut 4 large squares of aluminum foil, about 4×4 inches, and brush one side lightly using 1 tablespoon olive oil. Brush each breast with lemon juice.

2. In a large bowl, combine remaining olive oil, pecans, Dijon mustard, and raisins. Stir to coat all ingredients. Place a spoonful of pecan filling in the center of each foil square. Place a chicken breast over the filling. Sprinkle each breast with lemon pepper. Carefully fold in foil edges to make a sealed packet. Place packets on a cookie sheet. Bake 30 minutes.

3. Remove from the oven and carefully open each packet. Add equal portions of onions and carrots to each packet. Leave packets slightly open and bake another 20 minutes. Allow to cool slightly before serving.

Variation: Try almost any vegetable you like baked in these convenient, low-mess packets. Bell peppers, apples, sweet potatoes, mushrooms, corn, green beans, broccoli, and spinach all taste great with the spicy mustard and buttery nuts.

 Don't Get Burned

The steam that builds up in these packets is very hot, so be careful when opening them!

Curried Chicken and Rice Casserole

Spicy curry flavors chicken and rice with sweet raisins and carrots.

Yield: 4 chicken breasts and about 3½ cups rice and sauce	
Prep time: 10 minutes	
Cook time: 45 minutes	
Serves: 8	
Serving size: ½ chicken breast and about ¾ cup rice and sauce	
Each serving has:	
323 calories	
10.8 g fat	
2.7 g saturated fat	
103 mg sodium	
27.7 g carbohydrates	
1.4 g dietary fiber	
28 g protein	

2 TB. olive oil

4 (2-lb.) chicken breasts

¼ cup water

1 cup apple juice

1 TB. curry powder

¾ cup uncooked brown rice

½ cup raisins

1 carrot, shredded

1 cup low-fat plain yogurt

1. Preheat oven to 350°F. Lightly oil a 9×13-inch baking dish. Arrange chicken in a single layer in the baking dish.

2. In a large bowl, whisk together olive oil, water, apple juice, and curry powder.

3. Add rice, raisins, and carrots to the baking dish and cover with apple juice mixture. Cover with foil and bake 45 minutes. Top with yogurt. Serve immediately.

Variation: Apples, celery, bell peppers, and sweet potatoes taste wonderful in this curry sauce.

Chicken with Vegetables and Tarragon

Chicken is cooked with onions, carrots, and potatoes flavored with tarragon.

2 onions, peeled and sliced

1 (about 3-lb.) whole chicken, cut into pieces

6 small red potatoes

4 carrots, cut into 2-inch lengths

5 cups water

½ tsp. salt

¼ tsp. ground black pepper

2 tsp. dried tarragon

Yield: 1 chicken and 10 cups vegetables
Prep time: 10 minutes
Cook time: 45 minutes
Serves: 6
Serving size: ⅙ chicken and 1⅔ cups vegetables
Each serving has:
379 calories
5 g fat
1.4 g saturated fat
335 mg sodium
34.5 g carbohydrates
4.7 g dietary fiber
47.9 g protein

1. In a large saucepan, combine onions, chicken, potatoes, carrots, water, salt, thyme, pepper, and tarragon. Bring to a boil. Reduce heat, cover, and simmer 45 minutes.

2. Remove chicken from the saucepan and remove skin.

3. Place chicken and vegetables in a large serving bowl. Serve hot with skimmed broth from the saucepan.

Kitchen Wise

This simple chicken dinner provides all the nutrients you need for a meal in one pot. You can add a side salad if you prefer.

Southern Spiced Chicken

Garlic and pepper flavor this quick chicken dish.

Yield: 4 chicken breasts and about 1 cup sauce
Prep time: 10 minutes
Cook time: 30 minutes
Serves: 4
Serving size: 1 breast and about ¼ cup sauce
Each serving has:
167 calories
7.8 g fat
1.7 g saturated fat
341 mg sodium
6.4 g carbohydrates
0.6 g dietary fiber
17 g protein

2 TB. olive oil

4 (1-lb.) chicken breasts

¼ cup flour

1 TB. crushed red pepper flakes

1 tsp. ground black pepper

1 tsp. salt

1 small green or red bell pepper, sliced

½ cup water

1 TB. honey

2 TB. cider vinegar

1 tsp. minced garlic

1. Heat olive oil in a large skillet over medium-high heat. In a large bowl, combine flour, red pepper, black pepper, and salt. Dredge each breast in flour mixture and place in the hot skillet. Cook chicken 4 minutes on each side.

2. Add bell pepper, water, honey, vinegar, and garlic. Stir well and reduce heat to medium. Simmer 20 minutes, stirring often. Serve hot.

Variation: Try fresh basil in this recipe—tear it in small pieces and add it during the last 5 minutes of cooking.

 Tasty Tidbits

Honey and cider vinegar lend a slightly sweet and sour taste to this garlicky chicken dish.

Tangy Chicken and Fruit Kabobs

This quick chicken and vegetable dinner is flavored with soy sauce.

1 TB. soy sauce

2 TB. olive oil

1 TB. lemon juice

2 (about ½-lb.) chicken breasts, cut in large chunks

1 onion, cut in large chunks

2 medium firm tomatoes, cut in large chunks

2 cups small mushrooms

Yield: 4 skewers
Prep time: 10 minutes plus 30 minutes to marinate
Cook time: 15 minutes
Serves: 4
Serving size: 1 skewer
Each serving has:
200 calories
11.2 g fat
2.1 g saturated fat
280 mg sodium
6.8 g carbohydrates
1.6 g dietary fiber
18.6 g protein

1. Preheat the broiler. In a large bowl, combine soy sauce, olive oil, and lemon juice. Whisk well.

2. Split soy sauce mixture in half in separate bowls. Marinate chicken 30 minutes, covered in refrigerator. Cover remaining sauce and refrigerate until ready to use.

3. On each skewer, alternate between chicken chunks and chunks of onion, tomatoes, and mushrooms without crowding the skewers. Brush each skewer with sauce from refrigerator. Broil 15 minutes, turning once. Serve hot.

 Kitchen Wise

If you use wooden or bamboo skewers, soak them for 30 minutes in water before using to prevent them from burning.

Turkey and White Bean Skillet

Mellow flavors of thyme and mushrooms permeate this quick meal.

Yield: About 4½ cups
Prep time: 5 minutes
Cook time: 15 minutes
Serves: 6
Serving size: About ¾ cup
Each serving has:
170 calories
5.3 g fat
1.2 g saturated fat
247 mg sodium
12.2 g carbohydrates
3.8 g dietary fiber
18.3 g protein

1 TB. olive oil

2 cups roast turkey, cut in medium-size cubes

1 (7-oz.) can sliced mushrooms

1 (15-oz.) can great northern beans

1 cup frozen spinach

1 tsp. dried thyme

1 TB. red wine vinegar

1. Heat olive oil in a large skillet over medium heat. Add turkey and mushrooms and sauté for 8 minutes.

2. Add beans, spinach, thyme, and vinegar. Stir well and cook 5 more minutes until heated throughout. Serve hot.

 Kitchen Wise _____

This quick meal provides excellent nutrition in 15 minutes or less of cooking.

Herb Roasted Turkey

Soaking the turkey breast overnight in brine makes this main dish entrée juicy and flavorful.

1 (6-lb.) turkey breast, bone in	2 TB. olive oil
1 cup kosher salt	1 onion, thinly sliced
1 TB. minced garlic	2 stalks celery, cut in large chunks
1 TB. dried rosemary	2 carrots, cut in large chunks
2 tsp. dried oregano	4 new potatoes, cut in quarters
¼ cup lemon juice	
6 cups cold water	2 tsp. ground black pepper

> *Yield: 1 (6-lb.) turkey breast and about 5 cups vegetables*
>
> **Prep time:** 15 minutes and overnight brining
>
> **Cook time:** 2½ hours
>
> **Serves:** 24
>
> **Serving size:** About 4 oz. meat and ¼ cup vegetables
>
> **Each serving has:**
>
> 159 calories
>
> 3.1 g fat
>
> 0.6 g saturated fat
>
> 1,451 mg sodium
>
> 11.9 g carbohydrates
>
> 1.8 g dietary fiber
>
> 20.1 g protein

1. In a bowl large enough to hold the turkey breast and cover it completely with liquid, combine salt, garlic, rosemary, oregano, lemon juice, and cold water. Stir until salt is completely dissolved. Add turkey breast and more cold water to cover if necessary. Cover the bowl and brine turkey in refrigerator overnight or at least 6 hours.

2. Preheat oven to 375°F. Discard brining liquid and rinse turkey breast well. Rub turkey with olive oil and place in roasting pan. Add onion, celery, carrots, and potatoes. Sprinkle with pepper. Roast 2¹/₂ hours until juices run clear. Cool slightly before slicing and serving.

Variation: Use any herbs you prefer in the brine that flavors the turkey. Try coriander, fennel, dill, or thyme. You can also use lime juice or unsweetened grapefruit juice instead of lemon.

Kitchen Wise

This turkey recipe serves 24, so plan on plenty of leftovers for sandwiches as well as lunch or dinner entrées such as tacos or tamale pie.

Leftover Turkey and Vegetable Stir-Fry

Sweet pineapple and soy sauce compliment fresh vegetables and the turkey.

Yield: About 6 cups
Prep time: 5 minutes
Cook time: 55 minutes
Serves: 6
Serving size: About 1 cup
Each serving has:
375 calories
8.7 g fat
1.7 g saturated fat
192 mg sodium
54 g carbohydrates
3.3 g dietary fiber
19.4 g protein

2 TB. olive oil

1 tsp. minced garlic

2 cups diced cooked turkey

1 green or red bell pepper, sliced

1 cup broccoli florets

½ cup pineapple chunks

1 TB. soy sauce

¼ cup pineapple juice

1 tsp. crushed red pepper flakes

2 cups cooked brown rice

1. Heat olive oil in a large skillet over medium heat. Add garlic and turkey. Cook 5 minutes, stirring constantly. Add bell pepper, broccoli, and pineapple. Cook 5 more minutes.

2. In a medium bowl, whisk together soy sauce, pineapple juice, and red pepper. Pour carefully into the skillet. Stir well. Cook another 5 minutes. Serve hot with rice.

Variation: Use cauliflower, green beans, or carrots in place of the broccoli.

 Kitchen Wise _____

This is a pared-down version of the traditional Asian stir-fry. You'll enjoy terrific flavor without costly specialty ingredients.

Caesar Turkey with Mushrooms

Creamy Caesar dressing, tangy Parmesan cheese, and seasoned croutons are baked with leftover turkey and mushrooms.

| |
| 1 (12-oz.) package whole-wheat noodles |
| 2 TB. olive oil |
| 1 cup sliced mushrooms |
| 1 tsp. ground black pepper |

| |
| 2 cups diced cooked turkey |
| 1 cup Caesar dressing |
| ¼ cup grated Parmesan cheese |
| 1 cup seasoned croutons |

Yield: About 7 cups
Prep time: 10 minutes
Cook time: 25 minutes
Serves: 6
Serving size: About 1 cup
Each serving has:
333 calories
15.8 g fat
3 g saturated fat
522 mg sodium
28.3 g carbohydrates
1.8 g dietary fiber
19.3 g protein

1. Prepare noodles according to package directions. Drain well.

2. Preheat oven to 350°F. Lightly oil a 2-quart casserole dish.

3. In a skillet over medium-high heat, combine olive oil, mushrooms, pepper, and turkey. Cook 8 minutes, stirring often.

4. In the prepared casserole dish, combine noodles, turkey and mushroom mixture, Caesar dressing, and cheese. Sprinkle with croutons. Bake 25 minutes. Serve hot.

 Tasty Tidbits

If you don't have any leftover turkey, you can use leftover chicken, skirt steak, or pork tenderloin in this recipe.

Apricot Glazed Turkey Thighs

Turkey thighs are simmered with bell peppers and green beans in an apricot-flavored sauce.

Yield: 2 turkey thighs and about 2 cups vegetables with sauce
Prep time: 5 minutes
Cook time: 30 minutes
Serves: 10
Serving size: 4 to 5 oz. turkey and about ½ cup sauce and vegetables
Each serving has:
190 calories
6.2 g fat
1.5 g saturated fat
288 mg sodium
12.9 g carbohydrates
0.8 g dietary fiber
20.5 g protein

2 TB. olive oil

2 turkey thighs, skin removed (about 2½ lb. total)

1 green or red bell pepper, diced

1 cup frozen green beans

½ cup apricot jam

1 tsp. salt

1 TB. lemon pepper

¼ cup water

¼ cup apple juice

1. Heat olive oil in a skillet over medium-high heat. Brown turkey for 5 minutes on each side.

2. Reduce heat to medium. Add bell pepper, green beans, jam, salt, lemon pepper, water, and apple juice. Stir well. Simmer 20 minutes. Serve hot.

Variation: Does your family like their food spicy? If so, add a couple dashes of your favorite hot sauce before simmering.

Tasty Tidbits _____

Watch for turkey to go on sale and enjoy this recipe with turkey breasts as well as thighs. Substitute chicken thighs if you find them on sale.

Chapter 17

Seafood Main Dishes

In This Chapter

- ◆ Cooking with fish for health and nutrition
- ◆ Eating seafood without breaking the budget
- ◆ Enjoying regional seafood tastes and flavors

Eating seafood feels luxurious. It offers elegant taste, but that's not all. Fish is the only source of complete omega-3 fatty acids, a key element of a heart-healthy diet, while being a fantastic source of lean protein.

Seafood, both fish and shellfish, can fit into your meal plans and your budget. If you live in a land-locked part of the country, you may need to shop for sales on fresh and frozen seafood. The simple preparations we include in these recipes will enhance the flavor of good seafood to let you create delicious meals without a lot of fuss.

Don't Get Burned

Some seafood can contain high levels of mercury, so do some research and select your purchases carefully. If you can find sustainably farmed fish from local sources, you can minimize possible health risks.

Pay careful attention to when your favorite grocery store has sales on seafood. Frequently a store will have regular sales on seafood one day per week, typically Sunday. Shop for seafood on sale days to save money without limiting your meal plan.

Gumbo with Shrimp and Sausage

This genuine Southern favorite is flavored with garlic, oregano, and the distinctive taste of andouille sausage.

2 TB. olive oil

¼ cup diced onion

¼ cup diced celery

1 tsp. crushed garlic

1 tsp. dried oregano

1 tsp. dried thyme

1 tsp. dried parsley

1 tsp. ground black pepper

1 (16-oz.) can whole tomatoes, crushed and drained

½ lb. turkey andouille sausage, thinly sliced

2 tsp. Worcestershire sauce

6 cups water

½ lb. peeled raw shrimp, deveined

½ cup diced green bell pepper

1 lemon, cut in half

1 cup spinach

2 cups cooked basmati or long-grain rice

Yield: About 12 cups		
Prep time: 15 minutes		
Cook time: 30 minutes		
Serves: 8		
Serving size: About 1½ cups gumbo plus ½ cup rice		
Each serving has:		
306 calories		
8.8 g fat		
2.8 g saturated fat		
308 mg sodium		
39.6 g carbohydrates		
1.4 g dietary fiber		
15.3 g protein		

1. Heat olive oil in a large skillet over medium heat. Add onions and celery. Stir until softened.

2. Add garlic, oregano, thyme, parsley, and pepper. Stir well. Add tomatoes, sausage, Worcestershire sauce, and water. Bring to a boil, reduce heat, and simmer 15 minutes.

3. Add shrimp, bell pepper, and juice from half the lemon. Cover and simmer 10 minutes. Remove from heat.

4. In a medium skillet over medium-low heat, combine spinach and juice from remaining lemon half. Stir often until spinach wilts. Remove from heat.

5. Serve shrimp and sausage mixture over wilted spinach and rice.

Variation: Use canned Cajun shrimp in place of the raw shrimp to add even more authentic flavor from the Cajun seasonings.

Tasty Tidbits

This version of gumbo calls for spinach in place of the traditional okra. If you're a fan of okra, add it to the stew.

Herbed Salmon Cakes

These tangy and crispy cakes will please everyone in the family.

Yield: 16 cakes
Prep time: 15 minutes
Cook time: 20 minutes
Serves: 8
Serving size: 2 cakes
Each serving has:
203 calories
12.9 g fat
2.1 g saturated fat
71 mg sodium
5.6 g carbohydrates
1.7 g dietary fiber
16.7 g protein

2 cups chopped cauliflower

3 TB. water

1 cup finely diced celery

2 eggs

½ cup chopped walnuts

1 TB. dried dill

2 tsp. dried parsley

16 oz. canned or vacuum-packed salmon

¼ cup cornmeal

2 lemons, cut into wedges

1. Preheat oven to 375°F.

2. Place cauliflower and water in a medium microwave-safe bowl. Cover. Cook on high in the microwave 3 to 4 minutes until tender. Remove cauliflower, drain, and mash with a fork. Cool slightly. Add celery, eggs, walnuts, dill, and parsley. Stir gently to blend ingredients with eggs.

3. In a second bowl, flake salmon. Fold it gently into cauliflower mixture.

4. Form mixture into 16 patties, dust with cornmeal, and bake 20 minutes on a cookie sheet lined with parchment paper. Serve immediately with lemon wedges.

 Tasty Tidbits

Serve these cakes on a bed of spinach with chopped apple or tuck them into warmed pitas with coleslaw (see Chapter 14). You can also serve on stone-ground buns as a salmon-burger.

Tuna with Olives and Pasta

Tuna and vegetables are dressed with olive oil, capers, and red wine vinegar in this no-cook sauce.

1 (16-oz.) package spaghetti

3 TB. capers

1 TB. minced onion

½ tsp. lemon pepper

2 TB. red wine vinegar

1 TB. olive oil

½ cup chopped tomatoes

¼ cup sliced black olives

½ cup shredded carrots

¼ cup stuffed green olives, sliced

2 (6-oz.) cans tuna packed in oil, drained and flaked

½ cup shredded Parmesan cheese

Yield: 4 cups sauce plus cooked spaghetti
Prep time: 15 minutes
Cook time: 25 minutes
Serves: 8
Serving size: About ½ cup sauce and ⅛ pkg. of spaghetti
Each serving has:
293 calories
8.7 g fat
2.3 g saturated fat
267 mg sodium
0.6 g dietary fiber
32.4 g carbohydrates
20.3 g protein

1. In a large pot, cook spaghetti as package directs but only until barely al dente. Drain in colander. Run cold water over pasta to stop the cooking process. Place in serving bowl and set aside.

2. In a medium bowl, mix together capers, onion, lemon pepper, vinegar, and olive oil. Add tomatoes, black olives, carrots, green olives, and tuna. Toss well.

3. Add vegetable mixture to the spaghetti. Toss. Sprinkle with Parmesan cheese. Serve at room temperature.

Tasty Tidbits

Enjoy this warm-weather dish with a side salad of vegetables or fruit.

Lemon Halibut Kebabs

Lemon, thyme, and celery salt give a tangy herbed flavor to halibut and vegetables.

Yield: 8 skewers
Prep time: 10 minutes
Cook time: 15 minutes
Serves: 8
Serving size: 1 skewer
Each serving has:
212 calories
10.8 g fat
1.9 g saturated fat
41 mg sodium
9.5 g carbohydrates
2.8 g dietary fiber
20.3 g protein

1 (1-lb.) halibut steak, cut into large cubes

¼ cup lemon juice

1 TB. dried thyme, crushed

3 red or green bell peppers, thickly sliced

3 zucchini, cut into 1-inch chunks

24 button mushrooms

2 onions, cut in thick wedges

¼ cup olive oil

1 TB. lemon pepper

2 tsp. celery salt

1. Preheat broiler or grill.

2. In a medium bowl, mix halibut, lemon juice, and thyme and let stand to marinate.

3. In a separate large bowl, combine bell peppers, zucchini, mushrooms, and onions. Drizzle with olive oil and stir gently to coat. Add lemon pepper and celery salt. Stir well.

4. Using metal or bamboo skewers (see the following note on bamboo skewers), add alternating halibut and vegetables. Arrange skewers in a single layer on a cookie sheet lined with foil. If you're using an outdoor grill, place directly on grill. Brush each skewer with remaining olive oil dressing. Broil 15 minutes, turning once. Serve immediately.

Variation: Use fresh salmon or tuna in place of the halibut.

 Kitchen Wise _____

If you use wooden or bamboo skewers, soak them for 20 to 30 minutes in water to keep them from burning.

Oven-Sautéed Catfish

Serve this lighter version of the old Friday night favorite with Hot Cabbage Slaw and Sweet Potato Fries.

½ cup cornmeal
1 tsp. ground coriander
2 tsp. paprika

½ tsp. ground black pepper
2 TB. olive oil
4 (1-lb.) catfish fillets

Yield: 4 fillets
Prep time: 5 minutes
Cook time: 8 minutes
Serves: 4
Serving size: 4 oz.
Each serving has:
274 calories
16.1 g fat
2.6 g saturated fat
66 mg sodium
12.9 g carbohydrates
1.8 g dietary fiber
19.2 g protein

1. Preheat oven to 350°F.

2. In a large bowl, combine cornmeal, coriander, paprika, and pepper. Brush each fish fillet with olive oil and dredge in cornmeal mixture.

3. Line a 9×13-inch baking pan with aluminum foil. Place fish fillets in the pan. Bake 10 to 15 minutes until fish flakes and is cooked throughout. Serve immediately.

Variation: Use any white fish, such as trout or sole, in place of the catfish.

Tasty Tidbits _____

Serve Oven-Sautéed Catfish with steamed broccoli, a side salad, and boiled red potatoes for a balanced meal.

Paella-Style Seafood Bake

Vegetables, seafood, and rice are flavored with turmeric, garlic, and chili powder.

Yield: 14 cups
Prep time: 20 minutes
Cook time: 30 minutes
Serves: 8
Serving size: About 1¼ cups
Each serving has:
305 calories
6.3 g fat
1.1 g saturated fat
149 mg sodium
45 g carbohydrates
2.6 g dietary fiber
15.5 g protein

2 TB. olive oil

¼ cup diced onions

½ cup diced green or red bell pepper

1 tsp. turmeric

1 tsp. crushed garlic

1 tsp. chili powder

2 tsp. ground black pepper

2 cups uncooked rice

1 (14½-oz.) can diced tomatoes

6 cups water

8 oz. haddock or other mild fish, cut into bite-size chunks

1 (4-oz.) can shrimp, drained

1 (6½-oz.) can clams with liquid

1 cup frozen peas

1. Heat olive oil in a large stockpot over medium heat. Add onions and bell pepper. Sauté 5 minutes. Stir in turmeric, garlic, chili powder, and pepper. Add rice and coat well in olive oil. Heat 3 minutes.

2. Add tomatoes and water, bring to a boil, and then reduce heat to medium and simmer uncovered for 10 minutes. Do not stir, just give the pan a little shake every few minutes.

3. If the rice is already getting dry, add more water. Cook 5 minutes. Add fish, shrimp, clams, and peas. Cover stockpot and cook 12 minutes longer.

4. Remove from heat, keep covered, and let stand at least 5 minutes. Serve in large bowls with lemon wedges, 2 per person.

 Money Matters

Canned shrimp and clams keep the cost down and the flavor high.

Baked Seafood Casserole

Clams and fish are baked with sourdough breadcrumbs and vegetables and flavored with rosemary.

1 (6-oz.) can clams

½ cup sliced mushrooms

½ cup diced tomatoes

½ cup diced celery

1 cup chopped green beans

1 cup sourdough breadcrumbs

1 TB. dried thyme

⅛ tsp. salt

⅛ tsp. ground black pepper

1 (8-oz.) white fish, cut into bite-size pieces

Yield: About 6 cups
Prep time: 15 minutes
Cook time: 25 minutes
Serves: 4
Serving size: 1 bowl, about 1½ cups
Each serving has:
251 calories
6.3 g fat
1.3 g saturated fat
395 mg sodium
27.9 g carbohydrates
3.1 g dietary fiber
20 g protein

1. Preheat oven to 350°F.

2. In a large bowl, combine clams with their juice, mushrooms, tomatoes, celery, green beans, breadcrumbs, thyme, salt, and pepper. Gently fold in fish.

3. Transfer to 2-quart baking dish. Bake 25 minutes.

Variation: Try different combinations of your family's favorite vegetables in this dish. Get them to help with preparing the veggies, and they may eat more of them.

Don't Get Burned

Keep your eyes on this casserole toward the end of baking. Different fish contain different amounts of moisture. You don't want your casserole to dry out.

Fish Tacos

Soft, warm tortillas are wrapped around crisp cabbage and fish spiced with garlic, cumin, and chili powder.

Yield: 8 tacos
Prep time: 10 minutes
Cook time: 10 minutes
Serves: 4
Serving size: 2 tacos
Each serving has:
271 calories
9.6 g fat
1.4 g saturated fat
167 mg sodium
29.2 g carbohydrates
4.6 g dietary fiber
19 g protein

2 TB. olive oil

¼ tsp. crushed garlic

3 TB. lemon juice

1 tsp. ground cumin

½ tsp. chili powder

8 oz. red snapper or other white fish, cut into bite-size pieces

½ cup corn

¼ cup shredded carrots

1 cup shredded cabbage

8 (6-inch) soft corn tortillas

¼ cup salsa

1. In a large skillet, heat olive oil over medium heat. In a large bowl, combine garlic, lemon juice, cumin, chili powder, and fish. Stir gently to coat fish well.

2. Place fish in the skillet and sauté for 5 minutes. Add corn and carrots. Cook 3 minutes covered. Add cabbage, stir well, and cook until cabbage begins to wilt.

3. Spoon mixture into tortillas. Fold and serve immediately.

 Tasty Tidbits _____

Serve tacos with guacamole (see Chapter 13) and finish your meal with your favorite dessert recipe from Chapter 22.

Fish Baked in Bags

The fish is moist and tender with an island flavor of soy sauce and pineapple.

4 (3- to 4-oz.) fillets sole or trout	**8 tsp. soy sauce**
2 TB. olive oil	**½ cup crushed pineapple**

1. Preheat oven to 400°F.

2. Cut 4 large squares of aluminum foil approximately 4×4 inches. Brush center of foil lightly with olive oil. Place a fish fillet in the center of each square. Drizzle 2 teaspoons of soy sauce and place 2 tablespoons crushed pineapple on top of each fillet. Carefully fold foil into envelope, making sure the edges are all closed.

3. Place packets on a cookie sheet. Bake 12 minutes. Serve immediately, either in the foil envelopes or removed with sauce in bag to individual plates.

 Don't Get Burned

Be careful opening these foil envelopes, the steam is hot!

Yield: 4 fillets
Prep time: 5 minutes
Cook time: 12 minutes
Serves: 4
Serving size: 1 bag, about 4 oz. fish and 3 TB. sauce and fruit
Each serving has:
184 calories
8.2 g fat
1.2 g saturated fat
646 mg sodium
3.3 g carbohydrates
2.5 g dietary fiber
23.1 g protein

Fish Stew with Potatoes and Tomatoes

This hearty fish stew is flavored with bay leaves and fennel.

Yield: About 12 cups
Prep time: 15 minutes
Cook time: 25 minutes
Serves: 4
Serving size: 3 cups
Each serving has:
317 calories
8.2 g fat
1.2 g saturated fat
248 mg sodium
43.3 g carbohydrates
5.2 g dietary fiber
19 g protein

2 TB. olive oil

¼ cup diced celery

¼ cup chopped onions

6 cups water

1 (14½-oz.) can chopped tomatoes

4 red potatoes, cut in large wedges

2 bay leaves

¼ tsp. crushed fennel seeds

1 (½-lb.) flounder or bass, cut in bite-size pieces

1 (6-oz.) can clams

½ tsp. crushed garlic

1 TB. dried parsley

¼ tsp. ground black pepper

1. Heat olive oil in a stockpot over medium heat, add celery and onion, and stir until softened. Add water, tomatoes, potatoes, bay leaves, and fennel seeds. Bring to a boil, reduce heat to medium-low, and simmer 20 minutes.

2. Increase heat to medium-high. Add fish, clams, garlic, parsley, and pepper. Cook 5 minutes. Remove bay leaves. Serve immediately.

Variation: Use any fish or seafood you have on hand.

 Tasty Tidbits

Serve this tomato-based fish stew with crusty sourdough bread and a tossed green salad.

Chapter 18

Ground Meat Main Dishes

In This Chapter

- Stretching your food budget
- Varied tastes of ground meat, both ethnic and regional
- Using quality yet cost-saving ingredients to flavor ground meat

In this chapter, we offer you a wide range of recipes for ground meat. From classics like meatloaf basted with tangy honey mustard to homemade favorites like lasagna, these recipes quickly turn a pound of ground meat into a hearty, delicious meal.

We specify the kind of meat to use in each recipe, but you can substitute easily. Try turkey meatloaf instead of beef, or beef meatballs instead of turkey. Ground bison or ground chicken are also good in these recipes.

Honey Mustard Glazed Meatloaf

This vegetable-stuffed meatloaf is flavored with Dijon mustard, honey, and Worcestershire sauce.

Yield: 1 meatloaf, about 10 slices
Prep time: 10 minutes
Cook time: 90 minutes
Serves: 10
Serving size: 1 slice
Each serving has:
145 calories
5.2 g fat
1.7 g saturated fat
155 mg sodium
5.1 g carbohydrates
0.6 g dietary fiber
18.5 g protein

1½ TB. olive oil

1 lb. lean ground beef

½ cup breadcrumbs or cracker crumbs

1 egg

1 carrot, shredded

½ cup frozen spinach

1 medium tomato, diced

1 TB. Worcestershire sauce

3 TB. Dijon mustard

1 TB. honey

1. Preheat oven to 375°F. Lightly oil a 9×5×3-inch loaf pan.

2. In a large bowl, combine ground beef, breadcrumbs or cracker crumbs, egg, carrot, spinach, tomato, and Worcestershire sauce. Mix well to combine. Transfer mixture to the loaf pan and shape into rounded loaf. Bake 1 hour.

3. In a medium microwave-safe bowl, combine mustard and honey. Microwave 10 seconds. Whisk well. Remove meatloaf from the oven. Spread honey mustard over meatloaf using the back of a spoon. Bake an additional 30 minutes. Cool slightly before slicing and serving.

Variation: You can also use vegetables such as corn, zucchini, peas, bell peppers, or sliced olives.

 Tasty Tidbits

Leftover meatloaf tastes terrific. Serve hot or cold in sandwiches. Leftovers can be served hot with a slice of cheese melted on sourdough bread for a hearty lunch.

Enchilada Pie

A golden sweet cornbread crust covers a spicy meat, cheese, and vegetable medley.

1 lb. ground turkey or beef	**¼ cup water**
2 TB. olive oil	**½ cup shredded Cheddar cheese**
1 tsp. minced garlic	
1 green or red bell pepper, diced	**1 cup flour**
	¾ cup cornmeal
1 medium tomato, chopped	**2 tsp. baking powder**
½ cup corn (frozen, canned, or fresh)	**⅔ cup low-fat milk**
1 tsp. ground cumin	**1 egg, beaten**
1 tsp. crushed red pepper flakes	

Yield: About 6 cups

Prep time: 20 minutes

Cook time: 30 minutes

Serves: 8

Serving size: About ¾ cup

Each serving has:

318 calories

14.4 g fat

4.3 g saturated fat

121 mg sodium

25.7 g carbohydrates

2 g dietary fiber

21.1 g protein

1. Preheat oven to 400°F. Lightly oil a 9×13-inch baking dish.

2. In a large skillet over medium heat, brown ground beef or turkey in olive oil for 5 minutes.

3. Add garlic, bell pepper, tomatoes, corn, cumin, red pepper, and water. Bring mixture to a boil. Reduce heat to medium and simmer 10 minutes, stirring often. Stir in cheese until melted. Transfer to prepared baking dish.

4. In a large bowl, combine flour, cornmeal, and baking powder. Add milk and egg. Stir well. Spoon cornmeal mixture onto meat mixture and spread smooth with the back of a spoon.

5. Bake 30 minutes until topping is golden and crisp. Serve hot.

Variation: Add pinto or black beans to the vegetable mixture in place of the ground turkey or beef, or stir mild diced green chiles into the cornbread topping for more flavor.

Kitchen Wise

If your family likes red enchilada sauce, use it in place of water. You can also use salsa, Rotel, or tomato sauce.

Lasagna with Meat and Cheese

This quick version of the traditional Italian classic offers vegetables, ground beef, and mozzarella cheese.

Yield: 1 9×13-inch pan
Prep time: 15 minutes
Cook time: 30 minutes
Serves: 12
Serving size: 1 square, about 3×4 inches
Each serving has:
198 calories
5.9 g fat
2.3 g saturated fat
381 mg sodium
17.2 g carbohydrates
2.2 g dietary fiber
17.8 g protein

1 (12-oz.) package lasagna noodles

1 lb. lean ground beef

2 TB. olive oil

2 tsp. minced garlic

1 green or red bell pepper, diced

½ cup spinach, fresh or frozen

1 medium zucchini, shredded

1 cup low-fat cottage cheese

1 (26-oz.) jar pasta sauce

½ cup shredded or grated mozzarella cheese

1. Preheat oven to 350°F. Lightly oil a 9×13-inch baking dish.

2. Prepare lasagna noodles according to package directions. Drain well and set aside.

3. In a large skillet over medium-high heat, brown beef in olive oil 7 minutes until it's no longer pink. Drain. Add garlic, bell pepper, spinach, and zucchini. Cook 5 minutes.

4. Arrange a layer of half the noodles on the bottom of the baking dish. Spread half of cottage cheese over noodles, then half of meat and vegetables. Top with half of tomato sauce. Arrange remaining lasagna noodles on top of sauce. Spread rest of cottage cheese over noodles and top cottage cheese with rest of meat and vegetable mixture. Spread remaining tomato sauce and top with mozzarella cheese. Bake 30 minutes until cheese is bubbly.

 Don't Get Burned

Don't let your lasagna noodles get too dry. Cover them with a damp towel while you assemble this dish. You can also toss them gently with a tablespoon of olive oil to keep them moist.

Turkey Meatballs with Spaghetti Marinara

These zesty meatballs are flavored with pasta sauce and served with whole-wheat noodles.

2 tsp. olive oil

1 lb. ground turkey breast

½ cup breadcrumbs or cracker crumbs

1 tsp. garlic powder

½ tsp. dried oregano

¼ tsp. dried rosemary

1 egg

¼ cup shredded Parmesan cheese

2 (26-oz.) jars pasta sauce

1 (12-oz.) package whole-wheat spaghetti

Yield: 16 meatballs and 4 cups sauce
Prep time: 15 minutes
Cook time: 30 minutes
Serves: 8
Serving size: 2 meatballs, ½ cup sauce, and 1 cup pasta
Each serving has:
363 calories
12.4 g fat
3.4 g saturated fat
520 mg sodium
37.2 g carbohydrates
2.4 g dietary fiber
24 g protein

1. Preheat oven to 400°F. Line a deep cookie sheet with foil and brush foil lightly with olive oil.

2. In a large bowl, combine turkey, breadcrumbs, egg, garlic, oregano, rosemary, and Parmesan cheese. Mix well. Form mixture into 16 golf ball–size balls. Place meatballs on the prepared cookie sheet. Bake 25 minutes.

3. In a large saucepan, heat pasta sauce.

4. Prepare whole-wheat spaghetti according to package directions. Drain. Serve spaghetti and meatballs, spooning sauce over both. Serve hot.

Tasty Tidbits

You can make these meatballs for sandwiches, appetizers, or a quick snack for family game night. The meatballs freeze well—allow them to cool completely before wrapping and freezing.

Easy Sloppy Joes

Apple juice sweetens this delicious family favorite.

Yield: 6 sandwiches
Prep time: 10 minutes
Cook time: 30 minutes
Serves: 6
Serving size: 1 sandwich
Each serving has:
191 calories
5.2 g fat
1.9 g saturated fat
183 mg sodium
10.4 g carbohydrates
1.2 g dietary fiber
24.7 g protein

1 lb. lean ground beef

1 (6-oz.) can tomato paste

2 tsp. Worcestershire sauce

1 TB. Dijon mustard

¼ cup apple juice

6 whole-wheat buns, split and toasted

1. In a large skillet over medium-high heat, brown beef until no longer pink. Drain well and return to heat.

2. Add tomato paste, Worcestershire sauce, Dijon mustard, and apple juice. Stir well and bring to a boil. Reduce heat and simmer 15 minutes until sauce thickens.

3. Spoon onto toasted buns and serve hot.

Tasty Tidbits

Serve these saucy sandwiches open faced and eat with a fork. That way, they're less messy.

Beef and Potato Casserole

This easy beef casserole is flavored with onions and celery and topped with Cheddar cheese.

1 tsp. olive oil

6 medium new potatoes, cut in quarters

¼ tsp. salt

1 lb. lean ground beef

¼ cup diced onions

½ cup chopped celery

1 cup corn, frozen or canned

1 tsp. ground black pepper

2 TB. water

½ cup shredded Cheddar cheese

Yield: About 8 cups
Prep time: 10 minutes
Cook time: 35 minutes
Serves: 8
Serving size: About 1 cup
Each serving has:
214 calories
6 g fat
2.9 g saturated fat
129 mg sodium
16.2 g carbohydrates
2.1 g dietary fiber
22.8 g protein

1. Preheat oven to 375°F. Lightly oil a 2-quart casserole dish.

2. In a large pot, bring 6 cups salted water to boil. Add potatoes and cook 10 minutes. Drain and set aside.

3. In a large skillet over medium-high heat, brown beef in olive oil 7 minutes until no longer pink. Drain. Add onions, celery, corn, pepper, and water. Cook 8 minutes, stirring often.

4. In the casserole dish, arrange potatoes in a single layer. Pour meat mixture over potatoes, top with cheese, and bake 20 minutes. Serve hot.

Variation: Add sliced mushrooms for a different flavor.

Kitchen Wise _____

You don't need to peel the potatoes. Instead, wash them well before quartering.

Spicy Turkey and Vegetable Burritos

These quick wraps combine turkey, white beans, green chiles, and vegetables flavored with hot sauce.

Yield: 12 burritos
Prep time: 10 minutes
Cook time: 15 minutes
Serves: 12
Serving size: 1 burrito
Each serving has:
551 calories
10.7 g fat
2.1 g saturated fat
277 mg sodium
86.2 g carbohydrates
16.7 g dietary fiber
27.5 g protein

1 lb. ground turkey breast

2 tsp. olive oil

1 (15-oz.) can great northern beans

1 (10-oz.) can diced green chiles

1 carrot, shredded

1 medium tomato, chopped

2 tsp. hot sauce

¼ cup shredded Monterey Jack cheese

3 cups shredded iceberg lettuce

12 whole-wheat tortillas

2 cups cooked rice

1. In a large skillet over medium heat, brown turkey in olive oil for 7 minutes. Add beans and chiles, carrot, and tomato. Cook 8 minutes, stirring often. Stir in hot sauce and cheese. Stir until cheese begins to melt.

2. In each tortilla, spoon ⅙ cup rice, about ½ cup vegetables, ¼ cup shredded lettuce, and top with 1/12 turkey and vegetable mixture. Roll up tortillas. Keep warm before serving.

Variation: Try steamed cauliflower, zucchini, or mushrooms in these burritos. You can also use ground beef instead of turkey.

Tasty Tidbits

You can replace the tomatoes and chiles in this recipe with your favorite Rotel variety. Be sure to cook the filling long enough to keep it from being watery.

Stuffed Turkey Burgers

Tender and moist burgers surround a warm cranberry and
Monterey Jack cheese core.

1 TB. olive oil

1 lb. ground turkey breast

1 egg

1 tsp. dried thyme

¼ tsp. ground black pepper

¼ cup dried cranberries

½ cup shredded Monterey
Jack cheese

6 whole-wheat buns, split and
toasted

Yield: 6 burgers
Prep time: 10 minutes
Cook time: 25 minutes
Serves: 6
Serving size: 1 burger
Each serving has:
272 calories
16.4 g fat
5.2 g saturated fat
211 mg sodium
5.3 g carbohydrates
2.9 g dietary fiber
24.7 g protein

1. Preheat oven to 400°F. Lightly oil a 9×13-inch baking dish.

2. In a large bowl, combine turkey, egg, thyme, and pepper. Mix
   well.

3. In a small bowl, combine cranberries and cheese. Form 6
   patties of the turkey mixture. Create a hollow in each patty
   and fill with cheese mixture. Fold edges of patty over cheese
   mixture to create a tight seal. Place patties in the prepared
   baking dish. Bake 15 minutes. Turn burgers over. Bake
   additional 10 minutes. Serve hot on toasted buns.

Variation: Stuff these burgers with any cheese you like. Try cream
cheese with dill or Swiss with a little sage. You can also dice an
apple and make it part of the stuffing.

Tasty Tidbits _____

Serve these juicy burgers with potato salad or sweet potato
fries.

Creamy Beef Stroganoff

Sour cream and mushrooms are blended with beef and flavored with onions and paprika, then served on wide egg noodles.

Yield: About 3½ cups
Prep time: 10 minutes
Cook time: 30 minutes
Serves: 8
Serving size: About ½ cup plus 1½ oz. noodles
Each serving has:
240 calories
10.7 g fat
5.3 g saturated fat
77 mg sodium
14.6 g carbohydrates
1.1 g dietary fiber
20.8 g protein

1 (12-oz.) package wide egg noodles

¼ cup diced onions

1 cup sliced mushrooms

2 tsp. olive oil

1 lb. lean ground beef

2 TB. flour

¼ tsp. ground black pepper

¼ cup water

1 TB. Dijon mustard

1 cup sour cream

1. Prepare egg noodles according to package directions. Drain well and set aside.

2. In a large skillet over medium heat, sauté onions and mushrooms in olive oil 8 minutes. Remove to a side bowl. In the same skillet, brown beef until no longer pink. Drain well and return to heat.

3. Return onions and mushrooms to the skillet. Add flour and pepper. Stir well to coat meat, onions, and mushrooms. Add water and mustard. Cook 10 minutes, stirring often.

4. Reduce heat and stir in sour cream. Heat gently for 3 minutes. Serve hot over noodles.

Variation: Use sirloin beef chunks in place of ground beef.

 Don't Get Burned _____

Stir in the sour cream slowly and heat on low, stirring constantly. Don't let the sauce sit too long on the bottom of the skillet or it will scald.

Turkey Goulash

Smoky paprika and nutty caraway compliment mild sour cream in our take on the Hungarian classic.

1 (12-oz.) package whole-wheat macaroni

1 lb. ground turkey breast

1 TB. olive oil

¼ cup sliced onions

2 tsp. caraway seeds

1 TB. paprika

1 cup sour cream

Yield: About 6½ cups	
Prep time: 10 minutes	
Cook time: 20 minutes	
Serves: 6	
Serving size: About 1 cup	
Each serving has:	
373 calories	
16 g fat	
6 g saturated fat	
79 mg sodium	
34.1 g carbohydrates	
1.9 g dietary fiber	
22.2 g protein	

1. Prepare macaroni according to package directions. Drain well and set aside.

2. In a large skillet over medium heat, brown turkey in olive oil for 5 minutes. Add onion, caraway seeds, and paprika. Cook 8 minutes, stirring often. Reduce heat and add sour cream, stirring while heating an additional 3 minutes.

3. In a large serving bowl, combine pasta and sauce. Toss gently and serve hot.

Tasty Tidbits _____

Paprika, the signature flavor of this dish, is made from grinding dried bell peppers. Enjoy its light flavor and bright color.

Chapter 19

Vegetarian Main Dishes

In This Chapter

- ◆ Meatless meals offering high-quality nutrition
- ◆ Saving money with hearty ingredients
- ◆ Spicing up grains, beans, and veggies

Many people think eating vegetarian food means eating strange and unpleasant foods. Not here! The recipes in this chapter offer familiar ingredients and favorite flavors.

Meatless main dishes are economical. Enjoy lasagna, pizza, macaroni and cheese, and more. Keep vegetarian meals interesting by using different varieties of legumes, vegetables, and seasonings.

If you let children choose some of the vegetables they eat, you may find it easier to get them to help with making dinner. This can also serve as an opportunity to get your family involved in the work of living and eating on a budget.

Baked Macaroni with Two Cheeses

This cozy comfort food blends the tastes of Cheddar and Swiss cheeses with peas or corn and bell pepper.

Yield: About 8 cups
Prep time: 15 minutes
Cook time: 20 minutes
Serves: 8
Serving size: About 1 cup
Each serving has:
304 calories
8.2 g fat
4.6 g saturated fat
132 mg sodium
42.9 g carbohydrates
2.8 g dietary fiber
13.9 g protein

1 (13¼-oz.) package whole-grain macaroni

1 cup low-fat milk

2 TB. flour

¼ tsp. crushed red pepper flakes

¾ cup shredded Cheddar cheese

¾ cup shredded Swiss cheese

1 tsp. olive oil

1 cup frozen peas or corn, thawed

¼ cup diced red or green bell pepper

¼ cup crushed chips or crackers

1. Prepare pasta al dente according to package directions. Drain and set aside. Preheat oven to 350°F.

2. In a large saucepan over medium heat, combine milk, flour, and red pepper. Add shredded cheese ¹/₂ cup at a time and stir occasionally until cheese melts before adding next ¹/₂ cup. When all the cheese has melted, reduce heat to low.

3. In a lightly oiled 2-quart casserole dish, combine pasta, peas or corn, and bell pepper. Pour the cheese sauce over the pasta and vegetables. Spread crushed chips or crackers over the top.

4. Bake 20 minutes. Allow to cool slightly before serving.

Variation: Substitute other types of pasta for the macaroni. Try bowtie, fusilli, or broken lasagna noodles.

 Kitchen Wise _____

By eating just one vegetarian meal every week, a family of four can save from $150 to $250 dollars every year.

Nutty Brown Rice Burgers

Apples, black beans, and pecans sweeten these rice patties, while salsa keeps them tender and adds a spicy tang.

1 cup cooked brown rice	¼ cup shredded carrots
1 cup diced apple	⅓ cup salsa
1 (15-oz.) can black beans, drained and rinsed	1 TB. olive oil
½ cup chopped pecans	8 sourdough rolls

Yield: 8 burgers
Prep time: 10 minutes
Cook time: 5 minutes
Serves: 8
Serving size: 1 burger
Each serving has:
445 calories
8.2 g fat
1.2 g saturated fat
277 mg sodium
76.3 g carbohydrates
11 g dietary fiber
18.2 g protein

1. In a large bowl, combine rice, apple, black beans, pecans, carrots, and salsa. Mix well, crushing black beans, until ingredients begin to stick together.

2. In a large skillet over medium heat, warm olive oil. When oil is hot, spoon about ¾ cup rice mixture into skillet. Use the back of a spoon to flatten into a patty shape. Cook 5 minutes, turning once. Keep warm in the oven if you need to prepare them in batches. Serve hot on crusty sourdough rolls.

Variation: If you prefer cheese on your "burgers," Cheddar and Swiss taste great with these flavors.

Don't Get Burned

These patties will cook fast, much faster than meat. Don't turn away to do some laundry or answer the phone.

Vegetable and Tofu Stir-Fry

Soy sauce and lemon juice flavor the rainbow assortment of
vegetables in this quick stir-fry.

Yield: About 4 cups stir-fry, 3 cups rice

Prep time: 20 minutes

Cook time: 15 minutes

Serves: 6

Serving size: About ³/₄ cup stir-fry and ¹/₂ cup rice

Each serving has:

436 calories

9.2 g fat

1.6 g saturated fat

323 mg sodium

77.3 g carbohydrates

4.7 g dietary fiber

12.1 g protein

---

2 TB. soy sauce

2 TB. lemon juice

¼ tsp. crushed red pepper flakes

1 (10-oz.) package firm tofu, drained and cut in small cubes

2 TB. olive oil

1 tsp. minced garlic

¼ cup diced onions

½ cup thin strips red bell pepper

1 zucchini, cut into ½-inch sticks

½ cup sliced carrots

1 cup broccoli florets

3 cups cooked brown rice

1. In a medium bowl, combine soy sauce, lemon juice, and red pepper. Whisk briskly. Add tofu cubes, cover, and marinate 20 minutes.

2. Heat oil in a wok or in a large skillet over medium-high heat. When oil is hot, add garlic and onions. Cook 3 minutes, stirring often. Add bell pepper, zucchini, carrots, and broccoli. Cook 7 minutes, stirring often. Add tofu and marinade. Cook 3 minutes, stirring gently.

3. Serve hot over cooked rice.

Variation: Use bamboo shoots and chopped water chestnuts for authentic Asian flavor.

 Tasty Tidbits

Here's another option: cut tofu into 1-inch cubes. Marinate the tofu cubes as in this recipe but don't cook them. Instead, roll them in toasted sesame seeds to make a quick and flavorful vegetarian appetizer. Serve with toothpicks.

Nutty Fruity Lentil Loaf

Sharp Cheddar cheese blends lentils with crisp apples, tart cranberries, and buttery walnuts and pecans.

2 TB. olive oil

¼ cup chopped celery

½ cup chopped carrot

1½ cups cooked lentils

1 small apple, diced

¼ cup dried cranberries

½ cup chopped walnuts

½ cup chopped pecans

1 tsp. ground cumin

½ cup shredded Cheddar cheese

Yield: 1 loaf
Prep time: 15 minutes
Cook time: 25 minutes
Serves: 6
Serving size: 1 slice
Each serving has:
391 calories
20.9 g fat
3.6 g saturated fat
73 mg sodium
35.3 g carbohydrates
17.2 g dietary fiber
18.3 g protein

1. Preheat oven to 375°F. In a large skillet over medium heat, combine olive oil, celery, and carrots. Cook 5 minutes. Add lentils, apple, and cranberries. Cook 10 minutes. Add walnuts, pecans, cumin, and cheese. Stir well until cheese begins to melt.

2. Remove from heat. Spoon mixture into a lightly oiled glass 9×5×3-inch loaf pan. Bake 25 minutes. Cool 10 minutes before removing from pan to serve.

Variation: Try different combinations of fruits and nuts in this loaf. Dried apricots, pineapple, cherries, or raisins all work well. Nuts like almonds and peanuts (or even sunflower or pumpkin seeds) work, too.

Kitchen Wise

Watch for bulk nuts to go on sale and then plan several meals and desserts featuring those nuts. Nuts can be stored in the refrigerator for months and will retain their freshness.

Pick-Your-Own Pita Pizzas

Warm and crisp individual pizzas are topped with marinara sauce, mushrooms, and mozzarella for an authentic Italian flavor.

Yield: 8 pita pizzas
Prep time: 10 minutes
Cook time: 7 minutes
Serves: 6
Serving size: 1½ pizzas
Each serving has:
316 calories
5.9 g fat
2.8 g saturated fat
700 mg sodium
51.4 g carbohydrates
3 g dietary fiber
13.3 g protein

8 whole-grain pitas

1 cup marinara sauce

1 cup sliced mushrooms

1 cup shredded mozzarella cheese

1. Set the broiler to low. Arrange pitas on a foil-covered cookie sheet.

2. Top each pita with 2 tablespoons of marinara sauce, 2 tablespoons sliced mushrooms, and 2 tablespoons mozzarella cheese.

3. Cook under the broiler until cheese is bubbly, about 7 minutes. Cut each pita in quarters. Serve immediately.

Variation: Fruit and vegetables give pizza interesting tastes. Try apples and pineapple with marinara sauce, raisins and asparagus with hummus, and mango and carrots with salsa. Choose a cheese that compliments your choices.

 Tasty Tidbits

Get your kids involved in the kitchen. Engage them in food preparation so that they learn how to prepare a healthy meal every day. Staying on budget and eating well are easy when everyone in the family does his or her share.

Vegetarian Barbecue Bake

Sweet potatoes, tomatoes, and carrots lend flavor to garbanzo
beans in a mustard sauce.

1 tsp. olive oil	½ cup diced red or green bell pepper
1 (15-oz.) can garbanzo beans, drained and rinsed	⅛ cup honey
1 small sweet potato, diced	2 tsp. Dijon mustard
1 medium tomato, chopped	1 TB. cider vinegar
¼ cup diced onion	2 TB. ketchup
1 carrot, sliced	

Yield: About 5½ cups
Prep time: 10 minutes
Cook time: 30 minutes
Serves: 5
Serving size: About 1 cup
Each serving has:
338 calories
5.3 g fat
0.6 g saturated fat
124 mg sodium
57.9 g carbohydrates
15.9 g dietary fiber
17.1 g protein

1. Preheat oven to 350°F.

2. In a lightly oiled 2-quart casserole dish, combine beans, sweet
   potatoes, tomatoes, onions, carrots, bell pepper, honey, Dijon
   mustard, cider vinegar, and ketchup. Stir well.

3. Bake 30 minutes. Serve immediately or cool completely before
   freezing.

Tasty Tidbits _____

Use seasonally abundant produce to stretch your budget.
Serve this delicious casserole with Hot Caraway Cabbage
(see recipe in Chapter 20) in the autumn and winter and with
Crunchy Coleslaw (see recipe in Chapter 14) in the spring and
summer.

Barley-Stuffed Peppers

Nutty barley adds earthy flavor to this favorite vegetable dish.

Yield: 6 peppers
Prep time: 20 minutes
Cook time: 25 minutes
Serves: 6
Serving size: 1 pepper
Each serving has:
285 calories
8.1 g fat
1.4 g saturated fat
361 mg sodium
46.9 g carbohydrates
11.8 g dietary fiber
7.4 g protein

3 cups water

6 large green bell peppers

2 TB. olive oil

¼ cup diced onions

1 cup barley, soaked overnight, drained, and rinsed

1 carrot, shredded

2 medium tomatoes, chopped

2 cups favorite marinara sauce (or sauce from Spaghetti with Meatballs recipe)

1. Preheat oven to 350°F.

2. In a large saucepan, bring water to a boil. Cut off bell pepper tops, remove seeds and ribs, and immerse in boiling water. Boil 5 minutes until bell peppers are bright and just starting to soften. Remove from water, drain well, and set aside.

3. Heat olive oil in a large skillet over medium heat. Add onion, barley, carrots, and tomatoes and stir well. Cook 5 minutes. Remove from heat.

4. Arrange bell peppers in a lightly oiled 2-quart baking dish. Spoon barley mixture into bell peppers. Top each bell pepper with marinara sauce and spoon sauce around the base of each bell pepper. Bake 25 minutes. Serve immediately.

Variation: Add ½ cup shredded Parmesan or Swiss cheese to the barley mixture.

 Kitchen Wise _____

Save yourself time with stuffed vegetables. Make this a midweek meal and use vegetable or grain leftovers from prior meals to stuff the vegetables.

Zucchini Lasagna

You'll enjoy classic Italian flavor in this vegetarian version of lasagna.

½ (1-lb.) box dried lasagna noodles

2 cups low-fat cottage cheese

¼ tsp. minced garlic

1 green or red bell pepper, diced

¼ cup chopped mushrooms

1 tsp. dried oregano

1 tsp. dried rosemary

¼ tsp. ground black pepper

1 tsp. olive oil

2 large zucchini, sliced lengthwise

2 cups favorite marinara sauce

½ cup shredded mozzarella cheese

Yield: 1 9×9-inch dish
Prep time: 20 minutes
Cook time: 25 minutes
Serves: 9
Serving size: 1 slice, 3×3 inches
Each serving has:
201 calories
4.4 g fat
1.8 g saturated fat
473 mg sodium
27.1 g carbohydrates
2.7 g dietary fiber
13.6 g protein

1. Preheat oven to 350°F. Prepare lasagna noodles al dente according to package directions. Drain and set aside.

2. In a large bowl, combine cottage cheese, garlic, bell pepper, mushrooms, oregano, rosemary, and pepper. Mix gently.

3. In a lightly oiled 9×9-inch baking pan, arrange a layer of lasagna noodles on the bottom. Top noodles with sliced zucchini, then gently spread on a layer of cottage cheese mixture. Top cheese mixture with another layer of noodles, then about ½ cup marinara sauce, then zucchini. Gently spread on remaining cheese mixture and top with zucchini slices. Pour remaining marinara sauce over zucchini. Sprinkle with mozzarella cheese.

4. Bake 25 minutes. Let stand for 5 to 10 minutes before serving. Allow to cool completely before freezing.

Variation: If you have fresh herbs on your windowsill, add fresh-snipped basil to the cheese mixture.

 Don't Get Burned

Check the label of your favorite marinara sauce. Is it full of the healthy ingredients you want to feed your family? If not, choose another.

Mushroom Ragout on Spaghetti Squash

Earthy mushrooms in a creamy herb sauce bring out the sweetness of roasted spaghetti squash.

1 medium spaghetti squash	⅛ **tsp. nutmeg**
½ **cup water**	½ **tsp. dried parsley**
3 TB. olive oil	¼ **tsp. salt**
¼ **cup sliced green onions**	**1 cup heavy cream**
2 cups sliced mushrooms	

Yield: About 6 cups

Prep time: 20 minutes

Cook time: 25 minutes

Serves: 6

Serving size: About 1 cup

Each serving has:

164 calories

14.3 g fat

5.6 g saturated fat

109 mg sodium

9.1 g carbohydrates

1.4 g dietary fiber

1.8 g protein

---

1. Preheat oven to 350°F. Split squash in half, remove seeds, and put squash in a microwave-safe dish with water. Microwave on high for 10 minutes. Remove and allow to cool slightly. Use a fork to scrape the cooked flesh into a large bowl. Toss gently with 1 tablespoon olive oil and set aside.

2. In a large skillet, heat 2 tablespoons olive oil over medium heat. When hot, add green onions and mushrooms. Cook 7 minutes, stirring often. Add nutmeg and parsley. Cook 5 minutes.

3. Add cream, stir well, and cook 10 minutes.

4. Arrange spaghetti squash on individual plates and top with mushroom ragout. Serve immediately.

Variation: Serve mushroom ragout over egg noodles or pan-fried polenta.

Kitchen Wise

Spaghetti squash can be baked or boiled as well as microwaved. Use the method easiest for your schedule, supplies, and kitchen.

Five Bean, Tofu, and Vegetable Bake

Savory thyme, garlic, and coriander flavor this hearty vegetable and bean casserole.

1 (15-oz.) can black beans, drained and rinsed

1 (15-oz.) can red kidney beans, drained and rinsed

1 (15-oz.) can cannellini beans, drained and rinsed

1 cup frozen green beans

1 cup water

2 medium tomatoes, chopped

2 carrots, sliced

1 (10-oz.) package firm tofu, drained and diced

½ tsp. dried thyme

¼ tsp. minced garlic

½ tsp. ground coriander

Yield: About 10 cups
Prep time: 10 minutes
Cook time: 25 minutes
Serves: 10
Serving size: About 1 cup
Each serving has:
461 calories
2.7 g fat
0.5 g saturated fat
31 mg sodium
81.1 g carbohydrates
24.7 g dietary fiber
31.5 g protein

1. Preheat oven to 375°F.

2. In a 2-quart casserole dish, combine black beans, kidney beans, cannellini beans, green beans, water, tomatoes, carrots, tofu, thyme, garlic, and coriander. Stir gently to combine well.

3. Bake 25 minutes. Serve hot.

Variation: Almost any combination of beans works well. Try garbanzo, pinto, great northern, or butter beans.

Tasty Tidbits _____

Coriander adds delectable flavor to this dish. If you, or your family, are unfamiliar with this aromatic seed, use a little less than the recipe recommends. Next time you make it, use the full amount.

Chapter 20

Vegetable Side Dishes

In This Chapter

- ◆ Preparing succulent and enticing vegetables
- ◆ Using in-season, on-sale, or frozen vegetables
- ◆ Adding healthful vegetables to your meals

Eating five to seven daily servings of vegetables and fruit will be easy when you cook with these recipes. They offer you many choices and combinations of tastes and textures.

Some recipes use simple sauces to enhance the natural sweetness of vegetables like corn, carrots, green beans, peas, and bell peppers. Roasting root vegetables, like carrots and beets, brings out their soft, savory-sweet goodness. Stir-fry, or quick skillet cooking, is perfect for broccoli, snap peas, and bell peppers.

Mix and match the flavors of these vegetable recipes with the flavors of your main courses to create fresh-tasting meals.

Fruit-Glazed Carrots

Sweet and tangy jam sauce jazzes up roasted carrots.

Yield: About 4 cups
Prep time: 5 minutes
Cook time: 25 minutes
Serves: 4
Serving size: About 1 cup
Each serving has:
103 calories
3.6 g fat
0.5 g saturated fat
79 mg sodium
17.4 g carbohydrates
3.2 g dietary fiber
1.1 g protein

4 cups sliced carrots

2 TB. water

2 TB. fruit jam or jelly— peach, strawberry, or apricot

½ tsp. red wine vinegar

1 TB. olive oil

Dash salt and ground black pepper

1. Preheat oven to 350°F. Place carrots in a microwave-safe bowl with water. Cover and microwave on high for 8 minutes. Drain well. Add jam, vinegar, and olive oil. Mix gently.

2. Transfer carrots to a lightly oiled 8×8×2-inch or 9×9×2-inch baking dish. Season with salt and pepper. Bake 15 minutes. Serve hot or chill 20 minutes before serving.

Variation: Try orange marmalade or chutney to intensify the flavor of the carrots. For a spicy taste, substitute ½ teaspoon hot sauce for the vinegar.

 Kitchen Wise

The sauce for these carrots tastes great on other vegetables as well, such as broccoli, snap peas, and spinach. You can also serve the sauce on the side for dipping.

Black Bean and Sweet Potato Bake

Tangy lemon pepper enhances the natural flavors of sweet potatoes and black beans.

2 TB. olive oil	**1 tsp. honey**
2 TB. water	**2 tsp. lemon pepper**
4 cups diced sweet potatoes	**½ tsp. salt**
1 TB. lemon juice	**1 (15-oz.) can black beans, drained and rinsed**

Yield: About 5½ cups
Prep time: 10 minutes
Cook time: 45 minutes
Serves: 8
Serving size: About ⅔ cup
Each serving has:
304 calories
4.3 g fat
0.7 g saturated fat
155 mg sodium
55.1 g carbohydrates
11.3 g dietary fiber
12.7 g protein

1. Preheat oven to 350°F. Lightly oil a 9×13-inch baking dish.

2. Place sweet potatoes in a large microwave-safe bowl with water. Cover and microwave on high for 8 minutes.

3. In a large bowl, combine remaining olive oil, lemon juice, honey, lemon pepper, and salt. Whisk briskly. Add beans and stir well. Gently stir in sweet potatoes and bean mixture.

4. Place mixture in the prepared baking dish. Bake 35 minutes. Serve hot.

Tasty Tidbits _____

This recipe offers enough protein that you can serve this as a substantial vegetarian entrée.

Herbed Roasted Roots

This is a medley of earthy vegetables, tangy vinegar, and aromatic rosemary.

Yield: About 4 cups
Prep time: 10 minutes
Cook time: 45 minutes
Serves: 6
Serving size: About ⅔ cup
Each serving has:
137 calories
4.7 g fat
0.7 g saturated fat
95 mg sodium
22.2 g carbohydrates
3.9 g dietary fiber
2.5 g protein

2 TB. olive oil

2 carrots, thickly sliced

3 potatoes, scrubbed and cut in large chunks

2 beets, peeled and cut in large chunks

1 TB. cider vinegar

⅛ tsp. salt

1 tsp. dried rosemary

1. Preheat oven to 400°F. Lightly oil a 9×13-inch baking dish.

2. In a large bowl, combine carrots, potatoes, beets, remaining olive oil, cider vinegar, salt, and rosemary. Stir until well coated. Transfer to the baking dish.

3. Bake uncovered for 45 minutes. Serve hot or cool completely before serving.

Variation: Try turnips and parsnips in this dish or any combination of your favorite root vegetables.

 Tasty Tidbits

Roasting brings out the natural sweetness of these vegetables. Enjoy this dish in a variety of ways. Serve it as a side dish for dinner, add scrambled eggs for a delicious brunch, or serve cold over fresh spinach for a lunch salad.

Rosemary Spaghetti Squash

Aromatic rosemary flavors nutty sweet squash "noodles."

2 medium spaghetti squash

2 TB. olive oil

½ tsp. ground black pepper

1 tsp. dried rosemary

1. Preheat oven to 350°F.

2. Cut off stem end of each squash and split in two lengthwise. Clean out seeds and place each half on a cookie sheet. Bake 90 minutes. Remove from oven and cool slightly.

3. Use a fork to scrape the flesh of the squash into long, noodle-like strands. Place squash noodles into a baking dish. Toss with olive oil, pepper, and rosemary. Bake uncovered 15 minutes. Serve hot.

Tasty Tidbits

If you have fresh rosemary, use 1 tablespoon of fresh herb instead of 1 teaspoon dried herb.

Yield: About 6 cups
Prep time: 5 minutes
Cook time: About 2½ hours
Serves: 6
Serving size: About 1 cup
Each serving has:
98 calories
4.7 g fat
0.7 g saturated fat
5 mg sodium
15.1 g carbohydrates
2.2 g dietary fiber
1.2 g protein

Slow-Cooked Onions with Apples and Sour Cream

Something almost magical happens to onions that simmer for hours. Their flavor mellows and sweetens.

Yield: About 4 cups
Prep time: 10 minutes
Cook time: 8 hours
Serves: 8
Serving size: About $\frac{1}{2}$ cup
Each serving has:
108 calories
6.5 g fat
2.4 g saturated fat
83 mg sodium
12.4 g carbohydrates
1.8 g dietary fiber
1.2 g protein

2 TB. olive oil

4 medium sweet onions, peeled and cut in quarters

1 tsp. dried thyme

$\frac{1}{4}$ tsp. salt

$\frac{1}{4}$ tsp. ground black pepper

$\frac{1}{2}$ cup apple juice

2 apples, sliced

$\frac{1}{2}$ cup sour cream

1. In a large skillet over medium heat, combine olive oil and onions. Cook 7 minutes until onions begin to brown, stirring often. Add thyme, salt, and pepper. Cook 3 more minutes.

2. Transfer onions to slow cooker. Add apple juice. Stir and cover. Cook on low for 8 hours or more until onions are translucent and tender. Serve with sliced apples and sour cream.

Variation: Add $\frac{1}{4}$ cup grated Swiss cheese about 15 minutes before serving.

Kitchen Wise

You can make this dish without a slow cooker. Place the ingredients in a covered casserole dish in the oven at 250°F for 3 to 4 hours.

Tart and Nutty Green Beans

Sweet, tart cranberries and buttery walnuts dress up crunchy green beans.

2 TB. water

4 cups fresh or frozen green beans

1 TB. butter

1 cup raw cranberries

1 TB. balsamic vinegar

½ cup chopped walnuts

Pinch salt

Yield: About 5½ cups
Prep time: 5 minutes
Cook time: 20 minutes
Serves: 6
Serving size: About 1 cup
Each serving has:
112 calories
8.2 g fat
1.6 g saturated fat
45 mg sodium
8.2 g carbohydrates
3.9 g dietary fiber
3.9 g protein

1. Place green beans in a microwave-safe bowl with water. Cover and microwave on high for 5 minutes. Drain well and set aside.

2. In a large skillet over medium heat, combine butter, cranberries, and balsamic vinegar. Stir well and cook 5 minutes until cranberries soften. Add walnuts and cook 5 minutes, stirring often.

3. Add green beans and salt to taste. Stir well to coat. Cook 5 more minutes. Serve hot or cold.

Variation: Cashews, peanuts, and almonds taste great in this sauce. You can also use broccoli instead of green beans.

Don't Get Burned

Be careful not to overcook the green beans. They should stay crisp and bright green.

Basil Broccoli with Cashews

Aromatic basil pairs with cashews as a sauce for broccoli.

Yield: About 4½ cups
Prep time: 10 minutes
Cook time: 15 minutes
Serves: 4
Serving size: About 1 cup
Each serving has:
190 calories
15 g fat
2.5 g saturated fat
36 mg sodium
11.6 g carbohydrates
2.8 g dietary fiber
5.2 g protein

4 cups broccoli florets

2 cups cold water

2 TB. cider vinegar

2 TB. olive oil

¼ cup fresh basil leaves, washed and roughly torn

½ cup chopped cashews

1. Soak broccoli florets in cold water and cider vinegar for 10 minutes. Drain and place in a medium microwave-safe bowl. Add 2 tablespoons water. Cover and microwave on high for 5 minutes.

2. In a large skillet over medium heat, combine olive oil and basil. Cook 5 minutes until basil wilts. Add cashews and cook 3 minutes. Add broccoli and cook 5 more minutes, stirring. Serve hot.

Tasty Tidbits

If you can't find fresh basil, use 1 tablespoon dried basil for a comparable taste.

Broccoli with Oranges and Rhubarb

Mandarin oranges and steamed broccoli are glazed with a sweet and sour sauce.

1 cup chopped rhubarb	**1 TB. cider vinegar**
1 cup plus 2 TB. water	**4 cups broccoli florets**
2 TB. honey	**1 (10-oz.) can Mandarin oranges, drained**

Yield: About 6 cups
Prep time: 10 minutes
Cook time: 25 minutes
Serves: 6
Serving size: About 1 cup
Each serving has:
63 calories
0.3 g fat
0 g saturated fat
24 mg sodium
15.1 g carbohydrates
2.2 g dietary fiber
2.2 g protein

1. In a medium saucepan, combine rhubarb, 1 cup water, honey, and cider vinegar. Bring mixture to a boil, then reduce heat and simmer for 15 minutes.

2. Place broccoli florets in medium microwave-safe bowl. Add 2 tablespoons water. Cover and microwave on high for 8 minutes. Drain well.

3. Add broccoli and oranges to the saucepan and stir lightly to coat with sauce. Serve hot.

Tasty Tidbits

This delicious, tangy sauce tastes great with carrots, zucchini, bell peppers, sweet potatoes, or onions.

Southwestern Succotash

Sweet corn and black beans are flavored with mild chiles and tomatoes.

Yield: About 5½ cups
Prep time: 5 minutes
Cook time: 20 minutes
Serves: 10
Serving size: About ½ cup
Each serving has:
268 calories
2.7 g fat
0 g saturated fat
34 mg sodium
53.1 g carbohydrates
15.7 g dietary fiber
13.4 g protein

1 tsp. olive oil

2 cups corn, drained

1 (15-oz.) can black beans, drained and rinsed

2 medium tomatoes, chopped

¼ cup diced green bell pepper

1 (10-oz.) can diced green chiles

1 TB. fresh chopped cilantro or 1 tsp. dried

1. Preheat oven to 375°F. In a lightly oiled 9×13-inch baking dish, combine corn, black beans, tomatoes, bell pepper, and chiles. Stir gently to mix.

2. Bake 20 minutes. Serve hot with cilantro garnish.

 Tasty Tidbits

Succotash usually contains lima beans, though the bean in this dish varies across the country. Use your favorite beans, such as green beans, pintos, or kidneys, in this recipe.

Spinach and Carrot Kugel

Apple juice flavors this colorful noodle dish.

2 tsp. olive oil

1 (12-oz.) package whole-wheat noodles

3 eggs

½ cup apple juice

2 carrots, shredded

¼ cup diced red bell pepper

¼ tsp. ground black pepper

2 cups frozen chopped spinach, thawed

Yield: About 8 cups	
Prep time: 10 minutes	
Cook time: 45 minutes	
Serves: 8	
Serving size: About 1 cup	
Each serving has:	
104 calories	
3.2 g fat	
0.8 g saturated fat	
42 mg sodium	
14.6 g carbohydrates	
1.2 g dietary fiber	
4.4 g protein	

1. Preheat oven to 375°F. Lightly oil a 9×13-inch baking dish. Prepare noodles al dente according to package directions. Drain well and set aside.

2. In a large bowl, combine eggs, apple juice, and remaining olive oil. Whisk briskly. Stir in shredded carrots, bell pepper, and pepper.

3. Place noodles in the bottom of the baking dish. Top with spinach. Pour egg-vegetable mixture over noodles and spinach. Stir gently. Bake 45 minutes. Cool slightly before serving.

Variation: Top the kugel with your favorite cheese about 15 minutes before the end of the baking time. Swiss cheese is especially good with this vegetable mix.

 Tasty Tidbits

Try different combinations of vegetables or add a diced apple for more intense flavor.

Cheesy Vegetable Polenta

Cornmeal and Cheddar cheese flavor colorful, fresh vegetables.

Yield: About 5 cups
Prep time: 10 minutes
Cook time: 20 minutes
Serves: 10
Serving size: About ½ cup
Each serving has:
114 calories
3.2 g fat
1.8 g saturated fat
293 mg sodium
12.6 g carbohydrates
1.4 g dietary fiber
8.8 g protein

4 cups water

¼ tsp. salt

1 cup coarse cornmeal (white or yellow)

½ cup shredded Cheddar cheese

1 medium tomato, diced

¼ cup diced celery

2 carrots, shredded

2 cups low-fat cottage cheese

1. In a large saucepan, bring water and salt to a boil. Add cornmeal and reduce heat to medium. Stir constantly for 15 minutes until mixture thickens to a doughlike consistency.

2. Add cheese, tomato, celery, and carrots. Stir well. Continue cooking 5 minutes. Serve hot, topped with cottage cheese.

Variation: For a southwestern flavor, substitute Monterey Jack cheese for the Cheddar and add one 10-ounce can of diced green chiles.

 Don't Get Burned

The secret to cooking polenta is to keep stirring the whole time it's cooking. Don't get too distracted or you could have a mess.

Baked Zucchini with Mozzarella

Mild mozzarella, savory garlic, and oregano complement the delicate flavor of zucchini.

1 tsp. olive oil

4 medium zucchini

½ cup shredded mozzarella cheese

2 tsp. minced garlic

½ tsp. dried oregano

Yield: 8 zucchini halves
Prep time: 10 minutes
Cook time: 20 minutes
Serves: 8
Serving size: 1 zucchini half
Each serving has:
49 calories
2.3 g fat
1.4 g saturated fat
66 mg sodium
4 g carbohydrates
1.1 g dietary fiber
4 g protein

1. Preheat oven to 350°F. Line a cookie sheet with aluminum foil and lightly brush with olive oil.

2. Wash and dry zucchini, and remove stem. Slice each zucchini in half lengthwise. Use a small spoon to carve a shallow groove into each half. Place halves on the cookie sheet.

3. In a medium bowl, combine cheese, garlic, and oregano. Pack cheese mixture into grooves in zucchini. Bake 20 minutes. Serve hot.

Variation: Try Parmesan, Cheddar, or Swiss cheese for variety.

 Don't Get Burned

You may need to trim the bottoms of each zucchini half so that they will remain upright and not spill when baking.

Hot Caraway Cabbage

Caraway seeds flavor hot shredded cabbage.

Yield: About 4 cups
Prep time: 5 minutes
Cook time: 15 minutes
Serves: 6
Serving size: About ⅔ cup
Each serving has:
56 calories
4.7 g fat
0.6 g saturated fat
35 mg sodium
3.3 g carbohydrates
1.6 g dietary fiber
0.8 g protein

2 TB. olive oil

4 cups shredded green or red cabbage

1 TB. caraway seeds

1 TB. red wine vinegar

Pinch salt

1. Heat olive oil in a large skillet over medium heat. Add cabbage. Cook 10 minutes, stirring often, until cabbage wilts.

2. Add caraway seeds, vinegar, and salt. Stir well and cook an additional 5 minutes. Serve hot or chill 1 hour before serving.

 Tasty Tidbits _____

Caraway has a mild, slightly nutty flavor. Allowing the seeds to heat through releases their wonderful fragrance and flavor. You can toast the seeds for an even deeper, more complex flavor.

Red Cabbage and Zucchini Skillet

Red wine vinegar and honey intensify the flavor of the cabbage and zucchini in this warm dish.

2 TB. olive oil	**¼ tsp. salt**
2 cups shredded red cabbage	**½ tsp. ground black pepper**
2 cups sliced zucchini	**2 TB. red wine vinegar**
1 TB. honey	

1. In a large skillet over medium heat, warm olive oil. Add cabbage and cook until cabbage wilts, stirring often, about 7 minutes. Add zucchini, honey, salt, and pepper. Stir gently. Cook 8 minutes.

2. Add vinegar and stir gently to coat. Serve hot.

Yield: About 4 cups
Prep time: 5 minutes
Cook time: 15 minutes
Serves: 6
Serving size: About ⅔ cup
Each serving has:
74 calories
4.6 g fat
0.6 g saturated fat
105 mg sodium
8.4 g carbohydrates
1 g dietary fiber
0.8 g protein

Mashed Cauliflower with Cheese

Cauliflower is mashed and flavored with a rich Cheddar cheese sauce.

Yield: About 4 cups
Prep time: 10 minutes
Cook time: 25 minutes
Serves: 6
Serving size: ⅔ cup
Each serving has:
153 calories
10.9 g fat
6.8 g saturated fat
205 mg sodium
7.3 g carbohydrates
1.8 g dietary fiber
7.4 g protein

4 cups chopped cauliflower

2 TB. water

2 TB. butter

2 TB. flour

1 TB. Dijon mustard

¾ cup low-fat milk

1 cup shredded Cheddar cheese

1. Place cauliflower and water in a microwave-safe bowl. Cover and microwave on high for 8 minutes. Drain well. Gently mash cauliflower with the back of a spoon, leaving slightly lumpy.

2. In a medium saucepan, melt butter over medium heat. Reduce heat to low and then add flour and mustard. Whisk until smooth. Add milk slowly. Stir often for 10 minutes while sauce thickens.

3. Add cheese and cook 5 additional minutes, stirring often, until sauce is thick and smooth. Pour cheese sauce over smashed cauliflower. Serve hot.

Variation: This cheese sauce makes a wonderful topping for steamed broccoli or asparagus.

 Tasty Tidbits

Mashed cauliflower is a great substitute for mashed potatoes. If you prefer to eat fewer high-glycemic carbohydrates, use mashed cauliflower in place of mashed potatoes. They taste great with gravy, butter, or garlic.

Chapter 21

Grains and Side Dishes

In This Chapter

- ◆ Preparing energy-giving, nutritious carbohydrates
- ◆ Easy-on-the-budget side dishes
- ◆ Family-favorite selections

Use these dishes to complement the flavors and textures of your main course. Some foods just seem to go together, like baked beans and Crunchy Coleslaw (see Chapter 14) with Oven Barbecued Beef (see Chapter 15) or cornbread with Red Chili (see Chapter 12). Other flavors we've included, like cheesy risotto and barley pilaf, pair wonderfully with almost any main dish.

Some of these recipes are really just ways to soak up delicious sauces, soups, and stews. Feel free to experiment—you know what your family likes, and many of these recipes can be adapted to accommodate a range of preferences. If your family likes white beans but not red beans, make substitutions where necessary.

Sides are great places to use dried beans and rice purchased in bulk. It's faster to use canned beans or converted rice, but it's not necessarily cheaper. Compare the prices on packaged goods and bulk goods at several stores around you to determine the most economical buying strategy for your family.

Barley Pilaf with Mushrooms

Nutty barley is delicately flavored with garlic and parsley.

Yield: 6 cups
Prep time: 10 minutes
Cook time: 40 minutes
Serves: 6
Serving size: 1 cup
Each serving has:
244 calories
0.9 g fat
0 g saturated fat
123 mg sodium
53.7 g carbohydrates
11.1 g dietary fiber
7.2 g protein

2 cups pearled barley

¼ cup chopped onions

1 cup chopped mushrooms

1 cup chopped celery

2 cups water

¼ tsp. crushed garlic

2 tsp. dried thyme

2 tsp. dried parsley

¼ tsp. salt

1 tsp. ground black pepper

1. Preheat oven to 375°F.

2. Lightly oil a 2-quart casserole dish. Add barley, onions, mushrooms, celery, water, garlic, thyme, parsley, salt, and pepper. Stir gently.

3. Bake 40 minutes until barley and mushrooms absorb all the liquid. Gently fluff barley with a fork. Serve immediately.

 Tasty Tidbits

Shop for fresh parsley or grow some of your own in a sunny window or porch. The flavor is worth it! Tear or snip the parsley from the stem and add it to the barley 3 minutes before the end of cooking.

Sweet Potato Oven Fries

A little egg white and olive oil make velvety sweet potatoes deliciously crispy.

2 large sweet potatoes, peeled

2 TB. olive oil

1 egg white

1. Preheat oven to 400°F.

2. Cut sweet potatoes into 1-inch thick strips about 3 inches long. In a large bowl, beat together olive oil and egg white. Add sweet potato strips and stir gently to coat.

3. Arrange strips in a single layer on a cookie sheet lined with parchment paper or aluminum foil.

4. Bake 40 minutes, shaking the pan every 10 minutes to keep fries from sticking. Cool slightly before serving.

Tasty Tidbits _____

You can make oven fries from new potatoes this same way. Scrub them well and you don't even need to peel them.

Yield: 2 sweet potatoes
Prep time: 10 minutes
Cook time: 40 minutes
Serves: 4
Serving size: About ½ potato
Each serving has:
91 calories
4.6 g fat
0.6 g saturated fat
13 mg sodium
11.2 g carbohydrates
1.7 g dietary fiber
1.8 g protein

Risotto with Green Peas and Parmesan

Creamy rice gives you Italian aroma and flavorings.

Yield: 6 cups
Prep time: 10
Cook time: 35 minutes
Serves: 6
Serving size: 1 cup
Each serving has:
247 calories
6.1 g fat
1.4 g saturated fat
72 mg sodium
40.7 g carbohydrates
1.9 g dietary fiber
6.3 g protein

2 TB. olive oil

½ tsp. crushed garlic

¼ cup sliced mushrooms

1½ cups basmati rice or long-grain brown rice

4 cups hot water

⅛ tsp. salt

⅛ tsp. ground black pepper

2 tsp. dried basil, crushed

1 cup frozen green peas

¼ cup grated Parmesan cheese

1. In a large saucepan, heat olive oil over medium-high heat. Sauté garlic briefly. Add mushrooms. Cook 3 minutes. Add rice and stir well to coat rice in oil. Reduce heat to medium.

2. Add hot water ½ cup at a time, stirring until all liquid is absorbed before adding more water. With last ½ cup water, add salt, pepper, basil, and peas. Keep stirring.

3. Just as rice begins to dry, add Parmesan cheese. Stir until cheese melts. Remove and serve immediately.

Variation: Asparagus is also wonderful in this dish.

 Don't Get Burned

You will be tempted to turn away for just a second, but you must not! The success of your risotto depends on stirring and attention. The delicious results make every second worth it!

Baked Beans

Honey and molasses sweeten creamy white beans.

8 oz. turkey bacon

2 (15-oz.) cans great northern beans, drained

½ cup diced apples

¼ cup finely diced onions

¼ cup finely diced celery

1 (15-oz.) can crushed tomatoes

¼ cup honey

¼ cup molasses

2 TB. dried yellow mustard

2 TB. Worcestershire sauce

1 tsp. ground cumin

½ tsp. paprika

¼ tsp. chili powder

Yield: 1 casserole
Prep time: 10 minutes
Cook time: 40 minutes
Serves: 8
Serving size: ½ cup
Each serving has:
407 calories
8.9 g fat
2.9 g saturated fat
582 mg sodium
60 g carbohydrates
15.8 g dietary fiber
23.6 g protein

1. Preheat oven to 350°F.

2. In a large skillet, fry bacon until crisp. Crumble and set aside.

3. In a large bowl, combine beans, apples, onion, celery, tomatoes, honey, molasses, mustard, Worcestershire sauce, cumin, paprika, and chili powder. Stir well.

4. Transfer bean mixture to a 2-quart casserole dish and sprinkle with bacon. Cover and bake 30 minutes.

Tasty Tidbits

For a fruity twist, try fresh or canned chopped pineapple and dried or fresh apricot in this dish.

Grandma's Rice and Beans with Spinach

This reliable staple dresses up with colorful, nutritious spinach, smoky bacon, and a spicy finish.

Yield: About 4 cups
Prep time: 5 minutes
Cook time: 40 minutes
Serves: 8
Serving size: ½ cup
Each serving has:
357 calories
15.8 g fat
4.5 g saturated fat
743 mg sodium
35 g carbohydrates
4.9 g dietary fiber
18.6 g protein

8 oz. turkey bacon

2 TB. olive oil

¼ cup diced onions

¼ cup diced celery

1 cup basmati rice or long-grain brown rice

2½ cups water

1 cup red kidney beans, soaked in water overnight and drained

1 (12-oz.) package frozen spinach, thawed

1 TB. hot sauce

1. In a large skillet, fry bacon until crisp. Crumble and set aside.

2. Heat olive oil in a large saucepan over medium-high heat. Add onions and celery and sauté 5 minutes, stirring often. Add rice, stirring well to coat rice in oil. Add water and bring to a boil.

3. Reduce heat and add beans, bacon, spinach, and hot sauce. Simmer covered for 35 minutes until all liquid is absorbed.

 Tasty Tidbits _____

Canned beans of many varieties taste great in this recipe. Try garbanzo, pinto, or black beans for variety.

Quick Drop Biscuits

These moist and fluffy biscuits are perfect for breakfast and dinner. Their taste goes well with both sweet and savory foods.

1 cup white all-purpose flour

1 cup all-purpose wheat flour

1 TB. baking powder

¼ tsp. salt

¾ cup low-fat milk

¼ cup oil (canola or olive)

1. Preheat oven to 400°F. Line a cookie sheet with parchment paper or coat thinly with butter.

2. In a large bowl, combine white flour, wheat flour, baking powder, and salt. Make a hollow in the dry ingredients. Add milk and oil to the hollow. Stir gently until the dough just begins to stick together. Drop batter in 12 spoonfuls onto the baking sheet.

3. Bake 20 minutes until biscuit edges are golden brown and crispy. Serve warm.

Yield: 12 biscuits
Prep time: 5 minutes
Cook time: 20 minutes
Serves: 12
Serving size: 1 biscuit
Each serving has:
125 calories
5.1 g fat
0.8 g saturated fat
56 mg sodium
17.2 g carbohydrates
0.6 g dietary fiber
2.7 g protein

Tasty Tidbits

You can add many tasty tidbits to this basic biscuit recipe. Try berries, cheese and chiles, or rosemary. If the additions are wet or moist, like strawberries, reduce the amount of milk a little.

Buttermilk Corn Bread

This light, sweet pan bread made with whole corn is perfect partnered with bean dishes and main dish salads.

Yield: 1 8×8-inch pan (9 sliced squares)
Prep time: 5 minutes
Cook time: 25 minutes
Serves: 9
Serving size: 1 2-inch square
Each serving has:
180 calories
3.9 g fat
0.8 g saturated fat
100 mg sodium
32.5 g carbohydrates
2.2 g dietary fiber
5.5 g protein

½ cup all-purpose flour

1½ cups cornmeal

2 tsp. baking powder

⅛ tsp. salt

1½ cups buttermilk (or 1½ cups milk and 4 tsp. lemon juice)

2 eggs

1 TB. canola oil

1 cup frozen corn, thawed

3 TB. honey

1. Preheat oven to 375°F.

2. In a large bowl, combine flour, cornmeal, baking powder, and salt. Stir with a fork to break up any lumps. Add buttermilk, eggs, canola oil, corn, and honey. Mix well with a fork until smooth.

3. Pour into a buttered 8×8-inch baking dish. Bake 25 minutes. Cool before cutting and serving.

Variation: Use ¼ cup diced green chiles or ½ cup sliced strawberries to dress up this bread. Add with the buttermilk and other wet ingredients.

 Kitchen Wise

Before you spend a dime on a boxed corn bread mix, check out the ingredient list for preservatives or artificial flavorings. Choose the mixes that have the healthiest ingredients. We like baking corn bread from scratch because it tastes better.

Cheese Grits Casserole

Creamy Swiss cheese and eggs are baked with corn grits.

1½ cups low-fat milk	2 eggs
1½ cups water	¼ tsp. cayenne pepper
1½ cups instant grits	¼ cup shredded Swiss cheese

1. Preheat oven to 375°F.

2. In a large saucepan, bring milk and water to a boil. Stir in grits. Reduce heat to medium and stir continually until thickened, about 3 to 4 minutes. Remove from heat and allow to cool slightly.

3. In a medium bowl, gently beat eggs. Add cayenne pepper and cheese. Stir well. Add grits. Transfer mixture to 1-quart casserole dish. Bake 30 minutes.

Variation: Use Cheddar, Gouda, or Monterey Jack cheese. If you prefer a hotter taste, use Pepper Jack.

Yield: About 4 cups
Prep time: 5 minutes
Cook time: 45 minutes
Serves: 4
Serving size: 1 cup
Each serving has:
147 calories
6.4 g fat
3.1 g saturated fat
214 mg sodium
13.6 g carbohydrates
1.5 g dietary fiber
8.5 g protein

Tasty Tidbits

Watch for sales on cheese or check the "bits and pieces bin" at the deli counter or the cheese bin at the grocery store.

Chapter 22

Desserts

In This Chapter

- ◆ Satisfying a sweet tooth and your budget
- ◆ Preparing late-day treats
- ◆ Desserts for special occasions

A delicious dessert can be inexpensive and satisfying. Homemade cookies simply taste better than those that come out of a box.

Prepare the slow cooker cake for a special weekend treat or bake a quick fruit cobbler for busy weeknights.

The ingredients in our dessert recipes are already stocked in your pantry, like jam, flour, cornmeal, oatmeal, sugar, apples, and bananas. Others you will want to watch for sales and specials on, like fresh or frozen berries and other seasonal fruits.

Dessert should be a treat, especially for the person who makes it. Enjoy these simple recipes in blissful moderation.

Pear Cobbler

The tangy topping of this cobbler contrasts with the sweetness of the fruit.

Yield: About 6 cups
Prep time: 10 minutes
Cook time: 30 minutes
Serves: 9
Serving size: About ⅔ cup
Each serving has:
196 calories
7.2 g fat
4.3 g saturated fat
182 mg sodium
33.2 g carbohydrates
2.5 g dietary fiber
2.1 g protein

5 TB. softened butter

4 to 5 medium pears, cored and cut in narrow wedges

¼ cup honey

½ tsp. ground nutmeg

¼ cup sugar

½ cup flour

½ cup oatmeal

1 tsp. baking powder

½ tsp. baking soda

½ tsp. salt

½ cup low-fat milk plus ½ TB. vinegar, or ½ cup buttermilk

1. Preheat oven to 425°F. Lightly grease a 9×9-inch baking dish with 1 teaspoon of butter.

2. Arrange pears evenly on the bottom of the baking dish. Drizzle with honey and sprinkle with nutmeg. Bake 12 minutes.

3. In a medium bowl, combine sugar, flour, oatmeal, baking powder, baking soda, and salt. Use a fork to work in remaining butter. Slowly add milk or buttermilk to form crumbly dough.

4. Remove pears from the oven. Gently drop spoonfuls of dough on fruit. Return to the oven and bake 15 minutes until golden. Serve hot.

Variation: Substitute berries, apples, or peaches for the pears.

 Kitchen Wise

You can easily make a substitute for buttermilk by adding ½ tablespoon vinegar to ½ cup milk.

Baked Stuffed Apples

Cinnamon, raisins, and walnuts compliment the flavor of sweet, hot apples.

4 large apples

¼ **cup apple juice**

½ **cup finely chopped walnuts**

½ **tsp. ground cinnamon**

½ **cup raisins**

2 TB. butter

2 TB. sugar

Yield: 4 apples
Prep time: 15 minutes
Cook time: 25 minutes
Serves: 4
Serving size: 1 apple
Each serving has:
298 calories
15.3 g fat
4.2 g saturated fat
45 mg sodium
41.3 g carbohydrates
5 g dietary fiber
4.7 g protein

1. Preheat oven to 300°F. Wash apples and pat dry. Use a sharp knife or apple corer to carefully remove most of the core from each apple. Be careful not to cut all the way through the apples. Arrange apples on a cookie sheet covered with parchment paper or aluminum foil.

2. In a large bowl, combine apple juice, walnuts, cinnamon, raisins, butter, and sugar. Mix well and spoon into hollowed apples. Bake 25 minutes. Serve hot.

Variation: Try dried cranberries, apricots, or mango to replace the raisins.

 Don't Get Burned _____

These tasty treats are very hot in the center when they come out of the oven. Cool apples more quickly by cutting the apple in half before serving.

Sweet Potato Fritters with Apples

Apple and sweet potato are spiced with cinnamon and pan fried.

Yield: About 16 fritters
Prep time: 15 minutes
Cook time: 30 minutes
Serves: 8
Serving size: About 2 fritters
Each serving has:
195 calories
5.1 g fat
2.9 g saturated fat
127 mg sodium
32.8 g carbohydrates
2.2 g dietary fiber
5.4 g protein

1 cup cooked and mashed sweet potato

½ cup low-fat cottage cheese

1 apple, cored and diced

½ cup all-purpose flour

1 tsp. ground cinnamon

1 egg

¼ cup sugar

1 tsp. baking powder

2 TB. butter

¼ cup powdered sugar

1. In a large bowl, combine sweet potato, cottage cheese, apple, flour, cinnamon, egg, sugar, and baking powder. Stir well until smooth. Use a spoon to form 16 balls of dough.

2. In a large skillet over medium-high heat, heat butter until hot. Place 4 balls of dough in skillet. Flatten with a spatula. Fry the balls for 2 to 3 minutes per side. Remove to paper towels to drain. Continue frying dough until all the balls are cooked. You may need to add more butter to fry all the balls. Sprinkle with powdered sugar.

 Money Matters

To use fewer paper towels, set down a ¼-inch thick layer of newspaper. Top with a single layer of paper towels. Use this surface to drain the fritters.

Sweet Fruit and Noodle Pudding

Cottage cheese adds creamy texture to a vanilla-flavored fruit and noodle pudding.

1 TB. olive oil

1 (12-oz.) package whole-wheat noodles

¼ cup sugar

1 egg

½ cup low-fat milk

1 TB. vanilla extract

1 cup low-fat cottage cheese

1 cup sliced peaches, canned or frozen

1 cup frozen berries, such as strawberries or blackberries

Yield: About 9 cups
Prep time: 10 minutes
Cook time: 1 hour
Serves: 9
Serving size: About 1 cup
Each serving has:
135 calories
3.6 g fat
1 g saturated fat
118 mg sodium
18.5 g carbohydrates
1.6 g dietary fiber
6.6 g protein

1. Preheat oven to 350°F. Lightly oil a 9×13-inch baking dish. Prepare noodles according to package directions. Drain well and set aside.

2. In a large bowl, stir together sugar, egg, milk, and vanilla. Add cottage cheese and stir gently. Fold in peaches and blackberries. Gently fold in noodles.

3. Transfer mixture to the baking dish and cover with aluminum foil. Bake 30 minutes. Remove foil and bake 25 more minutes until golden. Cool slightly before cutting.

Variation: Use the fruit combination of cherry with apple or pineapple with apricot for this sweet noodle pudding.

 Tasty Tidbits

Serve this pudding for brunch along with eggs and sausage.

Raspberry Banana Bread

Tangy berries and sweet bananas mingle with chocolate in this easy, attractive loaf.

Yield: 1 loaf, about 8 slices
Prep time: 10 minutes
Cook time: 55 minutes
Serves: 8
Serving size: 1 slice
Each serving has:
325 calories
14.1 g fat
2.9 g saturated fat
127 mg sodium
48.2 g carbohydrates
2.1 g dietary fiber
3 g protein

1 tsp. butter

1½ cups all-purpose flour

½ tsp. baking powder

1 cup sugar

½ tsp. salt

3 bananas, mashed

½ cup raspberries, fresh or frozen

2 eggs, lightly beaten

½ cup canola oil

½ cup semisweet chocolate chips

1. Preheat oven to 350°F. Butter a 9×5×3-inch loaf pan.

2. In a medium bowl, combine flour and baking powder, using a fork to stir well. Add sugar and salt. Stir well.

3. In a large bowl, combine bananas, raspberries, eggs, and oil. Add flour mixture and stir until almost smooth. Stir in chocolate chips. Pour batter into the prepared loaf pan. Bake 55 minutes until firm and golden. Remove from the pan carefully by loosening around edges with a knife then inverting gently onto a cooling rack. Allow to cool slightly before slicing and serving.

Variation: Strawberries, blueberries, or blackberries work well in this bread, too.

 Tasty Tidbits _____

Make this bread for dessert early in the week, then use the leftovers for French toast over the weekend after the bread dries out a little.

Slow-Cooked Pudding and Fruit Cake

This creamy and sweet vanilla cake is lightly spiced with cinnamon and apricots.

2 tsp. olive oil

1 (3½-oz.) package vanilla instant pudding mix

2 cups boiling water

2½ cups all-purpose flour

½ cup sugar

1 TB. baking powder

⅛ tsp. salt

1½ cups milk

¼ cup butter, softened

1 tsp. vanilla extract

½ tsp. ground cinnamon

½ cup diced dried apricots

Yield: About 8 cups
Prep time: 10 minutes
Cook time: 6 hours
Serves: 8
Serving size: About 1 cup
Each serving has:
329 calories
8.3 g fat
4.5 g saturated fat
279 mg sodium
58 g carbohydrates
1.3 g dietary fiber
5.7 g protein

1. Lightly oil slow cooker. In a medium heat-proof bowl, combine pudding mix and boiling water. Stir well and set aside.

2. In a large bowl, combine flour, sugar, baking powder, and salt. Stir well. Add milk, butter, vanilla, and cinnamon. Stir well. Add apricots and stir well.

3. Transfer mixture to the slow cooker. Pour pudding over cake batter. Do not stir. Cover and cook on low 6 hours. Serve warm.

Variation: Use any flavor of pudding your family likes. Try chocolate, lemon, or even pistachio. You can also use almost any dried fruit. Try dates, mango, or pineapple.

 Kitchen Wise

Desserts made in the slow cooker are perfect for summertime. Prepare the ingredients early in the day and then enjoy the results when the temperature cools down in the evening.

Brown Sugar Ginger Shortbread

A shortbread cookie is flavored with brown sugar and ginger.

Yield: About 12 pieces
Prep time: 10 minutes
Cook time: 20 minutes
Serves: 12
Serving size: 1 piece
Each serving has:
140 calories
7.8 g fat
4.9 g saturated fat
81 mg sodium
16.2 g carbohydrates
0 g dietary fiber
1.5 g protein

1 stick of butter (½ cup)
1¼ cups all-purpose flour
½ cup packed brown sugar

1 TB. ground ginger
⅛ tsp. salt

1. Preheat oven to 350°F. Butter a 9×9-inch baking dish.

2. In a large saucepan over medium-low heat, melt remaining butter. Stir constantly until butter begins to darken. Remove from the heat.

3. Add flour, brown sugar, ginger, and salt. Stir well. Pour batter into the prepared baking dish. Bake 20 minutes.

4. Remove shortbread from the oven and gently score the shortbread with a sharp knife (do not cut all the way through), making 12 squares. Allow shortbread to cool in the pan 20 minutes before breaking up and serving.

Variation: Add ¹/₂ teaspoon lemon or orange zest to the batter before baking for a special treat.

 Tasty Tidbits _____

Serve this super-sweet cookie for dessert or wrap a couple and put them in lunchboxes.

Cookies Flavored with Tea

These simple cookies are flavored with your favorite tea and honey.

1 cup softened butter

1 cup sugar

1 egg

2 TB. honey

2½ cups all-purpose flour

2 tsp. tea leaves (2 teabags of your favorite flavor)

⅛ tsp. salt

Yield: About 2 dozen	
Prep time: 10 minutes	
Cook time: 10 minutes	
Serves: 12	
Serving size: 2 cookies	
Each serving has:	
311 calories	
16 g fat	
9.9 g saturated fat	
139 mg sodium	
39.5 g carbohydrates	
0.7 g dietary fiber	
3.3 g protein	

1. Preheat oven to 375°F. Line a cookie sheet with parchment paper.

2. In a large bowl, cream butter and ¾ cup of sugar. Add egg and honey. Mix well.

3. In a medium bowl, combine flour, tea, and salt. Stir gently with a fork to combine. Slowly add flour mixture to wet ingredients. Stir until well mixed.

4. Shape dough into a log and wrap tightly in plastic wrap or waxed paper. Chill 1 hour. Unwrap log and slice into 24 rounds. Place rounds on a cookie sheet and bake 10 minutes until golden. Sprinkle warm cookies with remaining sugar. Cool slightly before serving.

Variation: You can use any tea you like in these cookies. Try Lady Gray, Earl Grey, green tea, chai, or chamomile.

Kitchen Wise

By varying the flavors of tea you use to make these cookies each time, these can be a very different treat every time you bake them.

Chocolate Chip Cookies

This is a timeless, home-baked classic made simple.

Yield: About 2 dozen cookies
Prep time: 10 minutes
Cook time: 12 minutes
Serves: 12
Serving size: 2 cookies
Each serving has:
322 calories
17 g fat
10.6 g saturated fat
166 mg sodium
38.8 g carbohydrates
0.8 g dietary fiber
3.6 g protein

1 cup softened butter

1 cup sugar

1 egg

1 TB. vanilla extract

2½ cups all-purpose flour

¼ tsp. salt

¼ cup chocolate chips

1. Preheat oven to 375°F. Line a cookie sheet with parchment paper.

2. In a large bowl, cream together butter and sugar. Add egg and vanilla. Mix well.

3. In a medium bowl, combine flour and salt. Stir gently with a fork to combine. Add chocolate chips and stir well. Add flour and chocolate mixture to wet ingredients slowly. Stir until well mixed.

4. Spoon dough onto the cookie sheet with a tablespoon, about 12 to a cookie sheet. Bake 12 minutes. Remove cookies from the sheet with a spatula gently and transfer to a wire rack. Cool 5 minutes before serving.

Variation: Add ½ cup chopped nuts such as walnuts, pecans, or macadamia nuts.

 Tasty Tidbits

You can use these cookies to make ice-cream sandwiches. Slightly thaw your favorite flavor ice cream, spread about ¼ cup on top of one cookie and place a second cookie upside down on top of the ice cream. Chill 1 hour before serving.

Chocolate Not-Quite-Fudge Pâté

This dessert is so easy, you don't even have to bake it. Chocolaty, nutty, and sweet.

1 cup semisweet chocolate chips

2 TB. heavy cream

½ cup butter

¼ cup brown sugar

½ cup chopped walnuts or pecans

1 TB. vanilla extract

1. Line a 9×9-inch baking dish with parchment paper or aluminum foil, making sure the edges are covered with paper.

2. In a large saucepan over medium-low heat, combine chocolate, heavy cream, butter, and sugar. Stir often until all ingredients are melted and mixture is smooth. Add nuts and vanilla and stir well.

3. Pour mixture into the lined baking dish. Cool in the refrigerator at least 1 hour before slicing and serving.

Variation: Add ½ cup chopped dried apricots, dates, or shredded coconut with the nuts.

Yield: 9 pieces
Prep time: 15 minutes
Cook time: None
Serves: 9
Serving size: 1 piece, about 3×3 inches
Each serving has:
287 calories
22.9 g fat
12.1 g saturated fat
75 mg sodium
21.1 g carbohydrates
2.4 g dietary fiber
2.5 g protein

Kitchen Wise

This pâté makes even inexpensive chocolate chips taste elegant and special.

Brownies with Walnuts

This is a classic chocolate brownie with buttery walnuts.

Yield: 9 brownies
Prep time: 15 minutes
Cook time: 35 minutes
Serves: 9
Serving size: 1 brownie, about 3×3 inches
Each serving has:
353 calories
19.2 g fat
9.4 g saturated fat
119 mg sodium
42.4 g carbohydrates
2.1 g dietary fiber
5.6 g protein

1 stick butter

½ cup semisweet chocolate chips

1 cup sugar

1 TB. vanilla extract

2 eggs

1 cup all-purpose flour

⅛ tsp. salt

2 TB. unsweetened cocoa powder

½ cup chopped walnuts

1. Preheat oven to 350°F. Lightly butter an 8×8-inch baking dish.

2. Place remaining butter and chocolate in a large heatproof bowl over a pan of simmering water. Stir often until chocolate melts. Remove bowl from the heat carefully and cool slightly.

3. Add sugar and vanilla. Mix well until sugar dissolves. Add eggs and mix thoroughly.

4. In a separate bowl, combine flour, salt, and cocoa. Use a fork to mix. Add dry ingredients to wet ingredients. Mix well. Fold in walnuts.

5. Pour batter into the prepared baking dish. Bake 35 minutes. Cool before cutting and serving.

Variation: Vary the flavor of these brownies by adding ½ teaspoon instant coffee, ¼ teaspoon crushed red pepper flakes, or ¼ teaspoon ground black pepper. For a special taste treat, omit the salt in the recipe. When the brownies come out of the oven, sprinkle the top with ⅛ teaspoon sea salt.

 Tasty Tidbits

Freeze any leftover brownies. Next time you or your family wants ice-cream sundaes, pull out the frozen brownies and chop them. Heat a small amount of strawberry jam in the microwave. For each serving, use one scoop of ice cream, a heaping spoonful of chopped brownie, and drizzle with hot strawberry jam. This is so good that you can serve it to guests, too.

Appendix A

Glossary

al dente   Italian for "against the teeth." Refers to pasta or rice that's neither soft nor hard but just slightly firm against the teeth.

all-purpose flour   Flour that contains only the inner part of the wheat grain. Usable for all purposes from cakes to gravies.

almonds   Mild, sweet, and crunchy nuts that combine nicely with creamy and sweet food items.

andouille sausage   A sausage made with highly seasoned pork chitterlings and tripe, or pork shoulder. A standard component of many Cajun dishes.

artichoke hearts   The center part of the artichoke flower, often found canned in grocery stores.

arugula   A spicy-peppery garden plant with leaves that resemble a dandelion and have a distinctive—and very sharp—flavor.

au gratin   The quick broiling of a dish before serving to brown the top ingredients. When used in a recipe name, the term often implies cheese and a creamy sauce.

bake   To cook in a dry oven. Dry-heat cooking often results in a crisping of the exterior of the food being cooked. Moist-heat cooking, through methods such as steaming, poaching, etc., brings a much different, moist quality to the food.

balsamic vinegar   Vinegar produced primarily in Italy from Trebbiano grape juice and aged in wood barrels. It is heavier, darker, and sweeter than most vinegars.

bamboo shoots   Crunchy, tasty white parts of the growing bamboo plant, often purchased canned.

barbecue   To quick-cook over high heat, or to cook something long and slow in a rich liquid (barbecue sauce).

basil   A flavorful, almost sweet, resinous herb that is delicious with tomatoes and used in all kinds of Italian and Mediterranean-style dishes.

baste   To keep foods moist during cooking by spooning, brushing, or drizzling with a liquid.

beat   To quickly mix ingredients.

black pepper   A biting and pungent seasoning, freshly ground pepper is a must for many dishes and adds an extra level of flavor.

blanch   To place a food in boiling water for about 1 minute (or less) to partially cook the exterior and then submerge in or rinse with cool water to halt the cooking.

blend   To completely mix something, usually with a blender or food processor, more slowly than beating.

boil   To heat a liquid to the point where water is forced to turn into steam, causing the liquid to bubble. To boil something is to insert it into boiling water. A rapid boil is when a lot of bubbles form on the surface of the liquid.

bok choy (also **Chinese cabbage**)   A member of the cabbage family with thick stems, crisp texture, and fresh flavor. It's perfect for stir-frying.

bouillon   Dried essence of stock from chicken, beef, vegetable, or other ingredients. This is a popular starting ingredient for soups as it adds flavor (and often a lot of salt).

braise   To cook in liquid over low heat, usually over an extended period of time.

breadcrumbs   Tiny pieces of crumbled dry bread, often used for topping or coating.

brine   A highly salted, often seasoned, liquid used to flavor and preserve foods. To brine a food is to soak, or preserve, it by submerging it in brine. The salt in the brine penetrates the fibers of the meat and makes it moist and tender.

broil   To cook in a dry oven under the overhead high-heat element.

broth   *See* stock.

brown   To cook in a skillet, turning, until the food's surface is seared and brown in color, to lock in the juices.

brown rice   Whole-grain rice, including the germ, with a characteristic pale brown or tan color; more nutritious and flavorful than white rice.

bulgur   A wheat kernel that's been steamed, dried, and crushed and is sold in fine and coarse textures.

Cajun cooking   A style of cooking that combines French and Southern characteristics and includes many highly seasoned stews and meats.

caramelize   To cook sugar over low heat until it develops a sweet caramel flavor. The term is increasingly used to describe cooking vegetables (especially onions) or meat in butter or oil over low heat until they soften, sweeten, and develop a caramel color.

caraway   A distinctive spicy seed used for bread, pork, cheese, and cabbage dishes. It is known to reduce stomach upset, which is why it is often paired with, for example, sauerkraut.

carbohydrate   A nutritional component found in starches, sugars, fruits, and vegetables that causes a rise in blood glucose levels. Carbohydrates supply energy and many important nutrients, including vitamins, minerals, and antioxidants.

cardamom   An intense, sweet-smelling spice common to Indian cooking and used in baking and coffee.

cayenne   A fiery spice made from (hot) chile peppers, especially the cayenne chile, a slender, red, and very hot pepper.

Cheddar   The ubiquitous hard cow's milk cheese with a rich, buttery flavor that ranges from mellow to sharp. Originally produced in England, Cheddar is now produced worldwide.

chevre   French for "goat milk cheese," chevre is a typically creamy-salty soft cheese that's delicious by itself or paired with fruits or chutney. Chevres vary in style from mild and creamy to aged, firm, and flavorful.

chiles (or **chilies**)   Any one of many different "hot" peppers, ranging in intensity from the relatively mild ancho pepper to the blisteringly hot habañero.

chili powder   A seasoning blend that includes chili pepper, cumin, garlic, and oregano. Proportions vary among different versions, but they all offer a warm, rich flavor.

Chinese five-spice powder   A seasoning blend of cinnamon, anise, ginger, fennel, and pepper.

chives   A member of the onion family, chives grow in bunches of long leaves that resemble tall grass or the green tops of onions and offer a light onion flavor.

chop   To cut into pieces, usually qualified by an adverb such as "*coarsely* chopped" or by a size measurement such as "chopped into $1/2$-inch pieces." "Finely chopped" is much closer to mince.

chorizo   A spiced pork sausage eaten alone or as a component in many recipes.

chutney   A thick condiment made with fruits and/or vegetables cooked with vinegar, sugar, and spices. Often served with Indian curries.

cider vinegar   Vinegar produced from apple cider, popular in North America.

cilantro   A member of the parsley family used in Mexican cooking (especially salsa) and some Asian dishes. Use in moderation as the flavor can overwhelm. The seed of the cilantro is the spice coriander.

cinnamon   A sweet, rich, aromatic spice commonly used in baking or desserts. Cinnamon can also be used for delicious and interesting entrées.

clove   A sweet, strong, almost wintergreen-flavor spice used in baking and with meats such as ham.

coriander   A rich, warm, spicy seed used in all types of recipes, from African to South American, from entrées to desserts.

count   In terms of seafood or other foods that come in small sizes, the number of that item that compose 1 pound. For example, 31 to 40 count shrimp are large appetizer shrimp often served with cocktail sauce; 51 to 60 count are much smaller.

couscous   Granular semolina (durum wheat) that is cooked and used in many Mediterranean and North African dishes.

crimini mushrooms   A relative of the white button mushroom but brown in color and with a richer flavor. The larger, fully grown version is the portobello. *See also* portobello mushrooms.

croutons   Chunks of bread, usually between $1/4$ and $1/2$ inch in size, sometimes seasoned and baked, broiled, or fried to a crisp texture and used to garnish soups and salads.

cumin   An earthy-tasting spice popular in Middle Eastern and Indian dishes. Cumin is a seed; ground cumin seed is the most common form used in cooking.

curd   A gelatinous substance derived from coagulated milk, used to make cheese. Curd also refers to dishes of similar texture, such as dishes made with egg (lemon curd).

curing   A method of preserving uncooked foods, usually meats or fish, by either salting and smoking or pickling.

curry   Rich, spicy, Indian-style sauces and the dishes prepared with them. A curry uses curry powder as its base seasoning.

curry powder   A ground blend of rich and flavorful spices used as a basis for curry and many other Indian-influenced dishes. Common ingredients include hot pepper, nutmeg, cumin, cinnamon, black pepper, and turmeric. Some curry can also be found in paste form.

custard   A cooked mixture of eggs and milk popular as a base for desserts.

dash   A few drops, usually of a liquid, released by a quick shake of, for example, a bottle of hot sauce.

deglaze   To scrape up the browned bits of meat and seasoning left in a pan or skillet after cooking. Usually this is done by adding a liquid such as wine or broth and creating a flavorful stock that can be used to create sauces.

devein   The removal of the dark vein from the back of a large shrimp with a sharp knife.

dice   To cut into small cubes about $1/4$-inch square.

Dijon mustard   Hearty, spicy mustard made in the style of the Dijon region of France.

dill   An herb perfect for eggs, salmon, cheese dishes, and, of course, vegetables (pickles!).

dollop   A spoonful of something creamy and thick, like sour cream or whipped cream.

double boiler   A set of two pots designed to nest together, one inside the other, and provide consistent, moist heat for foods that need delicate treatment. The bottom pot holds water (not quite touching the bottom of the top pot); the top pot holds the ingredient you want to heat.

dredge   To cover a piece of food with a dry substance such as flour or cornmeal.

drizzle   To lightly sprinkle drops of a liquid over food, often as the finishing touch to a dish.

dry   In the context of wine, a wine that contains little or no residual sugar, so it's not very sweet.

fennel   In seed form, a fragrant, licorice-tasting herb. The bulbs have a much milder flavor and a celerylike crunch and are used as a vegetable in salads or cooked recipes.

feta   A white, crumbly, sharp, and salty cheese popular in Greek cooking and on salads. Traditional feta is usually made with sheep milk, but feta-style cheese can be made from sheep, cow, or goat milk.

fillet   A piece of meat or seafood with the bones removed.

flake   To break into thin sections, as with fish.

floret   The flower or bud end of broccoli or cauliflower.

flour   Grains ground into meal. Wheat is perhaps the most common flour. Flour is also made from oats, rye, buckwheat, soybeans, etc.

fold   To combine a dense mixture, such as a batter, with a light mixture, such as beaten egg whites, using a gentle, circular stirring action from the bottom of the bowl.

frittata   A skillet-cooked mixture of eggs and other ingredients that's not stirred but is cooked slowly and then either flipped or finished under the broiler.

fritter   A food such as apples or corn coated or mixed with batter and deep-fried for a crispy, crunchy exterior.

fructose   Sugar naturally found in fruit, slightly sweeter than table sugar.

fry   *See* sauté.

garbanzo beans (or **chickpeas**)   A yellow-gold, roundish bean used as the base ingredient in hummus. Chickpeas are high in fiber and low in fat.

garlic   A member of the onion family, a pungent and flavorful element in many savory dishes. A garlic bulb contains multiple cloves. Each clove, when chopped, provides about 1 teaspoon of garlic. Most recipes call for cloves or chopped garlic by the teaspoon.

garnish   An embellishment not vital to the dish but added to enhance visual appeal.

ginger   Available in fresh root or dried, ground form, ginger adds a pungent, sweet, and spicy quality to a dish.

glucose   The simplest natural sugar.

Gorgonzola   A creamy and rich Italian blue cheese. "Dolce" is sweet, and that's the kind you want.

grate   To shave into tiny pieces using a sharp rasp or grater.

grind   To reduce a large, hard substance, often a seasoning such as peppercorns, to the consistency of sand.

grits   Coarsely ground grains, usually corn.

handful   An unscientific measurement; the amount of an ingredient you can hold in your hand.

Havarti   A creamy, mild Danish cow's milk cheese perhaps most often enjoyed in its herbed versions such as Havarti with dill.

hazelnuts (also **filberts**)   A rich nut popular in desserts and, to a lesser degree, in savory dishes.

hearts of palm   Firm, elongated, off-white cylinders from the inside of a palm tree stem tip.

high-glycemic foods   Carbohydrates that are quickly digested by the stomach into simple sugars. These cause a quick lift in blood sugar levels and in insulin levels. Eating high-glycemic foods—such as simple starches, high-fructose corn syrup, and sugars—causes weight gain and leads to insulin resistance and metabolic syndrome, and may lead to type 2 diabetes.

horseradish   A sharp, spicy root that forms the flavor base in many condiments from cocktail sauce to sharp mustards. Prepared horseradish contains vinegar and oil, among other ingredients. Use pure horseradish much more sparingly than the pre-pared version or try cutting it with sour cream.

hummus   A thick, Middle Eastern spread made of puréed garbanzo beans, lemon juice, olive oil, garlic, and often tahini (sesame seed paste).

infusion   A liquid in which flavorful ingredients such as herbs have been soaked or steeped to extract that flavor into the liquid.

Italian seasoning   A blend of dried herbs, including basil, oregano, rosemary, and thyme.

jicama   A crunchy, sweet, large, round Central American vegetable. If you can't find jicama, try substituting sliced water chestnuts.

julienne   A French word meaning "to slice into very thin pieces."

kalamata olives   Traditionally from Greece, these medium-small long black olives have a smoky rich flavor.

Key limes   Very small limes grown primarily in Florida and known for their tart taste.

knead   To work dough to make it pliable so that it holds gas bubbles as it bakes. Kneading is fundamental in the process of making yeast breads.

kosher salt   A coarse-grained salt made without any additives or iodine.

lentils   Tiny, lens-shape pulses used in European, Middle Eastern, and Indian cuisines.

marinate   To soak meat, seafood, or other food in a seasoned sauce, called a marinade, which is high in acid content. The acids break down the muscle of the meat, making it tender and adding flavor.

medallion   A small round cut, usually of meat or vegetables such as beef tenderloin or carrots.

meld   To allow flavors to blend and spread over time. Melding is often why recipes call for overnight refrigeration and is also why some dishes taste better as leftovers.

meringue   A baked mixture of sugar and beaten egg whites, often used as a dessert topping.

miso   A fermented, flavorful soybean paste, key in many Japanese dishes.

nutmeg   A sweet, fragrant, musky spice used primarily in baking.

olive oil   A fragrant liquid produced by crushing or pressing olives. Extra-virgin olive oil—the most flavorful and highest quality—is produced from the first pressing of a batch of olives; oil is also produced from later pressings.

olives   The fruit of the olive tree commonly grown on all sides of the Mediterranean. Black olives are also called ripe olives. Green olives are immature, although they are also widely eaten. Olives are always brined or cured before eating. *See also* kalamata olives.

oregano   A fragrant, slightly astringent herb used in Greek, Spanish, and Italian dishes.

orzo   A rice-shape pasta used in Greek cooking.

paella   A grand Spanish dish of shellfish, vegetables, meats, herbs, and rice flavored with a rich broth.

paprika   A rich, warm, earthy red spice that also lends a red hue to many dishes.

Parmesan   A hard, dry, flavorful cheese primarily used grated or shredded as a seasoning for Italian-style dishes.

parsley   A fresh-tasting green leafy herb, often used as a garnish.

pâté   A savory loaf that contains finely ground meats, poultry, or seafood; spices; and often a lot of fat, served cold and spread or sliced on crusty bread or crackers.

pecans   Rich, buttery nuts, native to North America, that have a high unsaturated fat content.

peppercorns   Large, round, dried berries ground to produce pepper.

pesto   A thick spread or sauce made with fresh basil leaves, garlic, olive oil, pine nuts, and Parmesan cheese. Some newer versions are made with other herbs.

pickle   A food, usually a vegetable such as a cucumber, that's been pickled in brine.

pilaf   A rice dish in which the rice is browned in butter or oil and then cooked in a flavorful liquid such as a broth, often with the addition of meats, vegetables, or herbs. The rice absorbs the broth, resulting in a savory dish.

pinch   An unscientific measurement term, the amount of an ingredient—typically a dry, granular substance such as an herb or seasoning—you can hold between your finger and thumb.

pine nuts (also **pignoli** or **piñon**)   Grown on pine trees, these nuts are rich (read: high fat), flavorful, and a bit piney. Pine nuts are a traditional component of pesto and add a wonderful hearty crunch to many other recipes.

pita bread   A flat, hollow bread often used for sandwiches or sliced, pizza style, into wedges. It's terrific eaten soft with dips or baked or broiled as a vehicle for other ingredients.

pizza stone   Preheated in the oven, a pizza stone cooks a crust to a delicious, crispy, pizza-parlor texture. It also holds heat well, so a pizza (or other food) removed from the oven on the stone stays hot for as long as a half hour at the table.

poach   To cook a food in simmering liquid, such as water, wine, or broth.

porcini mushrooms   Rich and flavorful mushrooms used in rice and Italian-style dishes.

portobello mushrooms   A mature and larger form of the smaller crimini mushroom, portobellos are brownish, chewy, and flavorful. Often served as whole caps, grilled, and as thin sautéed slices. *See also* crimini mushrooms.

preheat   To turn on an oven, broiler, or other cooking appliance in advance of cooking so that the temperature will be at the desired level when the assembled dish is ready for cooking.

prosciutto   Dry, salt-cured ham that originated in Italy.

purée   To reduce a food to a thick, creamy texture, usually using a blender or food processor.

reduce   To boil or simmer a broth or sauce to remove some of the water content, resulting in more concentrated flavor and color.

rice vinegar   Vinegar produced from fermented rice or rice wine, popular in Asian-style dishes. Different from rice wine vinegar.

ricotta   A fresh Italian cheese that's smoother than cottage cheese with a slightly sweet flavor.

risotto   A popular Italian rice dish made by browning arborio rice in butter or oil and then slowly stirring in liquid to cook the rice, resulting in a creamy texture.

roast   To cook something uncovered in an oven, usually without additional liquid.

rosemary   A pungent, sweet herb used with chicken, pork, fish, and especially lamb. A little of it goes a long way.

roux   A cooked mixture of butter or another fat and flour, used to thicken sauces and soups.

saffron   A spice made from the stamens of crocus flowers, saffron lends a dramatic yellow color and distinctive flavor to a dish. Use only tiny amounts of this expensive herb.

sage   An herb with a musty yet fruity, lemon-rind scent and "sunny" flavor.

salsa   A style of mixing coarsely chopped fresh vegetables and/or fruit. Salsa can be spicy or not, fruit based or not, and served as a starter on its own (with chips, for example) or as a companion to a main course.

sauté   To pan-cook on the stove using a small amount of fat such as oil or butter.

savory   A popular herb with a fresh, woody taste.

sear To quickly brown the exterior of a food, especially meat, over high heat to preserve interior moisture.

sesame oil An oil, made from pressing sesame seeds, that's tasteless if clear and aromatic and flavorful if brown.

shellfish A broad range of seafood, including clams, mussels, oysters, crabs, shrimp, and lobster. Some people are allergic to shellfish, so take care with its inclusion in recipes.

shiitake mushrooms Large, dark brown mushrooms with a hearty, meaty flavor. Can be used either fresh or dried, grilled or as a component in other recipes, and as a flavoring source for broth.

shred To cut or tear into many long, thin pieces.

simmer To boil gently so the liquid barely bubbles.

skewers Thin wooden or metal sticks, usually about 8 to 12 inches long, used for assembling kebabs, dipping food pieces into hot sauces, or serving single-bite food items with a bit of panache.

skillet (also **frying pan**) A generally heavy, flat-bottomed metal pan with a handle designed to cook food over heat on a stovetop or campfire.

skim To remove fat or other material from the surface of a liquid.

slice To cut into thin pieces.

steam To suspend a food over boiling water and allow the heat of the steam (water vapor) to cook the food. A quick-cooking method, steaming preserves the flavor and texture of a food.

stew To slowly cook pieces of food submerged in a liquid. Also describes a dish that has been prepared by this method.

stir-fry To cook small pieces of food in a wok or skillet over high heat, moving and turning the food quickly to cook all sides.

stock A flavorful broth made by cooking meats and/or vegetables with seasonings until the liquid absorbs these flavors. The liquid is then strained and the solids discarded. Can be eaten alone or used as a base for soups, stews, sauces, etc.

succotash A cooked vegetable dish usually made of corn and peppers.

tahini A paste made from sesame seeds used to flavor many Middle Eastern recipes.

tarragon   A sweet, rich-smelling herb perfect with seafood, vegetables (especially asparagus), chicken, and pork.

teriyaki   A Japanese-style sauce composed of soy sauce, rice wine, ginger, and sugar that works well with seafood as well as most meats.

thyme   A minty, zesty herb.

toast   To heat something, usually bread, so that it's browned and crisp.

tofu   A cheeselike substance made from soybeans and soy milk.

tomatillo   A small, round fruit with a distinctive spicy flavor, often found in south-of-the-border dishes. To use, remove the papery outer skin, rinse off any sticky residue, and chop like a tomato.

turmeric   A spicy, pungent, yellow root used in many dishes, especially in Indian cuisine, for color and flavor. Turmeric is the source of the yellow color in many prepared mustards.

vegetable steamer   An insert for a large saucepan or a special pot with tiny holes in the bottom designed to fit on another pot to hold food to be steamed above boiling water. *See also* steam.

venison   Deer meat.

vinegar   An acidic liquid widely used as dressing and seasoning, often made from fermented grapes, apples, or rice. *See also* balsamic vinegar; cider vinegar; rice vinegar; white vinegar; wine vinegar.

walnuts   A rich, slightly woody-flavored nut.

water chestnuts   A tuber popular in many types of Asian-style cooking. The flesh is white, crunchy, and juicy, and the vegetable holds its texture whether cool or hot.

whisk   To rapidly mix, introducing air to the mixture.

white mushrooms   Button mushrooms. When fresh, they have an earthy smell and an appealing "soft crunch."

white vinegar   The most common type of vinegar, produced from grain.

whole-wheat flour   Wheat flour that contains the entire grain.

wild rice   Actually a grass with a rich, nutty flavor, popular as an unusual and nutritious side dish.

wine vinegar   Vinegar produced from red or white wine.

wok   A large pan with thin walls and sloped sides used for stir-frying.

Worcestershire sauce   Originally developed in India and containing tamarind, this spicy sauce is used as a seasoning for many meats and other dishes.

yeast   Tiny single-cell fungi that, when mixed with water, sugar, flour, and heat, release carbon dioxide bubbles, which, in turn, cause the bread to rise.

Resources

Listed here are some Internet resources you can explore to learn more about the information in this book.

Free online software for budgeting:

- Quicken.com online at http://quicken.intuit.com/personal-finance-software/free-online-money-management.jsp

- Mint.com at www.mint.com

- iPhone app at http://quicken.intuit.com/personal-finance-software/free-iphone-application.jsp

Computer software for budgeting (you work with data stored on your computer and can work offline):

- Quicken at www.quicken.com

- Money for Apple Computers at www.apple.com/downloads/macosx/business_finance/money.html

Websites for budget analysis and guidelines:

- www.betterbudgeting.com/budgetformsfree.htm

- http://consumerist.com/5059234/on-the-moneys-budget-calculator-helps-guide-your-monthly-spending

Shopping lists sites:

- www.grocerylists.org
- www.grocerywiz.com

Coupons:

- www.coupons.com

School lunch:

- www.fns.usda.gov/CND
- www.schoolnutrition.org

Growing herbs:

- http://gardening.about.com/od/herbs

Preserving food by canning, freezing, or drying:

- www.uga.edu/nchfp

Index

A

actual expenses versus budget comparison, 32
add-on foods, 12
after-school snacks, 28
amount of foods on plates, 10-11
appetizers. *See also* salads; soups
  after-school, 28
  Asian Chicken Appetizers, 155
  Avocado Kraut Cups, 161
  Baked Hot Drumsticks, 154
  Cool Dill Dip, 164
  Crunchy Jicama Snack, 157
  Deviled Eggs, 159
  Guacamole, 158
  Hot Spinach and Artichoke Dip, 162
  Hummus, 156
  Oven-Baked Potato Chips, 160
  Quick Fruit Salsa, 165
  Warm Onion and Mushroom Dip, 163
apples
  Baked Beans, 265
  Baked Chicken with Apples and Sweet Potatoes, 198
  Baked Cranberry Apple Oatmeal, 116
  Baked Stuffed Apples, 273
  Cottage Cheese and Fruit, 118
  Curried Fruit and Spinach Salad, 180

Fresh Fruit with Tangy Yogurt Sauce, 119
Mint and Melon Salad, 181
Nutty Brown Rice Burgers, 235
Nutty Fruit Parfait, 120
Nutty Fruity Lentil Loaf, 237
Quick Fruit Salsa, 165
Slow-Cooked Onions with Apples and Sour Cream, 250
Sweet Potato Fritters with Apples, 274
Turkey and Cranberry Wrap, 128
apricots
  Apricot Glazed Turkey Thighs, 208
  Slow-Cooked Pudding and Fruit Cake, 277
artichokes, 162
artificial sweeteners, 12
Asian Chicken Appetizers, 155
Autumn Salad, 171
avocados
  Avocado Kraut Cups, 161
  Guacamole, 158

B

bacon
  Savory Spinach and Bacon Bake, 110
  Tossed Chef's Salad, 182
bad food habits
  expired food, 54
  leftovers, 53
  packaging, 53

Baked Beans, 265
Baked Chicken with Apples and Sweet Potatoes, 198
Baked Cranberry Apple Oatmeal, 116
Baked French Toast with Honey Walnut Syrup, 117
Baked Hot Drumsticks, 154
Baked Italian Sausage and Peppers with Spaghetti, 195
Baked Macaroni with Two Cheeses, 234
Baked Salmon and Asian Cabbage Salad, 132
Baked Scotch Eggs, 114
Baked Seafood Casserole, 217
Baked South-Of-The-Border Tortillas, 130
Baked Stuffed Apples, 273
Baked Zucchini with Mozzarella, 257
baking, 51
bananas
  Banana Honey Oatmeal, 115
  Cottage Cheese and Fruit, 118
  Fresh Fruit with Tangy Yogurt Sauce, 119
  Grown-Up Peanut Butter and Jelly, 126
  Nutty Fruit Parfait, 120
  Raspberry Banana Bread, 276
barley
  Barley Pilaf with Mushrooms, 262
  Barley-Stuffed Peppers, 240

basic foods, 8
  butter and olive oil, 9
  condiments, 9
  dairy, 8
  fruits and vegetables, 8
  legumes, 8
  nuts, 9
  proteins, 8
  starchy vegetables, 8
  stone-ground breads, 9
  whole grains, 9
Basil Broccoli with Cashews, 252
bath soap/salts, 74
beef
  chuck roast, 38
  freezing, 101
  ground recipes
    Beef and Potato Casserole, 227
    Creamy Beef Stroganoff, 230
    Easy Sloppy Joes, 226
    Enchilada Pie, 223
    Honey Mustard Glazed Meatloaf, 222
    Lasagna with Meat and Cheese, 224
  recipes
    Beef Stew, 150
    Chili-Stuffed Potato Skins, 125
    Mediterranean Veggie Pockets, 122
    Orange Spiced London Broil, 186
    Oven Barbecued Beef, 188
    Pan-Seared Skirt Steak, 190
    Quick Beef Fajitas, 191
    Red Chili, 151
    Roast Beef, 189
    Slow-Cooked Pot Roast, 187

Beef and Potato Casserole, 227
Beef Stew, 150
beets, 248
benefits
  breakfast, 107-108
  coffee shops, 91
  fast food, 91
  high-end eateries, 92
  moderately priced sit-down restaurants, 91
  once a month food prep, 47
  once a week cooking, 49
  sporting events, 91
berries
  Grown-Up Peanut Butter and Jelly, 126
  Nutty Fruit Parfait, 120
  Sweet Fruit and Noodle Pudding, 275
beverages
  coffee/tea, 10
  cutting back tips, 27
  school lunches, 88
Big Pot Theory, 37-39
  beef chuck roast, 38
  ham, 38
  turkey, 37
black beans
  Black Bean and Sweet Potato Bake, 247
  Zesty Breakfast Burritos, 113
BOGO (buy one, get one free), 78
book-specific ingredients, 68-72
Bottom-of-the-Bag Chicken, 123
breads
  Baked French Toast with Honey Walnut Syrup, 117
  Brown Sugar Ginger Shortbread, 278

Buttermilk Corn Bread, 268
  Quick Drop Biscuits, 267
  Raspberry Banana Bread, 276
  stone-ground, 9
  storing, 54
  white, 9
breakfast
  benefits, 107-108
  cooking daily, 50
  eating, 37
  recipes
    Baked Cranberry Apple Oatmeal, 116
    Baked French Toast with Honey Walnut Syrup, 117
    Baked Scotch Eggs, 114
    Banana Honey Oatmeal, 115
    Chile Egg Puff, 109
    Cottage Cheese and Fruit, 118
    Fresh Fruit with Tangy Yogurt Sauce, 119
    Just Right Cheese Omelet, 112
    Nutty Fruit Parfait, 120
    Poached Eggs on Turkey, 111
    Savory Spinach and Bacon Bake, 110
    Zesty Breakfast Burritos, 113
  steel-cut oats, 50
broccoli
  Basil Broccoli with Cashews, 252
  Broccoli with Oranges and Rhubarb, 253
Brown Sugar Ginger Shortbread, 278
Brownies with Walnuts, 282

budgets
actual expenses versus goal comparison, 32
benefits, 4, 16
business principles, 4
calculating monthly, 17
categories, 19
controlling splurges, 5
don'ts, 29-30
emotional rewards, 5
families, 30-32
features, 6
managing, 21-22
misconceptions, 6
preliminary amounts, 16-18
recording purchases, 20-21
required items, 19
required supplies, 20
subcategories, 18
tools, 22-23
business principles of budgeting, 4
butcher shops, 80
butter, 9
Buttermilk Corn Bread, 268
buy one, get one free (BOGO), 78

C

cabbage
Baked Salmon and Asian Cabbage Salad, 132
Crunch Coleslaw, 176
Fish Tacos, 218
Hot Caraway Cabbage, 258
Red Cabbage and Zucchini Skillet, 259
Seven Layer Salad, 179
Caesar Turkey with Mushrooms, 207
calculating
calories needed per day, 6
monthly budget, 17

calories needed per day calculator, 6
calories per dollar, 6
canning food, 101-102
carrots
Cheesy Vegetable Polenta, 256
Fruit-Glazed Carrots, 246
Herbed Roasted Roots, 248
Spinach and Carrot Kugel, 255
casseroles
Baked Seafood Casserole, 217
Beef and Potato Casserole, 227
Caesar Turkey with Mushrooms, 207
Creamy Beef Stroganoff, 230
Curried Chicken and Rice Casserole, 200
categories
budgets, 19
food preferences, 26
weekly ingredient list, 60
catfish, 215
cauliflower, 260
cheese
Baked Macaroni with Two Cheeses, 234
Baked South-Of-The-Border Tortillas, 130
Baked Zucchini with Mozzarella, 257
Beef and Potato Casserole, 227
Cheese Grits Casserole, 269
Cheese Wraps with Vegetables and Herbs, 129
Cheesy Vegetable Polenta, 256
Enchilada Pie, 223

Hot Spinach and Artichoke Dip, 162
Just Right Cheese Omelet, 112
Mashed Cauliflower with Cheese, 260
Nutty Fruity Lentil Loaf, 237
Pick-Your-Own Pita Pizzas, 238
Risotto with Green Peas and Parmesan, 264
Stout Potato Cheese Soup, 146
Tossed Chef's Salad, 182
Zucchini Lasagna, 241
Cheese Grits Casserole, 269
cheese shops, 80
Cheese Wraps with Vegetables and Herbs, 129
Cheesy Vegetable Polenta, 256
Chef's Choice Salad, 183
chicken
Asian Chicken Appetizers, 155
Baked Chicken with Apples and Sweet Potatoes, 198
Baked Hot Drumsticks, 154
Bottom-of-the-Bag Chicken, 123
Chicken Noodle Soup with Vegetables, 140
Chicken Tortilla Soup, 144
Chicken with Vegetables and Tarragon, 201
Creamy Chicken and Raisin Salad, 131
Curried Chicken and Rice Casserole, 200
Curried Fruit and Spinach Salad, 180
freezing, 101
Lemon Pecan Stuffed Chicken, 199

Southern Spiced Chicken, 202

Tangy Chicken and Fruit Kabobs, 203

White Chili, 152

Chicken Noodle Soup with Vegetables, 140

Chicken Tortilla Soup, 144

Chicken with Vegetables and Tarragon, 201

Chile Egg Puff, 109

chili, 151

Chili-Stuffed Potato Skins, 125

chocolate
Brownies with Walnuts, 282
Chocolate Chip Cookies, 280
Chocolate Not-Quite-Fudge Pâté, 281

Chocolate Chip Cookies, 280

Chocolate Not-Quite-Fudge Pâté, 281

choosing
budget-wise healthy foods, 66
family favorites, 36-37
grocery stores, 79-81
restaurants, 91-92

cider vinegar, 70

clams
Baked Seafood Casserole, 217
Creamy Clam Chowder, 143
Fish Stew with Potatoes and Tomatoes, 220
Paella-Style Seafood Bake, 216

cleaning supplies, 73, 76

coffee, 10

coffee breaks, 27

coffee shops
cutting back tips, 27
pros/cons, 91

comparing actual expenses versus budget, 32

computer software, 20-21

condiments, 9, 70

controlling splurges, 5

cookies
Brown Sugar Ginger Shortbread, 278
Chocolate Chip Cookies, 280
Cookies Flavored with Tea, 279

Cookies Flavored with Tea, 279

cooking
baking, 51
daily, 49-51
equipment, 72-73
herbs
fresh versus dried, 97-98
planting, 98-99
improving skills, 96-97
neighborhood co-ops, 51-52
once a month, 47-48
once a week, 48-49

Cool Dill Dip, 164

core foods, 18

corn
Buttermilk Corn Bread, 268
Enchilada Pie, 223
Fish Tacos, 218
Mexican Vegetable Salad, 173
Seven Layer Salad, 179
Southwestern Corn Chowder, 145
Southwestern Succotash, 254

costs of school lunches, 86

cottage cheese
Cheesy Vegetable Polenta, 256
Cool Dill Dip, 164
Cottage Cheese and Fruit, 118
Garbanzo and Cottage Cheese Salad with Pita Chips, 133
Lasagna with Meat and Cheese, 224
Sweet Potato Fritters with Apples, 274
Zucchini Lasagna, 241

coupons, 78-79

cranberries
Autumn Salad, 171
Baked Cranberry Apple Oatmeal, 116
Fresh Fruit with Tangy Yogurt Sauce, 119
Nutty Fruity Lentil Loaf, 237
Stuffed Turkey Burgers, 229
Tart and Nutty Green Beans, 251
Turkey and Cranberry Wrap, 128

Creamy Beef Stroganoff, 230

Creamy Chicken and Raisin Salad, 131

Creamy Clam Chowder, 143

Creamy Potato Salad, 175

Crunchy Coleslaw, 176

Crunchy Jicama Snack, 157

cucumbers, 177

Curried Chicken and Rice Casserole, 200

Curried Fruit and Spinach Salad, 180

cutting back tips, 27-29

D

daily food prep, 49-51
daily requirements, 8
dairy, 8
  cheese
    Baked Macaroni with
      Two Cheeses, 234
    Baked South-Of-The-
      Border Tortillas, 130
    Baked Zucchini with
      Mozzarella, 257
    Beef and Potato
      Casserole, 227
    Cheese Grits Casserole,
      269
    Cheese Wraps with
      Vegetables and Herbs,
      129
    Cheesy Vegetable
      Polenta, 256
    Enchilada Pie, 223
    Hot Spinach and
      Artichoke Dip, 162
    Just Right Cheese
      Omelet, 112
    Mashed Cauliflower
      with Cheese, 260
    Nutty Fruity Lentil
      Loaf, 237
    Pick-Your-Own Pita
      Pizzas, 238
    Risotto with Green Peas
      and Parmesan, 264
    Stout Potato Cheese
      Soup, 146
    Tossed Chef's Salad, 182
    Zucchini Lasagna, 241
  cottage cheese
    Cheesy Vegetable
      Polenta, 256
    Cool Dill Dip, 164
    Cottage Cheese and
      Fruit, 118

Garbanzo and Cottage
  Cheese Salad with Pita
  Chips, 133
Lasagna with Meat and
  Cheese, 224
Sweet Potato Fritters
  with Apples, 274
Zucchini Lasagna, 241
daily requirements, 8
eggs
  Baked Scotch Eggs, 114
  Cheese Grits Casserole,
    269
  Chile Egg Puff, 109
  Deviled Eggs, 159
  Egg Salad with Red
    Pepper and Walnuts,
    134
  frying, 108
  Just Right Cheese
    Omelet, 112
  Poached Eggs on
    Turkey, 111
  Tossed Chef's Salad, 182
yogurt
  Autumn Salad, 171
  Baked Cranberry Apple
    Oatmeal, 116
  Cool Dill Dip, 164
  Creamy Potato Salad,
    175
  Fresh Fruit with Tangy
    Yogurt Sauce, 119
  Nutty Fruit Parfait, 120
desserts
  Baked Stuffed Apples, 273
  baking, 51
  Brown Sugar Ginger
    Shortbread, 278
  Brownies with Walnuts,
    282
  Chocolate Chip Cookies,
    280
  Chocolate Not-Quite-
    Fudge Pâté, 281

Cookies Flavored with Tea,
  279
ice-cream sundaes, 282
Pear Cobbler, 272
Raspberry Banana Bread,
  276
Slow-Cooked Pudding and
  Fruit Cake, 277
Sweet Fruit and Noodle
  Pudding, 275
Sweet Potato Fritters with
  Apples, 274
Deviled Eggs, 159
dips
  Cool Dill Dip, 164
  Guacamole, 158
  Hot Spinach and Artichoke
    Dip, 162
  Hummus, 156
  Quick Fruit Salsa, 165
  Warm Onion and
    Mushroom Dip, 163
disadvantages
  coffee shops, 91
  fast food, 91
  high-end eateries, 92
  moderately priced sit-down
    restaurants, 91
  neighborhood cooking
    co-ops, 52
  once a month cooking, 48
  sporting events, 91
discount store grocery stores,
  80
disposable plastic food
  containers, 73
dressing recipe, 168
dried herbs, 97-98
drying food, 102

E

Easy Sloppy Joes, 226
eating in groups, 29

eating out
   entertaining, 93
   restaurants
      choosing, 91-92
      money-saving tips, 92-93
   school lunches, 86-88
      costs, 86
      packing, 87-88
   work lunches, 89-90
eating styles, 26
   categories, 26
   cutting back tips, 27-29
   don'ts, 29-30
eggs
   Baked Scotch Eggs, 114
   Cheese Grits Casserole, 269
   Chile Egg Puff, 109
   Deviled Eggs, 159
   Egg Salad with Red Pepper and Walnuts, 134
   frying, 108
   Just Right Cheese Omelet, 112
   Poached Eggs on Turkey, 111
   Tossed Chef's Salad, 182
emotions
   eating, 29
   rewards, 5
Enchilada Pie, 223
entertaining, 93
equipment
   canning, 102
   cooking, 72-73
   food storage, 73
essential meals out
   school lunches, 86-88
      costs, 86
      packing, 87-88
   work lunches, 89-90
ethnic markets, 80
event eating, 28

expenses
   actual versus budget
      comparison, 32
   tracking, 20-21
expired food, 54

F

fabric softeners, 74
families
   budgeting, 30-32
      conversation, 31
      rewards, 32
   favorites, 36-37
farmers' markets, 80
fast food
   cutting back, 28
   eating style, 26
   pros/cons, 91
fats, 9
filling plates, 10-11
finding
   coupons, 79
   sales, 77-78
fish. *See* seafood
Fish Baked in Bags, 219
Fish Stew with Potatoes and Tomatoes, 220
Fish Tacos, 218
Five Bean, Tofu, and Vegetable Bake, 243
food. *See also* specific ingredients
   add-ons, 12
   basic
      butter/olive oil, 9
      condiments, 9
      dairy, 8
      fruits and vegetables, 8
      nuts, 9
      proteins, 8
      starchy vegetables, 8
      stone-ground bread, 9
      whole grains, 9

budget-wise, high nutrition, 66
   money wasters, 11-12
   nutrient-dense, 26
   preferences, 26
   preserving
      canning, 101-102
      drying, 102
      freezers, 100-101
   soy, 8
   staples, 66-68
   storage
      canning, 101-102
      containers, 73
      drying, 102
      refrigerators/freezers, 50, 100-101
   waste reduction
      expired food, 54
      leftovers, 53
      packaging, 53
forms, 64
freezing foods, 50, 100-101
Fresh Fruit with Tangy Yogurt Sauce, 119
fresh herbs, 97-98
fruit, 8
   daily requirements, 8
   freezing, 101
   growing, 99-100
   organic, 9
   sell-by dates, 78
   recipes
      Apricot Glazed Turkey Thighs, 208
      Autumn Salad, 171
      Baked Chicken with Apples and Sweet Potatoes, 198
      Baked Cranberry Apple Oatmeal, 116
      Baked Stuffed Apples, 273
      Banana Honey Oatmeal, 115

Broccoli with Oranges and Rhubarb, 253
Cottage Cheese and Fruit, 118
Creamy Chicken and Raisin Salad, 131
Crunchy Coleslaw, 176
Curried Fruit and Spinach Salad, 180
Fresh Fruit with Tangy Yogurt Sauce, 119
Grown-Up Peanut Butter and Jelly, 126
Mint and Melon Salad, 181
Nutty Brown Rice Burgers, 235
Nutty Fruit Parfait, 120
Nutty Fruity Lentil Loaf, 237
Orange Spiced London Broil, 186
Pear Cobbler, 272
Quick Fruit Salsa, 165
Raspberry Banana Bread, 276
Slow-Cooked Onions with Apples and Sour Cream, 250
Slow-Cooked Pudding and Fruit Cake, 277
Stuffed Turkey Burgers, 229
Summer Salad, 170
Sweet Fruit and Noodle Pudding, 275
Sweet Potato Fritters with Apples, 274
Tangy Chicken and Fruit Kabobs, 203
Tart and Nutty Green Beans, 251
Turkey and Cranberry Wrap, 128

Fruit-Glazed Carrots, 246
frying eggs, 108
funny colors of foods, 12

G

Garbanzo and Cottage Cheese Salad with Pita Chips, 133
gardens, 99-100
glass containers with plastic lids, 73
gourmet eating style, 26
grains
    Baked Cranberry Apple Oatmeal, 116
    Banana Honey Oatmeal, 115
    Barley Pilaf with Mushrooms, 262
    Bottom-of-the-Bag Chicken, 123
    Buttermilk Corn Bread, 268
    Curried Chicken and Rice Casserole, 200
    Grandma's Rice and Beans with Spinach, 266
    Gumbo with Shrimp and Sausage, 211
    Leftover Turkey and Vegetable Stir-Fry, 206
    Nutty Brown Rice Burgers, 235
    Paella-Style Seafood Bake, 216
    Quick Drop Biscuits, 267
    Risotto with Green Peas and Parmesan, 264
    Spicy Turkey and Vegetable Burritos, 228
    Vegetable and Tofu Stir-Fry, 236
Grandma's Rice and Beans with Spinach, 266

Greek Salad, 174
green beans, 251
grits, 269
grocery shopping
    checking home first, 76
    choosing grocery stores, 79-81
    coupons, 78-79
    in-store tactics, 82-83
    once a month cooking, 48
    once a week cooking, 49
    organic produce, 9
    prepared foods, 84
    purchasing guidelines, 83-84
    sales, 76
        finding, 77-78
        in-store unadvertised specials, 78
        pantry staples, 77
        saving versus wasting money, 76-77
    weekly trip, 81-82
grocery stores, 79-81
ground meat dishes
    Beef and Potato Casserole, 227
    Creamy Beef Stroganoff, 230
    Easy Sloppy Joes, 226
    Enchilada Pie, 223
    Honey Mustard Glazed Meatloaf, 222
    Lasagna with Meat and Cheese, 224
    Spicy Turkey and Vegetable Burritos, 228
    Stuffed Turkey Burgers, 229
    Turkey Goulash, 231
    Turkey Meatballs with Spaghetti Marinara, 225

group eating, 29
growing
    herbs, 98-99
    vegetables, 99-100
Grown-Up Peanut Butter and
    Jelly, 126
Guacamole, 158
Gumbo with Shrimp and
    Sausage, 211

H

habitual purchases, 18
halibut, 214
ham
    Ham and Noodle
      Casserole, 194
    Ham and White Bean
      Soup, 141
    Hawaiian Ham Rollups,
      135
    meal ideas, 38
    Mustard-Glazed Ham, 193
    Split Pea Soup, 147
    Tossed Chef's Salad, 182
Hawaiian Ham Rollups, 135
health food grocers, 80
Herb Roasted Turkey, 205
Herbed Roasted Roots, 248
Herbed Salmon Cakes, 212
herbs
    fresh versus dried, 97-98
    planting, 98-99
high-end eateries, 92
high-fructose corn syrup, 11
high-nutrition foods, 66
Honey Mustard Glazed
    Meatloaf, 222
Hot Caraway Cabbage, 258
Hot Spinach and Artichoke
    Dip, 162
household supplies, 73-74
Hummus, 156

I

ice-cream sundaes, 282
improving cooking skills,
    96-97
in-store shopping tactics,
    82-83
in-store unadvertised specials,
    78
independent grocers, 80
ingredient money wasters,
    11-12
Internet grocery stores, 81

J

jerky, 102
jicama
    Crunchy Coleslaw, 176
    snack, 157
junk foods, 18
Just Right Cheese Omelet,
    112

K

kids' school lunches
    costs, 86
    packing, 87-88
kitchen eating style, 26

L

Lasagna with Meat and
    Cheese, 224
laundry supplies, 74
Leftover Turkey and
    Vegetable Stir-Fry, 206
leftovers, 39, 53
legumes, 8
    Baked Beans, 265
    Baked South-Of-The-
      Border Tortillas, 130

Black Bean and Sweet
    Potato Bake, 247
Chicken Tortilla Soup, 144
Five Bean, Tofu, and
    Vegetable Bake, 243
Garbanzo and Cottage
    Cheese Salad with Pita
    Chips, 133
Grandma's Rice and Beans
    with Spinach, 266
Ham and White Bean
    Soup, 141
Hummus, 156
Mediterranean Veggie
    Pockets, 122
Mexican Vegetable Salad,
    173
Nutty Brown Rice Burgers,
    235
Red Chili, 151
Southwestern Succotash,
    254
Spicy Turkey and Vegetable
    Burritos, 228
Tomato Soup, 148
Turkey and White Bean
    Skillet, 204
Vegetarian Barbecue Bake,
    239
Warm or Cold Bean Salad,
    178
White Chili, 152
Winter Salad, 172
Zesty Breakfast Burritos,
    113
Lemon Halibut Kebabs, 214
Lemon Pecan Stuffed
    Chicken, 199
lentils
    Lentil Soup, 142
    Nutty Fruity Lentil Loaf,
    237
lunches
    money-saving tips, 50

recipes
Baked Salmon and Asian Cabbage Salad, 132
Baked South-Of-The-Border Tortillas, 130
Bottom-of-the-Bag Chicken, 123
Cheese Wraps with Vegetables and Herbs, 129
Chili-Stuffed Potato Skins, 125
Creamy Chicken and Raisin Salad, 131
Egg Salad with Red Pepper and Walnuts, 134
Garbanzo and Cottage Cheese Salad with Pita Chips, 133
Grown-Up Peanut Butter and Jelly, 126
Hawaiian Ham Rollups, 135
Mediterranean Veggie Pockets, 122
Rarebit and Turkey Sandwiches, 127
Tuna Salad with Vegetables, 124
Turkey and Cranberry Wrap, 128
school
costs, 86
packing, 87-88
work, 27, 89-90
luxury foods, 19

M

main dishes
beef
Orange Spiced London Broil, 186
Oven Barbecued Beef, 188
Pan-Seared Skirt Steak, 190
Quick Beef Fajitas, 191
Roast Beef, 189
Slow-Cooked Pot Roast, 187
chicken
Baked Chicken with Apples and Sweet Potatoes, 198
Chicken with Vegetables and Tarragon, 201
Curried Chicken and Rice Casserole, 200
Lemon Pecan Stuffed Chicken, 199
Southern Spiced Chicken, 202
Tangy Chicken and Fruit Kabobs, 203
ground meat
Beef and Potato Casserole, 227
Creamy Beef Stroganoff, 230
Easy Sloppy Joes, 226
Enchilada Pie, 223
Honey Mustard Glazed Meatloaf, 222
Lasagna with Meat and Cheese, 224
Spicy Turkey and Vegetable Burritos, 228
Stuffed Turkey Burgers, 229
Turkey Goulash, 231
Turkey Meatballs with Spaghetti Marinara, 225
pork
Baked Italian Sausage and Peppers with Spaghetti, 195
Ham and Noodle Casserole, 194
Mustard-Glazed Ham, 193
Pork Chops with Rosemary, 192
seafood
Baked Seafood Casserole, 217
Fish Baked in Bags, 219
Fish Stew with Potatoes and Tomatoes, 220
Fish Tacos, 218
Gumbo with Shrimp and Sausage, 211
Herbed Salmon Cakes, 212
Lemon Halibut Kebabs, 214
Oven-Sautéed Catfish, 215
Paella-Style Seafood Bake, 216
Tuna with Olives and Pasta, 213
turkey
Apricot Glazed Turkey Thighs, 208
Caesar Turkey with Mushrooms, 207
Herb Roasted Turkey, 205
Leftover Turkey and Vegetable Stir-Fry, 206
Turkey and White Bean Skillet, 204
vegetarian
Baked Macaroni with Two Cheeses, 234
Barley-Stuffed Peppers, 240
Five Bean, Tofu, and Vegetable Bake, 243
Mushroom Ragout on Spaghetti Squash, 242
Nutty Brown Rice Burgers, 235

Nutty Fruity Lentil
Loaf, 237
Pick-Your-Own Pita
Pizzas, 238
Vegetable and Tofu Stir-
Fry, 236
Vegetarian Barbecue
Bake, 239
Zucchini Lasagna, 241
major grocery store chains, 79
managing budgets, 21-22
Mashed Cauliflower with
Cheese, 260
Mason Jars, 102
meals
entertaining, 93
essential meals out
school lunches, 86-88
work lunches, 89-90
ideas, 38
planning, 10-11, 36
avoiding boredom, 44
Big Pot Theory, 37-39
choosing family
favorites, 36-37
creating, 39
samples, 39
worksheets, 36
preparing
daily, 49-51
neighborhood cooking
co-ops, 51-52
once a month, 47-48
once a week, 48-49
restaurants
choosing, 91-92
money-saving tips, 92-93
splitting at restaurants, 92
meatballs, 225
Mediterranean Veggie
Pockets, 122
menu planning, 36
avoiding boredom, 44
Big Pot Theory, 37-39

choosing family favorites,
36-37
creating, 39
Plate Method, 10-11
samples, 39
worksheets, 36
Mexican Vegetable Salad, 173
Mint and Melon Salad, 181
Miso Soup, 149
moderately priced sit-down
restaurants, 91
money waster ingredients,
11-12
money-saving tips, 27-29
household supplies, 73-74
lunches, 50
restaurants, 92-93
monthly budget calculation,
17
monthly food prep, 47-48
benefits, 47
disadvantages, 48
shopping, 48
movie theaters, 28
multiple meals from one meat,
37-39
beef chuck roast, 38
ham, 38
turkey, 37
Mushroom Ragout on
Spaghetti Squash, 242
mushrooms
Baked Seafood Casserole,
217
Barley Pilaf with
Mushrooms, 262
Caesar Turkey with
Mushrooms, 207
Creamy Beef Stroganoff,
230
Mushroom Ragout on
Spaghetti Squash, 242
Pick-Your-Own Pita Pizzas,
238

Risotto with Green Peas
and Parmesan, 264
Tangy Chicken and Fruit
Kabobs, 203
Turkey and White Bean
Skillet, 204
Warm Onion and
Mushroom Dip, 163
Mustard-Glazed Ham, 193
mystery ingredients, 12

N

neighborhood cooking co-ops,
51-52
Nine Vegetable Soup, 139
notebooks, 20
nutrient-dense foods, 26
nuts, 9
Autumn Salad, 171
Baked French Toast with
Honey Walnut Syrup, 117
Baked Stuffed Apples, 273
Basil Broccoli with
Cashews, 252
Chocolate Not-Quite-
Fudge Pâté, 281
Egg Salad with Red Pepper
and Walnuts, 134
Fresh Fruit with Tangy
Yogurt Sauce, 119
Herbed Salmon Cakes, 212
Lemon Pecan Stuffed
Chicken, 199
Nutty Brown Rice Burgers,
235
Nutty Fruit Parfait, 120
Nutty Fruity Lentil Loaf,
237
Tart and Nutty Green
Beans, 251
Turkey and Cranberry
Wrap, 128

O

oatmeal, 50
Baked Cranberry Apple
Oatmeal, 116
Banana Honey Oatmeal,
115
olive oil, 9
olives, 213
once a month food prep,
47-48
benefits, 47
disadvantages, 48
shopping, 48
once a week food prep, 48-49
onions, 250
online ordering for local
grocery stores, 80
oranges
Broccoli with Oranges and
Rhubarb, 253
Mint and Melon Salad, 181
Orange Spiced London
Broil, 186
Oven Barbecued Beef, 188
organic produce, 9
Oven Barbecued Beef, 188
Oven-Baked Potato Chips,
160
Oven-Sautéed Catfish, 215

P

packing lunches
school, 87-88
work, 90
Paella-Style Seafood Bake,
216
Pan-Seared Skirt Steak, 190
pantry staples, 66
book ingredients, 68-72
sale shopping, 77
spices, 67-68

pasta
Baked Italian Sausage and
Peppers with Spaghetti,
195
Baked Macaroni with Two
Cheeses, 234
Caesar Turkey with
Mushrooms, 207
Chicken Noodle Soup with
Vegetables, 140
Creamy Beef Stroganoff,
230
Ham and Noodle
Casserole, 194
Lasagna with Meat and
Cheese, 224
Spinach and Carrot Kugel,
255
Sweet Fruit and Noodle
Pudding, 275
Tuna with Olives and Pasta,
213
Turkey Goulash, 231
Turkey Meatballs with
Spaghetti Marinara, 225
Zucchini Lasagna, 241
peaches, 275
peanut butter
Cottage Cheese and Fruit,
118
Grown-Up Peanut Butter
and Jelly, 126
Pear Cobbler, 272
peas, 264
Pick-Your-Own Pita Pizzas,
238
pineapple
Crunchy Coleslaw, 176
Fish Baked in Bags, 219
Hawaiian Ham Rollups,
135
Leftover Turkey and
Vegetable Stir-Fry, 206

planning menus, 36
avoiding boredom, 44
Big Pot Theory, 37-39
choosing family favorites,
36-37
creating, 39
Plate Method, 10-11
samples, 39
worksheets, 36
planting, 99-100
plastic containers with lids, 73
plastic storage bags, 73
Plate Method, 10-11
Poached Eggs on Turkey, 111
pork
bacon
Savory Spinach and
Bacon Bake, 110
Tossed Chef's Salad, 182
Baked Italian Sausage and
Peppers with Spaghetti,
195
freezing, 101
ham
Ham and Noodle
Casserole, 194
Ham and White Bean
Soup, 141
Hawaiian Ham Rollups,
135
meal ideas, 38
Mustard-Glazed Ham,
193
Split Pea Soup, 147
Pork Chops with Rosemary,
192
potatoes
Baked Chicken with Apples
and Sweet Potatoes, 198
Beef and Potato Casserole,
227
Black Bean and Sweet
Potato Bake, 247
Chicken with Vegetables
and Tarragon, 201

Chili-Stuffed Potato Skins, 125
Creamy Potato Salad, 175
Fish Stew with Potatoes and Tomatoes, 220
Herb Roasted Turkey, 205
Herbed Roasted Roots, 248
Oven-Baked Potato Chips, 160
Stout Potato Cheese Soup, 146
Sweet Potato Fritters with Apples, 274
Sweet Potato Oven Fries, 263
Vegetarian Barbecue Bake, 239
poultry
  chicken
    Asian Chicken Appetizers, 155
    Baked Chicken with Apples and Sweet Potatoes, 198
    Baked Hot Drumsticks, 154
    Bottom-of-the-Bag Chicken, 123
    Chicken Noodle Soup with Vegetables, 140
    Chicken Tortilla Soup, 144
    Chicken with Vegetables and Tarragon, 201
    Creamy Chicken and Raisin Salad, 131
    Curried Chicken and Rice Casserole, 200
    Curried Fruit and Spinach Salad, 180
    Lemon Pecan Stuffed Chicken, 199
    Southern Spiced Chicken, 202

Tangy Chicken and Fruit Kabobs, 203
White Chili, 152
  freezing, 101
  turkey
    Apricot Glazed Turkey Thighs, 208
    Baked Scotch Eggs, 114
    Caesar Turkey with Mushrooms, 207
    Enchilada Pie, 223
    Gumbo with Shrimp and Sausage, 211
    Herb Roasted Turkey, 205
    Leftover Turkey and Vegetable Stir-Fry, 206
    meal ideas, 38
    Poached Eggs on Turkey, 111
    Rarebit and Turkey Sandwich, 127
    slow cooking, 37
    Spicy Turkey and Vegetable Burritos, 228
    Stuffed Turkey Burgers, 229
    Turkey and Cranberry Wrap, 128
    Turkey and White Bean Skillet, 204
    Turkey Goulash, 231
    Turkey Meatballs with Spaghetti Marinara, 225
    White Chili, 152
preferences, 26
preliminary budget amounts, 16-18
prepared foods, 84
preparing meals
  daily, 49-51
  neighborhood cooking co-ops, 51-52

once a month, 47-48
  benefits, 47
  disadvantages, 48
  shopping, 48
once a week, 48-49
preserving food
  canning, 101-102
  drying, 102
  freezers, 100-101
proteins, 8
purchasing
  guidelines, 83-84
  prepared foods, 84

Q

Quick Beef Fajitas, 191
Quick Drop Biscuits, 267
Quick Fruit Salsa, 165
Quicken, 21

R

raisins, 131
Rarebit and Turkey Sandwich, 127
Raspberry Banana Bread, 276
recording purchases, 20-21
Red Cabbage and Zucchini Skillet, 259
Red Chili, 151
refrigerating foods, 50, 100-101
refrigerator staples, 66
  book ingredients, 68-72
  spices, 67-68
requirements
  budgets, 19-20
  cooking equipment, 72-73
  neighborhood cooking co-ops, 52
restaurants
  budget category, 18
  choosing, 91-92

money-saving tips, 92-93
splitting meals, 92
rewards
emotional, 5
family budgets, 32
rhubarb, 253
rice
Curried Chicken and Rice Casserole, 200
Grandma's Rice and Beans with Spinach, 266
Gumbo with Shrimp and Sausage, 211
Leftover Turkey and Vegetable Stir-Fry, 206
Nutty Brown Rice Burgers, 235
Paella-Style Seafood Bake, 216
Risotto with Green Peas and Parmesan, 264
Spicy Turkey and Vegetable Burritos, 228
Vegetable and Tofu Stir-Fry, 236
Risotto with Green Peas and Parmesan, 264
roast
Oven Barbecued Beef, 188
Roast Beef, 189
slow cooking, 38
Slow-Cooked Pot Roast, 187
roast beef
Mediterranean Veggie Pockets, 122
Roast Beef, 189
roast meal ideas, 38
Rosemary Spaghetti Squash, 249
Rotel tomatoes and chiles, 158

S

salads
Autumn Salad, 171
Baked Salmon and Asian Cabbage Salad, 132
Chef's Choice Salad, 183
Creamy Chicken and Raisin Salad, 131
Creamy Potato Salad, 175
Crunchy Coleslaw, 176
Curried Fruit and Spinach Salad, 180
dressing, 168
Egg Salad with Red Pepper and Walnuts, 134
Garbanzo and Cottage Cheese Salad with Pita Chips, 133
Greek Salad, 174
Mexican Vegetable Salad, 173
Mint and Melon Salad, 181
Seven Layer Salad, 179
Sour Cream Cucumber Salad, 177
Spring Salad, 169
Summer Salad, 170
Tossed Chef's Salad, 182
Warm or Cold Bean Salad, 178
Winter Salad, 172
sales, 76
finding, 77-78
in-store unadvertised specials, 78
saving versus wasting money, 76-77
salmon
Baked Salmon and Asian Cabbage Salad, 132
Herbed Salmon Cakes, 212
sample menus, 39

sandwiches
Baked South-Of-The-Border Tortillas, 130
Easy Sloppy Joes, 226
Grown-Up Peanut Butter and Jelly, 126
Nutty Brown Rice Burgers, 235
Rarebit and Turkey Sandwich, 127
Stuffed Turkey Burgers, 229
Tuna Salad with Vegetables, 124
saving money
cutting back tips, 27-29
restaurants, 92-93
sales, 76-77
Savory Spinach and Bacon Bake, 110
school lunches, 86-88
costs, 86
packing, 87-88
School Nutrition Association, 86
seafood
Baked Salmon and Asian Cabbage Salad, 132
Baked Seafood Casserole, 217
Creamy Clam Chowder, 143
Fish Baked in Bags, 219
Fish Stew with Potatoes and Tomatoes, 220
Fish Tacos, 218
Gumbo with Shrimp and Sausage, 211
Herbed Salmon Cakes, 212
Lemon Halibut Kebabs, 214
Oven-Sautéed Catfish, 215
Paella-Style Seafood Bake, 216

Tuna Salad with Vegetables, 124
Tuna with Olives and Pasta, 213
sell-by dates, 78
setting budget amounts, 16-18
Seven Layer Salad, 179
shopping
  checking home first, 76
  choosing grocery stores, 79-81
  coupons, 78-79
  in-store tactics, 82-83
  once a month cooking, 48
  once a week cooking, 49
  organic produce, 9
  prepared foods, 84
  purchasing guidelines, 83-84
  sales, 76
    finding, 77-78
    in-store unadvertised specials, 78
    pantry staples, 77
    saving versus wasting money, 76-77
  weekly trip, 81-82
shopping lists
  budget-wise, healthy foods, 66
  forms, 64
  nonfood items, 64
  staples, 66
    book ingredients, 68-72
    spices, 67-68
  transferring ingredients, 64
  weekly ingredients, 60
    breakfast example, 60
    categories, 60
    daily example, 62
    dinner example, 61
    snack example, 62
    totaling ingredients, 63

shrimp
  Gumbo with Shrimp and Sausage, 211
  Paella-Style Seafood Bake, 216
side dishes
  Baked Beans, 265
  Baked Zucchini with Mozzarella, 257
  Barley Pilaf with Mushrooms, 262
  Basil Broccoli with Cashews, 252
  Black Bean and Sweet Potato Bake, 247
  Broccoli with Oranges and Rhubarb, 253
  Buttermilk Corn Bread, 268
  Cheese Grits Casserole, 269
  Cheesy Vegetable Polenta, 256
  Fruit-Glazed Carrots, 246
  Grandma's Rice and Beans with Spinach, 266
  Herbed Roasted Roots, 248
  Hot Caraway Cabbage, 258
  Mashed Cauliflower with Cheese, 260
  Quick Drop Biscuits, 267
  Red Cabbage and Zucchini Skillet, 259
  Risotto with Green Peas and Parmesan, 264
  Rosemary Spaghetti Squash, 249
  Slow-Cooked Onions with Apples and Sour Cream, 250
  Southwestern Succotash, 254

  Spinach and Carrot Kugel, 255
  Sweet Potato Oven Fries, 263
  Tart and Nutty Green Beans, 251
slow cookers
  beef chuck roast, 38
  turkey, 37
Slow-Cooked Onions with Apples and Sour Cream, 250
Slow-Cooked Pot Roast, 187
Slow-Cooked Pudding and Fruit Cake, 277
snacks
  after-school, 28
  Asian Chicken Appetizers, 155
  Avocado Kraut Cups, 161
  Baked Hot Drumsticks, 154
  Cool Dill Dip, 164
  Crunchy Jicama Snack, 157
  Deviled Eggs, 159
  Guacamole, 158
  Hot Spinach and Artichoke Dip, 162
  Hummus, 156
  Oven-Baked Potato Chips, 160
  Quick Fruit Salsa, 165
  Warm Onion and Mushroom Dip, 163
social eating, 28-29
sodas, 27
soups. *See also* stews
  Chicken Noodle Soup with Vegetables, 140
  Chicken Tortilla Soup, 144
  Creamy Clam Chowder, 143
  Ham and White Bean Soup, 141
  Lentil Soup, 142

Miso Soup, 149
Nine Vegetable Soup, 139
Red Chili, 151
Southwestern Corn
    Chowder, 145
Split Pea Soup, 147
Stout Potato Cheese Soup,
    146
Tomato Soup, 148
White Chili, 152
Sour Cream Cucumber Salad,
    177
Southern Spiced Chicken, 202
Southwestern Corn Chowder,
    145
Southwestern Succotash, 254
soy products, 8
spaghetti squash
    Mushroom Ragout on
        Spaghetti Squash, 242
    Rosemary Spaghetti
        Squash, 249
specialty food shops, 80
spices
    fresh versus dried, 97-98
    planting, 98-99
Spicy Turkey and Vegetable
    Burritos, 228
spinach
    Cheese Wraps with
        Vegetables and Herbs,
        129
    Curried Fruit and Spinach
        Salad, 180
    Grandma's Rice and Beans
        with Spinach, 266
    Gumbo with Shrimp and
        Sausage, 211
    Honey Mustard Glazed
        Meatloaf, 222
    Hot Spinach and Artichoke
        Dip, 162
    Lasagna with Meat and
        Cheese, 224

Savory Spinach and Bacon
    Bake, 110
Spinach and Carrot Kugel,
    255
Summer Salad, 170
Turkey and Cranberry
    Wrap, 128
Turkey and White Bean
    Skillet, 204
Warm or Cold Bean Salad,
    178
Split Pea Soup, 147
splitting meals in restaurants,
    92
splurges, 5
sporting events, 91
Spring Salad, 169
staple foods, 66
    book ingredients, 68-72
    sale shopping, 77
    spices, 67-68
starchy vegetables, 8
steak, 190
steel-cut oats, 50
    Baked Cranberry Apple
        Oatmeal, 116
    Banana Honey Oatmeal,
        115
stevia, 12
stews. See also soups
    Beef Stew, 150
    Fish Stew with Potatoes
        and Tomatoes, 220
stone-ground breads, 9
storing food
    bread, 54
    brownies, 282
    canning, 101-102
    containers, 73
    drying, 102
    refrigerators/freezers, 50,
        100-101
Stout Potato Cheese Soup,
    146
Stuffed Turkey Burgers, 229

styles. See eating styles
Summer Salad, 170
supplies
    budgets, 19-20
    canning, 102
    cooking equipment, 72-73
    food storage, 73
    household, 73-74
    packing lunches, 87
Sweet Fruit and Noodle
    Pudding, 275
Sweet Potato Fritters with
    Apples, 274
Sweet Potato Oven Fries, 263
sweets
    Baked Stuffed Apples, 273
    baking, 51
    Brown Sugar Ginger
        Shortbread, 278
    Brownies with Walnuts,
        282
    Chocolate Chip Cookies,
        280
    Chocolate Not-Quite-
        Fudge Pâté, 281
    Cookies Flavored with Tea,
        279
    ice-cream sundaes, 282
    Pear Cobbler, 272
    Raspberry Banana Bread,
        276
    Slow-Cooked Pudding and
        Fruit Cake, 277
    Sweet Fruit and Noodle
        Pudding, 275
    Sweet Potato Fritters with
        Apples, 274

T

takeout, 18
    cutting back, 28
    eating style, 26
    pros/cons, 91

Tangy Chicken and Fruit Kabobs, 203
taste boredom, 44
tea, 10
tofu
 Five Bean, Tofu, and Vegetable Bake, 243
 Miso Soup, 149
 Vegetable and Tofu Stir-Fry, 236
tomatoes
 Baked Beans, 265
 Baked Italian Sausage and Peppers with Spaghetti, 195
 Baked Seafood Casserole, 217
 Baked South-Of-The-Border Tortillas, 130
 Barley-Stuffed Peppers, 240
 Cheesy Vegetable Polenta, 256
 Chicken Tortilla Soup, 144
 Enchilada Pie, 223
 Fish Stew with Potatoes and Tomatoes, 220
 Five Bean, Tofu, and Vegetable Bake, 243
 Gumbo with Shrimp and Sausage, 211
 Honey Mustard Glazed Meatloaf, 222
 Mediterranean Veggie Pockets, 122
 Nine Vegetable Soup, 139
 Paella-Style Seafood Bake, 216
 Pork Chops with Rosemary, 192
 Red Chili, 151
 Slow-Cooked Pot Roast, 187
 Southwestern Succotash, 254

Tangy Chicken and Fruit Kabobs, 203
Tomato Soup, 148
Vegetarian Barbecue Bake, 239
Tossed Chef's Salad, 182
tuna
 Tuna Salad with Vegetables, 124
 Tuna with Olives and Pasta, 213
turkey
 Apricot Glazed Turkey Thighs, 208
 Baked Scotch Eggs, 114
 Caesar Turkey with Mushrooms, 207
 Enchilada Pie, 223
 freezing, 101
 Gumbo with Shrimp and Sausage, 211
 Herb Roasted Turkey, 205
 Leftover Turkey and Vegetable Stir-Fry, 206
 meal ideas, 38
 Poached Eggs on Turkey, 111
 Rarebit and Turkey Sandwich, 127
 slow cooking, 37
 Spicy Turkey and Vegetable Burritos, 228
 Stuffed Turkey Burgers, 229
 Turkey and Cranberry Wrap, 128
 Turkey and White Bean Skillet, 204
 Turkey Goulash, 231
 Turkey Meatballs with Spaghetti Marinara, 225
 White Chili, 152
TV eating, 28

U–V

Vegetable and Tofu Stir-Fry, 236
vegetables, 8
 daily requirements, 8
 freezing, 100
 growing, 99-100
 organic, 9
 recipes
  Autumn Salad, 171
  Beef Stew, 150
  Cheese Wraps with Vegetables and Herbs, 129
  Chef's Choice Salad, 183
  Chicken Noodle Soup with Vegetables, 140
  Chicken Tortilla Soup, 144
  Chicken with Vegetables and Tarragon, 201
  Chili-Stuffed Potato Skins, 125
  Creamy Potato Salad, 175
  Crunchy Coleslaw, 176
  Crunchy Jicama Snack, 157
  Greek Salad, 174
  Herb Roasted Turkey, 205
  Leftover Turkey and Vegetable Stir-Fry, 206
  Lentil Soup, 142
  Mediterranean Veggie Pockets, 122
  Mexican Vegetable Salad, 173
  Miso Soup, 149
  Nine Vegetable Soup, 139
  Red Chili, 151

Savory Spinach and Bacon Bake, 110

Seven Layer Salad, 179

Slow-Cooked Pot Roast, 187

Sour Cream Cucumber Salad, 177

Southwestern Corn Chowder, 145

Spicy Turkey and Vegetable Burritos, 228

Split Pea Soup, 147

Spring Salad, 169

Stout Potato Cheese Soup, 146

Summer Salad, 170

Tomato Soup, 148

Tossed Chef's Salad, 182

Tuna Salad with Vegetables, 124

Warm Onion and Mushroom Dip, 163

White Chili, 152

Winter Salad, 172

Zesty Breakfast Burritos, 113

sell-by dates, 78

side dishes

Baked Zucchini with Mozzarella, 257

Basil Broccoli with Cashews, 252

Black Bean and Sweet Potato Bake, 247

Broccoli with Oranges and Rhubarb, 253

Cheesy Vegetable Polenta, 256

Fruit-Glazed Carrots, 246

Herbed Roasted Roots, 248

Hot Caraway Cabbage, 258

Mashed Cauliflower with Cheese, 260

Red Cabbage and Zucchini Skillet, 259

Rosemary Spaghetti Squash, 249

Slow-Cooked Onions with Apples and Sour Cream, 250

Southwestern Succotash, 254

Spinach and Carrot Kugel, 255

Tart and Nutty Green Beans, 251

starch, 8

vegetarian recipes

main dishes

Baked Macaroni with Two Cheeses, 234

Barley-Stuffed Peppers, 240

Five Bean, Tofu, and Vegetable Bake, 243

Mushroom Ragout on Spaghetti Squash, 242

Nutty Brown Rice Burgers, 235

Nutty Fruity Lentil Loaf, 237

Pick-Your-Own Pita Pizzas, 238

Vegetable and Tofu Stir-Fry, 236

Vegetarian Barbecue Bake, 239

Zucchini Lasagna, 241

side dishes

Baked Zucchini with Mozzarella, 257

Basil Broccoli with Cashews, 252

Black Bean and Sweet Potato Bake, 247

Broccoli with Oranges and Rhubarb, 253

Cheesy Vegetable Polenta, 256

Fruit-Glazed Carrots, 246

Herbed Roasted Roots, 248

Hot Caraway Cabbage, 258

Mashed Cauliflower with Cheese, 260

Red Cabbage and Zucchini Skillet, 259

Rosemary Spaghetti Squash, 249

Slow-Cooked Onions with Apples and Sour Cream, 250

Southwestern Succotash, 254

Spinach and Carrot Kugel, 255

Tart and Nutty Green Beans, 251

vinegar, 70, 76

W

warehouse grocery stores, 80

Warm Onion and Mushroom Dip, 163

Warm or Cold Bean Salad, 178

waste reduction

expired food, 54

leftovers, 53

packaging, 53

wasting money, 76-77

websites

calories needed per day calculator, 6

freezing vegetables, 101

School Nutrition
   Association, 86
weekly food prep, 48-49
weekly ingredient lists, 60
   breakfast example, 60
   categories, 60
   daily example, 62
   dinner example, 61
   snack example, 62
   totaling ingredients, 63
weekly menu planning, 36
   avoiding boredom, 44
   Big Pot Theory, 37-39
      beef chuck roast, 38
      ham, 38
      turkey, 37
   choosing family favorites,
      36-37
   creating, 39
   samples, 39
   worksheets, 36
weekly shopping trip, 81-82
white breads, 9
White Chili, 152
white vinegar, 76
whole grains, 9
Winter Salad, 172
work lunches, 27, 89-90
worksheets, 36
wraps
   Baked South-Of-The-
      Border Tortillas, 130
   Cheese Wraps with
      Vegetables and Herbs,
      129
   Hawaiian Ham Rollups,
      135
   Turkey and Cranberry
      Wrap, 128
writing shopping lists
   budget-wise healthy foods,
      66
   forms, 64
   nonfood items, 64

staples, 66
   book ingredients, 68-72
   sale shopping, 77
   spices, 67-68
transferring ingredients, 64
weekly ingredients, 60
   breakfast example, 60
   categories, 60
   daily example, 62
   dinner example, 61
   snack example, 62
   totaling ingredients, 63

X–Y

yogurt
   Autumn Salad, 171
   Baked Cranberry Apple
      Oatmeal, 116
   Cool Dill Dip, 164
   Creamy Potato Salad, 175
   Fresh Fruit with Tangy
      Yogurt Sauce, 119
   Nutty Fruit Parfait, 120

Z

Zesty Breakfast Burritos, 113
zucchini
   Baked Zucchini with
      Mozzarella, 257
   Red Cabbage and Zucchini
      Skillet, 259
   Zucchini Lasagna, 241